Media Rare

Media Rare

*Adventures of a
Grass-roots Newsman*

Nat Boynton

CHANDLER PRESS

MAYNARD, MASSACHUSETTS

Printed in the United States of America.

International Standard Book Number: 0-944593-20-8

Library of Congress Catalog Card Number: 87-073179

9 8 7 6 5 4 3 2 1

To Barbara
and our three children

Contents

The unpaid cheering section
is heard from...

It was that fine actor-producer-writer, Peter Ustinov, who once observed that the English language is unique, because it offers the writer such great diversity in the choice of words and in the many meanings one can draw from a single word.

What flows from this sage conclusion is that the writer who is well acquainted with our language can provide the reader with style as well as substance, whenever he or she takes pen or word processor in hand. It also helps if the writer is endowed with unquestioned talent.

By now you have guessed that I am describing the Nat Boynton I know, whose story-telling style is at its finest in this work, so appropriately called *Media Rare*. To follow Nat Boynton's adventures as a young reporter for those proud little newspapers in upstate New York is to feel swallowed up by the clickety-clack of old manual typewriters, the smoky bustle of the city room, the smell of the pressroom, and the unrelenting pressures of the clock and a workaholic editor whose dedication to his profession runs true and deep.

The character portrayals throughout the pages of *Media Rare* are especially vivid, wonderful, kindly, brutish, and obviously indelible, and Nat's later experience working the Associated Press wire out of Albany helped develop his respect for considerable substance, as well. Write it fast, but write it right.

Nat spent a few years with the U.S. Army Air Corps in Newfoundland during World War II, and later wrote for a number of General Electric vice presidents. He treats those years as some sort of diversion from that great love of the newspaper business. Yet, these are happy diversions for the reader, during which we suspect that W.W. II may have been brought to a more rapid conclusion because Nat was busy grinding out a morale-building newspaper for the air base instead of tinkering with those old piston engines, and during that GE diversion, we can learn how to satisfy both the writing and egocentric whims of corporate executives.

Nat's return to the newspaper business when he might have been thinking of retirement is pure Horatio Alger, complete with good guys and bad guys. For anyone who has aspired to or endured a career in the communications business, *Media Rare* constitutes the next-best thing to on-the-job training.

Oh, yes. It is no trade secret that Nat Boynton enjoyed writing the true story of *Media Rare,* nor should you be surprised that I happened to belong to a dedicated group of believers who egged him onward. Your ticket to sharing the nostalgia of the great days of the newspaper business requires but the turning of the pages, and the willingness to witness the ups and downs, as only Nat Boynton can tell of them—compactly, but with style. At the risk of metaphoric mixing, we, Nat's unsolicited cheering section, can report that *Media Rare* is very well done.

John E. Duncan
Scotia, N.Y.

John E. Duncan is the author of *The Sea Chain, Picture Book of Old Connecticut,* and several Long Ago Books.

A note of caution from the author . . .

The episodes narrated herein are true, so clearly etched in mind that they could have been yesterday—or last week. I feel comfortable in relying on memory in the absence of notes, diaries, news clippings and file records. If there are sporadic inaccuracies, I am confident they are minor, and at worst inconsequential to the story lines. The characters in the cast are as I saw them at the time our paths crossed or merged; even those long gone I can see in my mind's eye and hear their voices.

Perhaps I might have become a big-time newspaperman, a high-salaried corporate executive or a prize-winning author if I had had more ambition and less aversion to geographic areas I didn't want to live in. My career advancement also suffered from the pure joy of the jobs I held. With a few notable exceptions, I was so happy in each job that I rejected the thought of moving to another, even at a higher level. As a result I have made a modest living from a typewriter all my life, never knowing wealth, but rich in satisfaction, family devotion and geographic setting. I promised myself at an early age I would never take a job south of Poughkeepsie, nor in a crowded urban area, and I never did.

I sometimes wonder what life would have been like if I hadn't resisted so firmly temptations that would have meant giving up the wonderful environment, climate, family lifestyle and community conviviality that meant so much to our household. Living in quiet, picturesque countryside twenty minutes from downtown Albany, we have the advantages of an established metropolitan center as well as quick and easy access to wooded hills, trails, major ski slopes and mountain lakes in all four directions. We are never conscious of restrictive traffic, yet we are barely three hours from New York, Boston and the seacoast.

This kind of living may have left some marks on the text that follows. Meanwhile, wherever you are, or wherever you've been, I hope you've had as much fun in your life as I have had in mine.

N. A. B.
New Scotland, N. Y.

... and a hatfull of kudos.

These chapters were launched at the urgings of my family and several friends. Once the work got underway, many good people provided valuable and enthusiastic help, especially friends who generously gave time to reading drafts, and friends who helped round up old photos, a difficult task.

My daughter-in-law, a prize-winning writer of awesome talent whose by-line, Meg Kissinger, is synonymous with "must" reading in the Milwaukee Journal, was a charter wine-taster. She pronounced an early draft appropriate to serve to innocent bystanders. Likewise Arlene Bruno, Martha Lawrence, Mary Steesy, Martin Yazijian, Kathy Kendall and my close friend and classmate, Bob Thum.

Pewilla Dick's astute perspective in word definitions, style, phrasing and other fine points saved this journeyman journalist from tumbling into countless literary traps. When this strict taskmaster spliced words of praise between rhetorical scoldings, I was inspired to press on.

Ralph Pettit spent retirement hours searching photo files at the Watertown Times, and my classmate, John Johnson, now publisher, made the Times library (nee "morgue") available. Arthur Westcott, Jr. loaned negatives that account for many of the Massena photos. The others are courtesy of Eleanor (Sis) Dumas at the Massena Historical Museum. The Geneva Times had no photo facilities during my tenure there, and, incredible as it may seem, has no photo of G. B. Williams on file. Eleanor Clise at the Geneva Historical Museum saved me from a shutout in that charming city.

Dorothy Leader, Henry's widow, graciously lent me her husband's scrapbook and memorabilia, a fourteen-carat treasure that plunged me into nostalgia. Dawn Force, Marie Randio, John Cusano and Fred Ricard also helped with photos. Vince Potenza, Terri Lawlor Westervelt and Gary VanDerLinden did a masterful job in the production end, and somehow Susanne Smith maintained a tolerant temperament doing page mechanicals during my peregrinations.

I cannot say too much in gratitude to Dick and Mary Ahlstrom of Newsgraphics of Delmar, Inc., incumbent publishers of the Spotlight, for many favors and strong support. I never would have attempted this nonsensical labor if Dick hadn't installed a word-processing keyboard, complete with typesetting commands, in my retirement retreat in rural New Scotland six miles from the newspaper. He did this so that I could write occasional stories outside the office without adding to the turbulent traffic during the Monday-Tuesday rush to get to press.

I also have boundless gratitude and love for my daughter, Cornelia (Cia) Ochsenbein, a career graphic artist and book designer. Hers is one of the busiest lives I know of, yet she managed to wedge generous counseling time into valuable off-hours. And my adorable wife, Barbara, who, besides drawing the map outlines, tolerated me around-the-clock throughout this travail. She deserves more love and appreciation than I can ever give her.

N. A. B.
New Scotland, N. Y.

Media Rare

I

The North Country

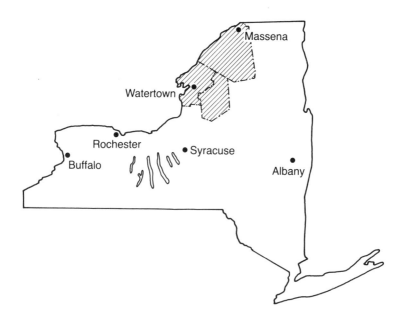

Massena

Watertown

Rochester

Buffalo

Syracuse

Albany

1

A New Cub for the Bear

Amidst the grime, clatter and clutter of the Watertown Times city room in 1940 was tingling excitement for a young reporter on his first newspaper job. At 7 a.m. the typewriters were clacking, the deskmen on the semi-circular rim of the copydesk were digging into the mountain of overnight stories in the mail and from the wire services. The copy boy was on his way to the railroad station behind the hotel on Public Square to pick up the stack of "baggage letters" from Times bureaus in St. Lawrence County, and the cupola bulbs on the bank of five phones hanging on spikes on the copydesk were starting to light up with incoming calls.

This was "upstate" New York, quite far upstate, 75 miles due north of Syracuse, 350 miles from Manhattan. We were two weeks into January, there was less than a foot of snow on the ground, not counting the piles stacked up by plows and drifts, and it was cold. On the first day of full-time employment, and in a vast projection of New York State that had more cows than people, I knew it was a good place to be. It might not be beautiful in January, but I had had some great times on the St. Lawrence River and in the Thousand Islands as a teenager, and I remembered how spectacular the North Country could be in July.

3

First day on the first job, one of life's major milestones. Across the North Country overnight people had died peacefully or accidentally, a barn had burned, town boards had resolved local issues or tried to, mishaps on a farm or roadways had sent several people to hospitals, word had come of the promotion of a local serviceman, and bids had been received for a new highway bridge. Among many other items that qualified in one way or another as news, babies had been born, a search was being organized for a trapper missing in the trackless Tug Hill wilderness, and a new candidate had declared for district attorney. In the elevated slot that anchored the copydesk crescent Gordon Bryant, city editor, was already halfway through his first White Owl cigar of the day.

At my newly assigned desk with its battered Underwood typewriter I was caught up in the vibrant pulse of people putting together another edition of a daily newspaper. Conversation was minimal; there was little time for chit-chat.

By 9 a.m. the newsroom was half empty as reporters started downstairs to fan out on their beats, covering city hall, police, banks, county and municipal courts, federal building, state agencies, chamber of commerce, highway department and a dozen other potential sources of news. Bryant's daily two-page list of continuing or upcoming story situations, with new and breaking stories added, had the name of the reporter assigned on each line. It would be another hour, probably two, before the reporters were back from their beats; in the meantime the staccato of typewriters came from the sports desk, women's desk, editorial writers, the obituary man and copy editors writing headlines.

Bryant, a perpetual-motion automaton, cigar butt wedged in a corner of his wide mouth, was consumed by the belief that there was a news story behind every tree, overturned trashcan, back porch, weedy lot and side alley in the city of 42,000. The same held true for scores of villages, hamlets and dairy farms stretching across the rural countryside in every direction. Any paper could cover the routine sources; Bryant knew there was much more. Any run-of-the-mill city editor could dispatch three reporters to cover every angle of a major downtown fire, but this

4

Gordon W. Bryant

was the Watertown Times, where it was just as important, perhaps more so, to report a small change in the sensitive price structure of milk pouring into dairy cooperatives by thousands of gallons before dawn each day, or that the most recent snow survey in the Adirondack foothills of Lewis County showed a greater depth this winter than last, thus posing possible flood watches on the Black River come spring.

It was Bryant who guided me into full-fledged membership in the newspaper fraternity. Years later, after a varied career in several aspects of journalism, I realized he had shaped my actions and performance more than any other associate in the industry. He was a stubby man of medium height with a permanent paunch that did not impede his status as one of the premier bowlers in the Class A City League. He had a full head of hair, gray despite his age in the early forties, parted unusually low on one side. His face was ruddy, nearly square, punctuated by blue eyes and a thin, wide mouth. He was rarely without a cigar, the supply of which was the responsibility of Neal Bintz, the cherubic copy boy, fresh out of Watertown High School.

"NEAL!" A roar from the city desk, like a howitzer shot.

"Yes, Mr. Bryant?" hurrying over from the bank of teletype machines in the corner.

"Dammit, Neal, you let me run out of cigars!"

"Gee, I'm sorry, Mr. Bryant. I only— "

"Never mind. Here, get me three, quick."

"Yessir." Heading for the stairs.

A step from the door Neal froze as Bryant roared again like an Army sergeant. The reporters looked up from their typewriters to watch the familiar ritual.

"NEAL!"

"Yes?"

"Yes what?"

"Yes, Mister Bryant?"

"That's better. What kind of cigars you gonna get?"

"White Owls."

"Why did you bring me Muriel Coronas yesterday?"

"I didn't— "

"Get going. Remember, WHITE OWLS!"

The beleaguered copyboy fled through the door as laughter, led by Bryant, spread across the room and the clacking of the keys resumed.

Neal, an overweight teenager, was genial and well liked. He retained his good humor despite relentless ribbing by Bryant and the older reporters. He lived with his family in a third-floor apartment in the city hall, where his father was the resident custodian. Neal later became a Times reporter, and to escape the hometown environment, and perhaps Bryant, moved to Utica.

There he rose steadily to managing editor of the Sunday Observer-Dispatch, a status and position loftier than that of his mentor and ex-tormentor. Bryant, as usual, had done his training work well.

Bryant was the jumpiest individual I ever met. In his swivel chair in the center of the crescent-shaped copydesk, elevated by a one-step platform, his movements were machine-gun, as if nervous energy was straining to escape. He jerked his copy pencil with lightning strokes, almost as if he were attacking the sheet of paper before him. His pudgy fingers flew so fast on the typewriter keyboard that the keys consistently bunched up at the throat. He talked the same way, words tumbling from his mouth so rapidly that only phrases and occasional words were audible. He was incapable of walking slowly. He was a jumping jack who couldn't remain in his chair more than a few minutes at a time, bounding off the step-high platform that elevated his desk and chair above the rim of the copydesk and pumping across the room to the door that opened to the composing room. Two minutes later the same door would fly open, Bryant would burst through, and in a dozen short piston strides would be back on his dais almost before the door clicked behind him.

He was gruff, but warm. He worked at bullying his young reporters to mold them into strict journalistic products, yet he often let his warmth toward them show through, if only for a moment. He was grim, serious and all-business until 11:15, when the noon edition closed. Then he swung out of his chair, jerked on his hat and coat without a word, and vanished down the stairs. A quick sandwich in the Arcade across the street, ten minutes at the pinball machine in the cigar store next door with a fresh White Owl in his countenance, a quick stop at the adjacent brokerage office to check the stock quotes, and he was back upstairs in "the slot" at 11:45.

The ritual never changed. The pace in the city room continued past two o'clock, when a mail edition, a remake of the noon edition, went downstairs early enough to make the mail trucks to Ogdensburg, Oswego and other distant points. Then the home stretch to the deadline for the final, Bryant's daily

Ex-cub Homer Baker.

Four of us had rooms in the Watertown Y, on Public Square one block from the Times.

8

pride, at 2:50. In the composing room he personally supervised the makeup of the Back Page, which proudly displayed the best North Country stories of the day—in effect, a local Page One.

*   *   *   *   *

My addition to the city staff that January meant an instant promotion for Homer Baker, who had been hired some eight weeks previously. Homer, a soft-spoken fellow two years out of Cornell, had grown up in Saranac Lake, where his father had a pharmacy. My arrival established for Homer an immediate seniority— he graduated to the bank beat, which included the Hotel Woodruff and the New York Central station. I replaced him on the federal building beat, the assignment traditionally given the newest cub.

Never mind. To me it was all part of the thrill of being on a newspaper at last, being part of the vibrancy, working alongside experienced editors and real-life reporters, absorbing the smell of hot lead and ink from the composing room, feeling the grimy wooden floor shake and throb when the big Hoe presses in the basement started their rhythmic rumbling and pounding deep downstairs just before noon, running the first edition for distant North Country outposts. Would any of the small items I had written make it into print? It was the whole world, more than romance, a deep-down love affair.

On my first day Homer had escorted me around the beat, introducing me as his successor to the occupants of half a dozen offices in the federal building barely a block from the Times. We toured the Farm Bureau, the Jefferson County Home Bureau and paid the daily call on the postmaster. Then over to another building for the state conservation office, a quick check to see if there was anything newly newsworthy at the library, and back to the Times to write the day's catch. Baptism completed, on Day 2 Homer and I again went down the narrow stairs to Arcade Street together at 9 a.m., but this time we split, he heading for the Square and I for Arsenal Street, on my own for the first time.

Back in the city room by 11 we pounded out as many stories as we could before breaking for a sandwich and milkshake at the lunch counter at Woolworth's, then raced to get every item

9

written before the last edition deadline. A few catch-up chores until 3:30 and liberation, tired and happy, once again in the fresh air of downtown Watertown. It was only a block's walk through the Arcade to Public Square, then across Washington Street to the YMCA where we paid $3.75 a week for a room.

Two contemporaries on the Times also lived at "the Y"— Tommy McHugh, a copyreader, and Ralph Pettit, a staff photographer. At age 22 and on the payroll for $19.75 a week, we found nighttime temptations were minimal or non-existent, so it was natural to gravitate back to the city room after an early supper. We knew that the only working occupant during evening hours, other than the regular night linotype operator, was Bryant. He had special dispensation from the Times hierarchy to "moonlight" as Watertown correspondent for the Syracuse Herald-Journal as a means of padding his salary (he was thought to be making as much as $45, a staggeringly lofty sum to us).

Except for his two bowling nights he regularly returned to the city room at 6 p.m., rewrote enough items from that day's Times to keep the Syracuse editors happy, and sent them down for the next day's Herald-Journal. Homer, Tommy, Ralph and I fell into the routine of dropping in each night, relaxing and reading all the other papers in the exchange pile. With no pocket money, no place to go and nothing else to do, we enjoyed shooting the breeze while Bryant rattled his keyboard at a speed that not only reflected his perpetual-motion charged-up energy, but left us in awe.

We also saw quickly that the nightside Bryant was a different person than the dayside Bryant. The White Owl was still scrunched in the corner of his wide mouth, but he was reasonably relaxed, extremely affable, and laughed and joked with us. It was a nice feeling to realize that the gruff, strictly business dynamo we knew as our domineering, demanding city editor was actually a pretty regular fellow suspected of having a warm heart and a friendly interest in us. After a while it became apparent that he enjoyed our evening visits, when the pressure was off, but we also knew that tomorrow morning he would be the prototype Bryant, passionately laying out his showpiece local pages, extorting stories out of every corner of the city room.

10

2

Wisdom from a White Owl

The Times format was unique. Whereas most papers used their best stories on Page One, local or otherwise, and devoted several inside pages or the front page of the second section as the display window for the day's other top local stories, the Times practiced strict and absolute segregation of local stories. The cream of North Country staff-written pieces and other stories of local interest were displayed on the back page, those from the rest of the state, nation and world on Page One and two "jump" pages— inside pages that accommodate runover of Page One stories.

The back page of the paper was an institution of its own, a local Page One. It was relatively inviolate to ads, and carried the top city and North Country stories and staff photos in careful makeup dictated by Bryant himself. There was no title flag across the top. In the upper left corner was a small weather box. Beneath it was a full column along the left margin under the heading in modest 12-point caps LOCAL PARAGRAPHS, a potpourri of one-paragraph items culled daily by reporters and correspondents at Bryant's incessant goading: calendar-type items, organization meetings, various notices, minor police

The Times occupied two merged buildings on Arcade Street. The city room was on the second floor, front, of the structure at the left, and was reached by the door nearest the third auto from the right. The large windows on the ground floor of the near building gave passersby a view of the press room. The publisher's office and his personal library occupied the floor above the press room.

items such as a stolen bicycle, a few personals and anything unworthy of a headline of its own.

Bryant was fiercely proud of the graphic composition of the hallowed back page as the showcase of Times staff excellence, the epitome of complete, total, all-embracing local news coverage. I never knew a local story to appear on Page One, and to my knowledge, even to this day more than forty-five years later, none has ever broken the barrier.

Immersed in the Times routine I found joy in my beat, the lowliest on the roster, rarely producing a story worth more than three paragraphs. I kept hoping that one of my daily calls would produce a decent story, but as the weeks went by I could only hope that perhaps the regional conservation officer who handled civil fines for taking game out of season, deer-jacking and poaching would come up with a string of felonious violations long enough to earn a "4-head" on the back page. I was, however, lucky that 1940 was a federal census year, and the first two or three times I had a story of any substance I got it from the Census Bureau's temporary quarters in the postoffice building, which was coordinating the entire North Country head count. Otherwise my daily rounds in this mundane arena were not likely to produce a back-page story, let alone make it "above the fold"— the top half of the page.

One day I had finished writing the meager output of my beat soon after lunch, which was unusual. I was trying to catch up with clippings when I heard Bryant's voice projected sharply in my direction. "Bucko!" he barked from his perch above the copydesk. "Whatcha got coming?"

Flustered at being singled out in front of everyone in the room, I could only answer meekly. "Nothing," I said, then with pride and new confidence, I added, "I'm all caught up."

That didn't pacify the old bear. "Get out of here and get me a story," he barked. "C'mon now, OUT!"

I reached for my coat, grabbed a pencil, stuffed some paper in a pocket and fled down the stairs. On the street I headed for Public Square, bewildered for only a moment. Looking at every store window, alleyway, passing truck, light pole and snowdrift, I found several broken parking meters, assaulted, no doubt, by passing plows. A sprint back to the office, a call to the Department of Public Works, and I had an official quote confirming that the city had counted seventeen damaged meters in a survey taken only three days earlier, and was putting them back in operation as quickly as possible. Three paragraphs and a 2-stub head on Bryant's proud page that day. I never knew whether he liked it, or even if he appreciated it; no comment was ever made.

On a similar occasion a short time later Bryant, apparently confronted with an unusual dearth of Local Paragraphs barely forty-five minutes before the city final was due to "go down,"

Back page of the Times, 1940. Local paragraphs at top left.

again bellowed at me from on high. This time he didn't ask what I was doing.

"Hey, Bucko! Go out and cover your beat again."

"What?" I was incredulous, having made my rounds barely two hours earlier.

"You heard me," he growled, making himself busy by glaring at his own desk. "I need copy."

It was bad enough knowing the meager cupboard on my beat was bare. It was embarrassing to poke my head through those same office doors for the second time that day, pleading for another item or two to satisfy my copy-hungry boss. But it turned out that since my visit that morning the Home Bureau unit in Chaumont had scheduled a quilt meeting at the home of

Mrs. Mabel Markley, and word had come from Albany that a traveling Farm Bureau representative would be demonstrating the art of disc harrowing at the Edgar Pike farm in Antwerp next Tuesday. Two local paragraphs for Bryant, a crisis averted and an embryonic professional reputation saved.

*   *   *   *   *

Even in my journalistic innocence I realized that the Times's passionate pursuit of blanket news coverage made it a first-rate newspaper, but it took a while for me to become aware that it was in a class by itself among upstate New York dailies. I was so preoccupied with Bryant and local stories I hardly had time to read other parts of the paper, notably national and world news on Page One, let alone editorials and columnists.

Although it had no competition in its own yard, Harold B. Johnson, editor-publisher, set his sights on giving his readers the same top-quality editorial excellence that was available to readers of the nation's top papers—New York Times, Washington Post, St. Louis Post-Dispatch, Kansas City Star, Montgomery Advertiser, Baltimore Sun and others, plus William Allen White's famous Emporia Gazette. If he hadn't quite achieved this lofty goal by 1940, he certainly had come close; the Watertown Times was perhaps the smallest daily in the nation that subscribed to all three major wire services (AP, UP and INS), plus the worldwide coverage of the Chicago Daily News syndicate, Reuters (British) and several others. As if that weren't enough, the Times maintained its own staff correspondent in Albany year-round and another in Washington. The only other upstate paper that could boast of such luxuries was the Buffalo Evening News; the Rochester, Albany and Utica papers used their Gannett capital bureaus while the Binghamton and Syracuse papers normally sent staffers to Albany only when the Legislature was in session.

The senior Johnson was a remarkable editor and publisher, accepted and respected among national leaders in both journalism and the political scene. Small wonder, then, that in

16

other parts of the nation scores of contemporary newspaper editors who kept a regular watch on their peers in other regions regularly scanned only three upstate New York papers—Buffalo Evening News, Albany Knickerbocker News and Watertown Times. If they had time for only two, it was Buffalo and Watertown. Such was the tribute earned and deserved by Harold B. Johnson, the small-town lad from Gouverneur who made an ordinary newspaper into a great one, employing the same zeal in covering the world and nation as he insisted Bryant use to cover New York's North Country.

*   *   *   *   *

In those training days in the Times city room in the bitter winter of 1940, one of the assigned functions of reporters was to take rewrites, i.e. stories phoned in from the legion of Times correspondents across the North Country. Except for the sports editor and women's editor, no staffer had a phone on his desk. A bank of five phones was aligned on spikes on the rim of the semicircular copy desk that formed the perimeter of Bryant's elevated station. Each incoming call lit a flashing bulb atop one of the five. The accepted practice by established newsmen was to ignore all rings and lights on the bank, leaving the cubs, Homer or me, to scramble across the room to the rewrite slot. This made for some pressurized moments when, pounding away at the day's catch of stories from the beat, we not only had to suffer the interruptions but write the caller's story, nine times out of ten an obituary, as deadlines loomed closer.

I had been toiling in this happy cauldron for some two months before hitting the jackpot, and I didn't even know I'd scored until I saw the final edition. It was a routine phone-in

This photo of the Times Editorial Department, taken in 1941, does not include bureau correspondents. Bryant is in "the slot." Assistant city editor Fred Kimball is seated at the far right station on the rim of the copydesk. Tommy McHugh is seated at the rewrite slot at Kimball's right, Homer Baker at McHugh's right. Harold B. Johnson is standing directly between McHugh and Baker, flanked by Harry Landon (behind Baker) and John B. Johnson.

from our man in Star Lake, a part-time correspondent in a remote hamlet deep in the Adirondacks. It was what newsmen call a "fatal" and as such a standard chore. A man walking along Route 3 had been struck by a car shortly after dark. He had been taken to the hospital in Tupper Lake, where he died the following morning. Our correspondent had the whole story within an hour, the obituary as well as the state police report of the accident.

From the scribbled notes I wrote the story in keeping with the finest of professional principles. "So-and-so, age 46, of Star Lake died today of injuries received last night when he was struck by a car while walking on Rt. 3 north of the village." It was a flawless piece of writing, I knew, and I was pleased to see that my lead survived Gordon's heavy black pencil intact en route to the linotype. An hour later my story appeared unscathed not only in print but under a 6-head, my first, on the inviolate back page, the lead story of the day. The top bank of Gordon's head stated,

STAR LAKE MAN
KILLED BY CAR

My elation was cut short by what I thought was a misleading headline. Was Bryant insensitive to the situation I had so carefully portrayed? I approached the great man boldly to complain.

"Gordon, this head— "

"What about it?" Gruffly.

"It's not right, he—"

"He what?" Patience getting thin.

"He died in the hospital. He was there about seven or eight hours. He wasn't killed on the road— "

"He wasn't killed by the car, that what you think?"

"Well, he died of injuries."

"Yeh, he did alright. Not a mark on him, eh, Bucko?"

And he was off to the composing room. End of discussion.

Public Square looking northwest. The Times was just off the photo to the left. The Y was on the southwest corner (near left).

A month or so later my incubation period had apparently been judged as complete. I was summoned to the glassed-in cubicle of the managing editor, where Harry F. Landon, a kindly senior with a remote, formal manner, told me I was being assigned to take over the Massena Bureau, a one-man operation on the Canadian border a hundred miles to the north. It was then that I knew I had passed the test of apprenticeship under that gruff old bear, Gordon W. Bryant. Now that my career as a newspaperman was assured, I was certain that the years ahead would be full of exciting adventures.

3

What Price Heritage

There is no explanation, logical or hereditary, for my unwavering decision, at an early age, to be a newspaperman. My father was a businessman, commuting from our New Jersey suburb to a stock brokerage firm on lower Broadway, Manhattan, where he handled his New Jersey accounts and personal clients. My mother might have been a concert pianist if she had pursued a career instead of a more traditional path that led to marriage and children. Neither parent was notably literary, although both were intelligent, articulate and well informed. Both had family trees with roots embedded deep in seventeenth century America, planted by settlers who had come from the British Isles. Both had been educated in first-rate private schools, but neither had gone to college. In the flow of nine generations their forebears had been craftsmen, tradesmen, manufacturers, teachers, preachers, soldiers, farmers, musicians, artists, housewrights, merchants, naval officers and civic officials. Not a writer, poet or publisher in the bunch, let alone a journalist.

Nor was there an uncle, cousin, friend, neighbor or teacher who might have weaned my journalistic tendencies in puberty or adolescence in the late 1920's in Orange, New Jersey, where I grew up. My early heroes were major league baseball players and sports writers. The New York Sun and the Sunday Herald-Tribune were the newspapers that best chronicled the deeds of Rogers Hornsby, Frankie Frisch, Pie Traynor, Travis Jackson, Max Wheat, Eddie Roush and my special Giants idols, Bill Terry, Mel Ott and Lefty O'Doul.

The Herald-Tribune was tossed on our porch steps every morning, but my father took it with him for the stock tables he needed. I rarely saw it except on Sundays, but he brought home The Sun each night. To me The Sun was the greatest paper in the world. It had Joe Vila, Will Wedge and Frank Graham writing baseball and George Trevor doing college football. With a varsity of this caliber, who needed Damon Runyon or Grantland Rice?

The Great Depression eliminated summer trips, so the young teenage boys in our crowded suburb spent their days playing dice baseball, stoop-ball or cotton-ball. Stoop-ball consisted simply of one player flinging a well-worn tennis ball against the porch steps, his opponent trying to field it on the fly or one bounce. (If you could hit the ridge of a step, the ball would explode into a double or a triple halfway across the street.) In cotton-ball, also a one-versus-one game, the pitcher threw a stuffed string-ball used by fathers who practiced golf in the garage. The batter, standing against the garage door in a gravel courtyard of rental garages, wielded with one hand a stubby sawed-off broom handle, striving to drive the little soft bird to spots in the gravel surface designated as a single, double, etcetera. (The curves and drops were murderous when you squeezed the soft pellet fairly flat and released it sidearm.)

By far our most popular Depression diversion—at least, with my three friends on Cleveland Street—was dice baseball. Each participant had his own roster of players personified by baseball cards from chewing gum distributors, and the rules were strict in regard to batting orders, pitching sequences, trading and record-keeping. I was the one who drew up the schedules, kept team standings and batting averages, and issued the newspaper for our league. I wrote the accounts of dozens of dice baseball games, each day laying out headlines and stories on graph paper in pencil.

DICE BASEBALL

Single

Home Run

Double

Single

Triple

Single

The rules of dice baseball are simple and basic: Double Ones, a single. Double Twos, two-base hit; Threes, a triple, Fours a home run. Double Fives and Double Sixes, single. Any throw with a One in it (except Double Ones) is an out. For all remaining combinations, odd number is a strike, even number a ball. In our version the baseball card of the player coming to bat was placed at home plate on our cardboard (or plywood) diamond before the dice were thrown. If he got on base, his card and subsequent cards were moved to each base as dictated by ensuing throws of the dice.

I also was the manager of the Pittsburgh Pirates in our league. I wanted desperately to have the New York Giants, but George Gardner, the smallest and sharpest of our foursome, won that coveted franchise in the organizational lottery.

Our four-team league had an exciting pennant race. For me, as the league scribe and editor-publisher of the league newspaper, maybe that's where all this newspaper business started.

* * * * *

At age 15 I was the winner in an arduous competition for the coveted job of newspaper correspondent for our school. Newark Academy, to which I commuted by trolley from Orange, played its football schedule on Friday afternoons rather than Saturdays. The 6 p.m. sports final of the Newark Evening News carried condensed play-by-play summaries of each scholastic game by quarters, taken by phone dictated by a student correspondent in each school in Essex County. We were paid fifteen cents a column inch for the Friday bulletins and for the regular account on the sports page the next day.

We had to phone in the play-by-play of the first two quarters at halftime. Then, after phoning in the fourth quarter, I had to run for the downtown trolley, race to the News office, knock out four or five paragraphs at an empty desk in the sports department, sprint two blocks to the Newark Star-Eagle to do one for them (they also paid fifteen cents an inch), then three more blocks to the Ledger, a morning tabloid. The Ledger was the grimiest, messiest and most exciting of the three plants. It was also the smallest, had the least space for school sports, and paid the least, ten cents an inch. On a good week I could earn forty cents from the Ledger.

If dice baseball on Cleveland Street planted the first seeds, perhaps it was the Ledger newsroom that nurtured the sprouting plant. The excitement of a newspaper office, reporters rattling typewriters, copy paper strewn everywhere, the distinctive smell of ink and hot lead, the musical tinkling of the linotype machines, the rumbling and shaking when the presses started to roll. The staffers paid little attention to me as I hacked at a typewriter at an unoccupied desk, an attitude I took as a sign of tacit acceptance. When one of them would venture, however casually, a "Hi, kid," I felt like one of the brethren in the lodge.

Everybody was always in a hurry. For me the pressure came not from deadlines for the next edition; I had to knock out my stories after the game and get home for supper. Daylight faded quickly on November football afternoons, and suburban mothers didn't like sons racing around downtown streets and standing on corners waiting for trolleys after dark. Luckily the three plants were within a radius of a few blocks.

One day in June I went around to the dingy, ramshackle office of The Daily Courier, the struggling little paper in Orange, three blocks from my house. Did they they need any teenage help for the summer? The young editor was friendly and receptive. The only help he could use was in sports. Did I know anything about baseball?

I couldn't have responded more quickly if he had asked me if a duck could swim or a bird fly. Would I write a story each week on the East Orange semipro team that played the big touring teams each Saturday afternoon? He couldn't pay me any money, but he could get me a season's pass to the Newark Bears in my own name. Deal. Ecstacy.

*   *   *   *   *

Two weeks into the assignment, the business manager of the East Orange team, a hustling promoter named Ray Oliver, offered me the job of official scorer and publicist at the astronomic stipend of five dollars a game! Five dollars to sit in the dugout with the players, a personal pass to the Newark Bears of the Triple A International League in my pocket, at age 16? Wow! And in the fall, with a lot of hustling on the football sidelines charting the flow of games with pencil and phone access to Newark papers, I was netting some weeks as much as two dollars, I was in an enviable fiscal position at a time when the nation's unemployment figures were at a disastrously historic high. Even my own father, at age 43, had been unable to find work since The Crash had shut down the brokerage firm he worked for in New York.

In this financial bonanza there was an added bonus. My addiction to baseball standings, statistics and strategies found a new dimension with the East Orange BBC. The initials stood for Base Ball Club, presumably a corporate appendage that rendered a nickname unnecessary. On Saturday afternoons in season I shared the dugout with a collection of top-flight ball players Ray Oliver had assembled to oppose famous touring teams, the "bearded wonders" of the House of David, the Detroit Clowns and others, primarily the legendary black teams that later formed the Negro National League.

This was high-caliber baseball, and I recall watching with awe the talent of the Pittsburgh Crawfords, Homestead Grays, Baltimore Black Sox and a Memphis team whose nickname is lost to mind. I can still see Satchel Paige on the mound for the Crawfords and Josh Gibson behind the plate, Satch with his pipestem legs, his long arm in a high arc whipping fastballs that looked like aspirin tablets, and Gibson, built like an Army tank, hitting a home run that cleared the centerfield fence and a row of trees beyond, landing in the parking lot of the Lackawanna station on Grove Street. There was Jimmy Woods, who probably stole four times as many bases as Ty Cobb.

Years later, when black ballplayers were accepted on major league teams, I got a special lift from nostalgic articles about the exploits of Paige, Gibson and others. It was especially pleasing when experts conceded that in his heyday (which was then) Satch was the equal of Matty, Three-Fingered Brown, Walter Johnson and such contemporaries as Dizzy Dean and Carl Hubbell, and that Josh Gibson might have been the greatest catcher who ever played the game. Some fifteen years later I was lucky enough to be in the stands in Cleveland Stadium when Satch, whose actual age was always a mystery, pitched in relief in the 1948 World Series against the Boston Braves. Gibson died before the major leagues lifted the color ban.

The home dugout in East Orange was no slouch. We had Bob Miller, a standout pitcher from Dartmouth who turned down a contract with the Yankees in favor of a steady job in New York City. We had Dutch Woerner, a second baseman sought by many big league teams who couldn't pry him loose from a secure job on Wall Street (even in Depression). There was Roy Tarr, an ex-Buffalo Bison whose thick mat of black hair curling out from the top button of his baseball shirt was a source of wonder to a light-complexioned teenager. Eddie Boland, the right fielder, after several years of profitable weekend ball with East Orange and the Bushwicks in Brooklyn, gave up his job with the New York City Sanitation Department to play for the Phillies and hit close to .300 for several seasons. Eppie Barnes, the slick first baseman, later had a respected career as director of athletics at Colgate, and Buck Lai, the leadoff man, did the same at Long Island University, where he also became a nationally known baseball coach and served as a scout for the Giants.

With my press pass from The Courier I went regularly to the stadium in Newark to see the Bears, the Yankees' No. 1 farm team. I was too awed to take full advantage of my access to the players' clubhouse and dugout, even though I knew the writers from the Newark News, Ledger and Star. The only player who ever spoke to me was a tall rookie pitcher named Charley Devens, who a few months earlier had received much publicity for being the first member of a Boston blue-blood family to defy tradition by becoming a professional baseball player. Charley had shocked his aristocratic family by signing a Yankee contract upon graduation from Harvard several weeks earlier. The Yankees were so impressed with his tremendous pitching record in college they assigned him to their highest minor league franchise. There his polished Beacon Street accent and fastidious manners set him a world apart from the cud-chewing pros in the locker room, and they ignored him, as they did me, in going about their work.

Charley treated me like a friend, and one blisteringly hot afternoon invited me to sit with him in the Bears dugout for the first game of a doubleheader against the Toronto Maple Leafs. He said I would have to go back to the stands between games, because he was the starting pitcher for the second game. It was a thrill I never have forgotten.

Charley did quite well in the highest minor league, but apparently found the life not to his taste. I assume the Devens clan was relieved when their prodigal returned to the ancestral fold to take his rightful place as a future bank president, head of a leading investment firm or governor of Massachusetts.

*   *   *   *   *

In 1935 I graduated from Newark Academy cum laude, but at Princeton I found myself inundated by a curricular load that was close to overwhelming. No time for the Daily Princetonian. I was a finalist in the intense competition for the Press Club, the collegiate counterpart of my Academy job as sports correspondent for Newark papers. I made it through four wonderful but gruelling years without scholarly distinction, but with a multitude of treasured friends and a diploma in political science, the ideal prep for a journalist. In the cold world of 1939 the economy was still depressed. There were no jobs on newspapers.

Through tragic circumstances my two younger sisters and I had been orphaned during my college days, and it was natural for

NEWARK

Batting Order / Uniform No.	1	2	3	4	5	6	7	8	9	10	AB	R	1B	SH	PO	A	E
1. Farrell, s. s. 1																	
2. Barton, r. f. 5																	
3. Hill, l. f. 3																	
4. Alexander, 1b. ...4																	
5. Carlyle, c. f. 2																	
6. Muller, 3b. 9																	
7. Glenn, c. 8																	
8. Schalk, 2b. 7																	
9. p.																	

Kies, c.—7
Brown, p.—14
McDonald, p.—19
LaRocca, p.—16

Devens, p.—18
Tamulis, p.—12
Duke, p.—15
Makosky, p.—20

Chandler, p.—17
Neun, inf.—10

Gibson, inf.—6
Mgr. Shawkey—21

D. E. Martino, mascot—23

The Newark Bears offered this lineup for a 1934 International League game against the Albany Senators. It was only the second year that players wore numbers. By coincidence the manager, Bob Shawkey, bobs up again 130 pages and 14 years later.

me to gravitate to upstate New York after finishing at Princeton. As a family we had always been close to my mother's sister and her five children in Geneva, and I constantly envied my contemporary cousins for what I viewed as a far better life socially, recreationally and geographically in the Finger Lakes of New York State than I had endured in flat, humid, crowded and urban New Jersey.

The president of the Wall Street firm my late father worked for in New York City, an alumnus of both Princeton and Newark Academy, offered me a job as a trainee in the lofty world of finance, but I rejected it on two counts— I was unwilling to accept the life of a commuter in a fiscal pressure-cooker like metropolitan New York, as had my father, and I was determined to be a newspaperman and not get enmeshed in the whirling circus of Wall Street. I had no money, little estate and was solidly in debt to Princeton, even with interest waived. In my post-graduate perspective, however, a low-paying news job was preferable to potential future wealth in a high-powered but unappealing stratum of the national economic structure.

Thereupon came stark reality. There were no news jobs in upstate New York, let alone low-paying ones. It was a long summer. Living with my loving aunt in the fresh air of the Finger Lakes, I started my employment quest with the hometown Geneva Daily Times. The Times was about as dreary a paper as could be found, but it was dependable in that it published six days a week. My interview with the venerable city editor, E. T. Emmons, was pleasant but unproductive. He was an affable Vermonter, a perfect part in his snow-white hair, and he was sympathetic to the plight of an aspiring young reporter, but there was simply no opening. Would he give me some low-level assignments if I worked for no pay? Oh, he wouldn't feel right about that. I can live with my aunt, I explained, and can survive without salary. No, he insisted, if he took me on, he would certainly pay me something. Awfully sorry, hope you understand.

I didn't understand, but three weeks later someone sent me to a fellow who was trying to set up a radio station in Geneva. Tex Waldorf was a salesman-entrepreneur with only enough capital to lease two hours of evening time from the Auburn station twenty-five miles to the east. He had rented space in the basement of Bolin's music store in downtown Geneva, had soundproofed and equipped a small broadcasting studio, and had hired a well-known local theatrical producer as an announcer while he hustled Geneva sponsors for spot commercials.

In his limited programming Tex needed a reporter to write and broadcast five minutes of Geneva news at 8 p.m. Monday through Friday. He was selling the program for six dollars, of which three would go to the newsman. He had commitments for three nights of the five, but the program had to be five nights. I could have the job, he said, but it was understood that there would be no pay on nights when there was no sponsor. In other words, I could count on nine dollars a week, fifteen whenever he was able to sell all five segments.

There followed four months of makeshift journalism. It was a pretty sad excuse for a job, but I hadn't written for a paper since my school days, and that was strictly sports. There was no one around to show me how to go about covering general news. Instinct, however, is a strong motivator, and in no time I was checking city hall, police station, fire chief, undertakers and others, writing the day's catch in radio format. At 8 I had to read it on the air.

It wasn't long before I discovered my homegrown approach was effective. Scanning the Geneva Times each afternoon to see what I'd missed, I realized I was, for the most part, a day ahead of them. The only exceptions were major overnight breaking stories, and even then the casual pace and attitude of the Times, unaccustomed to and disdainful of competition, often held them a day. After all, what difference did it make?

In that phase of its history the Geneva Times, among other concessions to mediocrity, did not feel committed to reporting police news. Whatever the reason for such an unorthodox policy, it came as a shock to realize that my eager-beaver reporting, beating the local paper at almost every turn, was making a zero impression on the people for whom I had offered to work for free. Either they didn't notice that I was a red-hot reporter, or they didn't care.

Meanwhile I kept pursuing newspaper employment in Rochester, Syracuse and Ithaca without success, and it was nearly Christmas, six months after college graduation, before an opening showed. My good friend and college classmate, Johnny Johnson, who was a reporter on a paper his father published in Watertown, N.Y., wrote to say there was a spot open, and to come up for an interview if interested.

Interested? I jumped, I went, I got the job. Thus began a string of adventures that hasn't stopped yet.

4

Competition Rears Its Head

A blustery overcast greeting me that heady Sunday morning in April was a far cry from the gaiety of the farewell party my Watertown friends threw at the Woodruff Hotel grill Saturday night on the eve of my departure for my new assignment. My 1937 Ford was packed to the gunwales with all my worldly goods, my expected hangover was surprisingly mild, and as I pointed the trusty old car north for Massena, a place that had all the earmarks of a wilderness frontier, I felt the kind of anticipatory thrill that might have come to an explorer setting off on the Amazon by canoe.

Three hours later, the sky still foreboding, I drove into the main business section of the most uninspiringly drab town I had ever seen. I could forgive the deserted streets— after all, it was Sunday noon— but it was hard to find any encouragement in a hodgepodge of tasteless storefronts, many needing paint or sprucing up. But then, let's be fair, I was on the Canadian border, in what seemed to be a peninsula of civilization, in mid-April after a rugged North Country winter, so why not forgive the architecture for appearing weatherbeaten and defeated?

*   *   *   *   *

Establishing a news beat in a habitat I had never seen before might have been intimidating if I hadn't been so fired up with the thrill of being on my own for the first time. Within two days of my arrival in this barren outpost nearly a hundred miles north of Watertown I was introduced to an aspect of the newspaper world I had not previously encountered— competition on the news beat.

During my three-month incubation in the city room it had never occurred to me that there was any serious threat from another newspaper. The two Syracuse papers that shared, to some extent, the newsstands in Watertown had local correspondents and carried stories from the Watertown area, but those stories were invariably at least one day behind. The Times coverage was so complete, so well organized and so sweeping that it was hard to believe anyone actually read those other papers, let alone subscribed to them. I automatically assumed that the only reason to scan the morning Post-Standard was to check baseball scores or stock market quotes, and I could think of no reason why anyone in the North Country would want to read the Herald-Journal if they had read last night's Times.

Thus it came as somewhat of a shock to have Harry Landon, our remote managing editor, call me into his sanctum the day

Harry F. Landon

before my departure for Massena to tender some fatherly advice. Harry (I called him Mr. Landon, of course) was a portly old-timer with an aura of seniority and sagacity that tended to inhibit young reporters, hence his words, even in his squeaky soprano voice, were to be respected as gospel. Passive and insulated as he seemed, he was, after all, Bryant's boss, and only one level below the supreme authority, Harold B. Johnson.

"Nat," he began, looking paternally at his youngest trainee, "we regard Massena as one of the most important bureaus we have. We are sending you up there because things have not been going well for us there. For some time now we have been dissatisfied with the coverage we are getting from Irving Carbino. Irving is a bright fellow, but he is the proprietor of a jewelry store in Massena and we feel he is not devoting enough time to taking care of our bureau. We also have reason to believe that he is in league with the Post-Standard man there, so we are not always getting our own stories and we're not always getting them in timely fashion. You have the intelligence and ability to get your own stories without any help from anyone else. Remember that. I know you'll do well."

A brief rundown of Massena's economic and demographic makeup and a dictum on the strong circulation enjoyed by our Massena edition closed out the interview. As I vacated my chair, my counselor repeated his primary thrust. "Remember, Nat, we're counting on you to give us good coverage. I don't want you to have anything to do with the Post-Standard man. Good luck!"

*   *   *   *   *

I hadn't been on my new beat two days before this counsel was put to test. Irving Carbino, a prosperous Main Street merchant apparently disgruntled at being deprived of an easy income writing for the Times on the side, was not much interested in showing me around town, so I picked my own way through town hall, which also housed village offices, police headquarters and a spacious second-floor auditorium-ballroom. I also made introductory contact with other basic news sources— fire department, state police, undertakers, schools, Chamber of Commerce.

On my second day I had a courtesy visit from, of all people, the resident Post-Standard correspondent. He was an old-timer with graying temples, a bouncy little fellow who charged fearlessly into my one-room office on the second floor of the Niagara Mohawk building that proclaimed in block letters on frosted glass that it was indeed the Massena Bureau of the Watertown Times. He was hardly five-six, and couldn't have weighed 120 pounds, probably in his fifties. He was wearing a dark suit that needed pressing and a fedora that had seen its best days, rakishly slanted on a full head of graying hair. The two things that struck me immediately were his springy step and his spontaneous smile. It was instantly apparent that he was a good fellow and that his visit was more of a welcoming than a declaration of war. He introduced himself as Fred Holliday of the Post-Standard, offered his hand in friendship, and plunked himself into one of the two other wooden office chairs in the semi-bare room. I was intrigued.

We exchanged brief biographical identifications, and he got right to the point. He and Carbino worked together, he explained, and each gave the other carbon copies of every piece of copy they typed. They divided the Massena beat, Fred checking the undertakers first thing each morning for obituaries, then our two local state troopers when they came to the Silver Grill for breakfast. Carbino took care of the village police, the mayor's office and town clerk. Holliday looked in each morning at the Andrews Street fire station. In this way they covered, between them, all sources of what was known in the trade as "spot news" with a minimum of effort.

This cheery little fellow, whom I warmed to on the spot, went on to say that now that Carbino was out of the picture, he hoped that I would continue the happy arrangement. His editors down in Syracuse, 175 miles distant, said Holliday, had never insisted on beating anybody to the news. They were satisfied, he explained, with a half dozen items each day in the mail, one or even two days late, showing enough of a scattering of Massena datelines along with stuff from Ogdensburg, Potsdam, Canton and environs to justify a North Country edition. Holliday, well aware of the Times's passion for instant publication of each

This view of Main Street was taken about two years before I saw Massena for the first time.

obituary as the highest news priority, would supply me with full notes of overnight deaths each morning, even before he wrote his own copy. In return he asked for carbons of my stuff, with full knowledge that all my stories would be in the Times a full day before his rewrites arrived in Syracuse.

It was a tailored, foolproof deal, an all-win no-lose proposition, insulated by long-distance geography from the nearest editor who might sniff collusion. But I was imbued with the purest of journalistic fidelity, barely four months on my first job, less than a week in my own new bailiwick. Much as I liked Fred Holliday and his obviously genuine approach, the austere and authoritative words of Harry Landon less than a week ago came crashing into my cranium. "You get your own stories," he had said. "Don't have anything to do with the Post Standard."

There was only one thing I could say to my smiling visitor. No deal, but I had to say it in a nice way, a friendly way. I tried to recount my dialogue with the lofty managing editor, adding that since we had to be competitors, we could still be friends and, perhaps, work together— discreetly— on special occasions.

Fred took the bad news well, in fact, perhaps too well. If he was disappointed he didn't show it. He gave an unmistakable impression that it would only be a matter of time before I saw the light. It was plain he was confident that wouldn't be long.

How right he was! Five or six weeks of working six days a week for a paper that printed daily except Sunday can be confining no matter how exciting and engrossing the new beat became as I got to know it better. I yearned to break away for a weekend with family and friends in Geneva, my home town, now 225 miles away by twisty, two-lane highways. There was only one way to escape without leaving the territory uncovered. I was haunted by the grim thought of some major story breaking— a big fire, the mayor suffering a fatal heart attack or getting himself assassinated, an explosion or a sudden strike at the big Aluminum Company plant . . . and I would be far away downstate as the paper went to press without the Big Story. End of newspaper career.

The one way out was collaboration with Fred Holliday. Would he cover for me if I took off, say 11 a.m. Saturday, with the

Massena edition about to hit the press in Watertown? More important, would he leave his weekend carbons in my office slot so that when I got back late Sunday night I could knock off those stories and run them out to the railroad station in a Baggage Letter before going to bed? That way I could still get my stories on the 7:05 a.m. train Monday, to be picked up by the copy boy in Watertown along with the packets from Potsdam, Canton and Gouverneur bureaus.

When I conceded to Fred that I had decided to yield to infidelity in the interests of practicality, he tilted his hat back on his bushy gray thatch, chuckled in glee and said he'd be glad to comply. To his everlasting credit he refrained from saying something like I-knew-you'd-come-around, or well-it's-about-time-you-saw-the-light. From that moment we were firm friends and co-conspirators.

In the days that followed Fred gave me many a tip that earned me a news beat, and his reliability, as well as his intimate knowledge of the town and its constituents, enabled me to take a number of weekends over the following two years. In return I banged out a few rewrites each Wednesday and mailed them at 4 p.m. in Fred's Post-Standard envelopes, an arrangement that permitted my new colleague to pursue his favorite recreation, a day of fishing on the St. Lawrence a few miles from town. It also gave the Times, in effect, a second reporter in the bureau and more comprehensive coverage than a single individual, no matter how talented or energetic, otherwise could have provided.

This close relationship, however illicit, endured until the day I left for military service two years later, courtesy of Massena Draft Board No. 413, and I kept in touch with Fred long after I had left the Times. If Harry Landon or anyone else on the Times ever suspected me of being lured into the Carbino Carbon Syndrome, it was never mentioned.

5

Fire, Ready or Not

There was another competitive aspect in Massena that my counselors in Watertown had not bothered to mention, the local paper. Weekly newspapers were a fixture in a dozen or so communities throughout Times territory, many of which dated back to the nineteenth century. The Massena Observer was a semi-weekly, appearing each Tuesday and Friday. Unlike the weeklies, which were independent, the Observer was owned by the people who put out the Ogdensburg Journal, the only other daily published in the three counties the Times blanketed.

The Massena Observer was a fairly compact operation housed in a small brick printing plant adjoining the rear of several Main Street stores. It was accessible from a paved pedestrian alleyway that ran between the mercantile building and the town hall, linking the sidewalk on Main Street with the municipal parking lot behind town hall. The editor was a middle-aged pipe-smoking fellow named Leonard Prince who had been there fifteen-plus years. The fact that we became good friends could be attributed to Leonard's total acceptance of the concept that only a daily could beat a daily to breaking news stories, and my realization that the Observer was content to take what came along rather than compete aggressively. In a small town our paths crossed frequently and we often sat together at community functions and swapped trade talk. In my second year in Massena Leonard hired a young reporter who considered me and the Times as an enemy, but his aggressiveness far outstripped his reportorial capacities and I was able to ignore whatever threat his presence posed to my daily rounds.

Much later in my career, when I became owner of a suburban weekly newspaper, I came to realize how deeply a local editor can resent the overpowering advantages an intruding out-of-town daily can bring to bear on the little hometown independent. But back in those days just prior to our involvement in World War II, it was I who held most of the aces, unaware— and probably uncaring— that the Times was the hated foe of the Potsdam Courier-Freeman, two weeklies in Canton, the Gouverneur Tribune-Press, the Carthage Republican and others.

*   *   *   *   *

If I was made aware of the competitive climate of the newsgathering business in my first few days in Massena, it took only ten days for a head-on collision with another facet of the newspaper world I had never encountered—the Big Story, or perhaps more accurately, the Breaking Story. On Thursday of my second week in a town I had never seen before, the largest and most pivotal commercial building in the business section was wrecked by a six-hour fire that still ranks as Massena's most historic of this century and one of the more spectacular blazes in North Country annals.

I was roused from my rented room on a quiet residential street by blaring fire horns shortly after 5 on a gray April morning. I rushed down to the main corner of town to see flames shooting from the second floor of the two-story Central Building. My first thought was the Times camera, an ancient boxlike Graflex a cubic foot in dimension. Carbino had taken less than three minutes to show me how to load the film packs, warning me to be sure to pull the "black slide" before snapping the trigger. (The present-day equivalent would be: remove lens cap before taking photo.)

Central Building ablaze. April, 1940. Hose is directed at window from which fireman fell. Arthur Westcott took this photo; the shots the Times used from my bulky Graflex have been lost to posterity.

My office was only a block away. I sprinted up the stairs, unlocked the door, grabbed the unwieldy box and a couple of film packs, and ran back to the fire scene with heart pounding. What a way to get my baptism in news photography, without a bit of practice, and zero training! It was early enough that only forty or fifty people had gathered at the scene. I was able to plant my feet firmly on the sidewalk in front of the Kinney Drug Store and point the cumbersome box directly across the intersection where a fireman was on a ladder trying to enter a second-floor window.

Peering down into the view finder with my right thumb on the shutter trigger I was able to twist the range knob with my left hand and bring the ladder and fireman into sharp focus. I was centering the scene on the view-finder when I heard the crowd gasp. Looking up quickly I saw the second-floor window sash give way. For a split second the man on the ladder tried to grasp the sill, but missed. In horror I watched as he plunged to the sidewalk. He landed in a crumpled heap at the foot of the ladder before I realized to my acute dismay that my errant digit was still on the camera trigger. If I had snapped the photo instead of watching the drama I would have caught his fall in mid-flight, which would have made a startling newsphoto. But such was not the fortune of this 22-year-old rookie. However, I did take some good shots of flames and smoke, enough to catch the blaze in action before turning to my reportorial chores.

Here the first order of business was to determine who and what occupied the embattled structure. In the nine working days I had been on the job in Massena I had been in the building only once, and that was to pick up several items in the Newberry 5-and-10 store that monopolized the first floor on the main corner of town. At the far end of the Andrews Street side I could see that the entrance to the stairway leading to the second-floor offices was relatively free of smoke and flames, and the door was ajar.

I dashed across the street, hopped over several snakes of firehose, and pulled the door open. On the wall just inside the entrance hallway I found what I had hoped to find, a directory with removable letters in a glassed-in metal frame. I was not about to become a hero, but it seemed safe to wrench the whole directory assembly from the wall and make off with it, which I did. Depositing that trophy and the camera in the security of my office a block down Main Street, I ran back to the scene to get as much official information from firemen and police as was available at the moment, learned the identity of the injured fireman and his emergency destination (Ogdensburg hospital). It was now 7 a.m. and I was beginning to think I had a possible back-page 6-head, a world apart from a cake-baking demon-stration by the Lafargeville unit of the Jefferson County Home Bureau. I sprinted back down Main Street to my office and grabbed the phone to notify Watertown.

The Central Building as it looked in 1928, top, and after the fire.

This time I was the one on the live end of the calls coming into the bank of phones at the rewrite slot on the Times copydesk in Watertown instead of on the receiving end. I got my story in by way of several phone calls, all handled expertly by Dominic Pepp, an experienced professional and a veteran of the police and fire beats in Watertown. He told me to hire a driver to speed my film pack to Watertown, which I did.

By 10 a.m. firemen had the blaze under control. When the Massena edition rolled in by Times truck shortly after 3:30 p.m., there it was, a four-column head and two big photos, miraculously captured by the clumsy Graflex, in a spread that dominated the back page. Later I learned that the story, substantially abridged and with only one photo, had also made Bryant's revered back page in the city final. Even more exciting to me was a one-paragraph note a day later, signed by Harold B. Johnson himself, commending me for the coverage. It was a memorable occasion, more vivid in my mind than fatal airline and highway crashes, major fires, political block-busters and investigative headliners that came along later.

6

Arms of the Law

As a boy devouring Stanley Walker's biographical narrations of the police beat in the heyday of New York City's fiercely competitive newspapers of the twenties, I grew up believing that the highest adventure and most thrilling drama in the world of journalism invariably befell the police reporter.

My romance with the newspaper profession got a jolt when I discovered that police headquarters in Massena occupied spanking clean, brightly illuminated and modernized quarters in a newly renovated basement of the town hall. The new linoleum floors were polished so freshly it seemed a pity to mar the wax by walking down the corridor. All these things, plus the antiseptic smell, seemed a far cry from the image of a police station in my youthful mind.

There was a shiny formica-topped counter at which to serve the public. In the spacious room behind it were new metal desks for the sergeant in charge and the uniformed clerk. In the far left corner was a water cooler, a coffee machine and an inkpad device for fingerprinting. In the far right corner a door opened into the chief's office, also roomy, modern and comfortable. The whole setup look more like an insurance agency than a police station.

From the outside the station was reached by a door opening from the macadam alleyway between the side of the town hall and the Observer office. There was also a rear door to the parking lot behind the building. Since I had daily deadlines of 11:15 for the noon (Massena) edition, 2 p.m. for the Watertown final and 6 p.m. for mailing the day's newscopy, I quickly fell into the habit of breezing through the station from side door to rear door, or vice versa, four or five times a day to ask Harold Manning, the desk sergeant, "Anything new?"

For most people the work day that began at 8 or 8:30 ended at 5 or 6. For a Times bureau correspondent it was a 24-hour job seven days a week. When not writing stories or covering the beat and public events, a newspaper correspondent is, in effect, on-call. To miss a "spot news" story before deadline was unthinkable, a Class A journalistic felony.

The routine stuff went down to Watertown by mail at 6 p.m. Anything in the evening— village board meeting, lecture, traffic accident, obit— had to be written that night. Before going to bed, I would tuck the night's production into one of the large re-usable manila envelopes imprinted in bold type BAGGAGE MASTER, WATERTOWN, N.Y., and take it out to the railroad station on the outskirts of town. There I would stash it in a small rack, where it would spend the rest of the night waiting to be plucked from the holder by a baggageman about to board the 7:05 the next morning. Anything after that would have to be wired or phoned to Watertown.

In this cycle I habitually checked the police station each evening after the movies, bowling, softball, date with a girl, party or picnic. I knew each cop well— there were only a dozen officers, two sergeants and the chief— and often was invited behind the front counter to swap small talk. On several occasions I got a call tipping me off to a breaking story.

The same camaraderie held true for the state troopers in Massena's two-man sub-station on the outskirts of town. Jim Smith, a short, barrel-chested strongman, and Walter Larkin, a slender Irishman with freckles, were always cooperative in giving us the routine stuff as well as an occasional tip. I well remember the day early in my first summer in Massena Jimmy and Walt, working on their regular coffee-and-Danish breakfast at the Silver Grill, asked me if I was going to the carnival local firemen were sponsoring in a field off East Orvis Street. When I

46

Massena's Main Street, looking south, circa 1937.

The same Main Street block looking north, circa 1942, showing the rebuilt Central Building, center. The Times bureau was in the Niagara Mohawk building at left, reached by a stairwell on the near side. The one-room office was in the near corner of the second floor, one window on the side, a double window in front. Town Hall is the large building to the right of the tree. The mayor's residence was between the two buildings.

said I'd been there twice that week, Jimmy suggested that I go again that night. I read that as a tip, and asked if 7:30 was early enough. "Sure," said Jimmy, in his tight-lipped Brooklyn semi-sneer, adding a wink. Sure enough, I was standing in front of the booth with the large spin-the-wheel when three troopers moved in from the darkness behind the tent, seized the cash box, exposed the foot pedal that controlled the wheel, and laid hands on an attendant trying to flee through a side exit. A short distance away I saw three more troopers occupying a booth with a roulette-type attraction. I enjoyed the spectacle, especially since no other reporter apparently had been tipped.

In all this fellowship the lone exception was Massena's chief of police. Darwin Shatraw not only avoided fraternization with his officers, but practiced what I like to call the Peacock Concept. He was so in love with his status and his uniform he habitually strutted and preened. He was a quiet man, perhaps 42, disciplined and formal. No one on the force had been to college,

Main Street in winter. Across the street are the town hall, mayor's house and Niagara Mohawk building housing the Times bureau.

but there was a suspicion that Shatraw's mental processes worked more slowly and absorbed less than most of the men under his command. His handwriting was somewhat juvenile, his written reports only semi-literate.

He was kind to me and often tried to make sure that my reporting reflected excellence and superior performance on the part of his department. In the enthusiastic pace of the daily routine I often was too busy or too distracted to rescue my car from the grasp of parking meters on Main Street or the municipal lot behind town hall, which led to a collection of parking tickets. Cops on the beat or at the desk regularly nullified them or, recognizing my battered gray Ford, overlooked the overtime and didn't write tickets as an accepted courtesy to the press. Chief Shatraw let the former go on for a while, but his tolerance had a limit.

On one of my several daily visitations to the police blotter on the counter, Shatraw summoned me into his private office. Here he showed me three sheets of lined yellow tablet paper, each covered with a listing of local citizens, laboriously composed in his familiar round handwriting. Opposite each name was a number.

This was, he explained in characteristic dignity, a tabulation of parking tickets issued to local residents. The figure "1" was most prevalent, occupying fully half the list. A goodly number were down for the figure 2, a dozen or so had a 3, and one unfortunate soul was pegged with the numeral 5. Midway on one list he placed his finger on the name Nathaniel Boynton, then moved it to the column on the right border of the sheet, where the number 15 was inscribed.

Such disregard of law and order, even for the privileged press, must stop, he declared, apparently setting the stage for some kind of negotiation. He permitted a short discussion of possible penalties before pronouncing sentence. "Come with me," he said, moving through the door.

He walked past the sergeant's desk, went around the counter and crossed the corridor to the door leading to the small block of jail cells. I had a moment of panic, but it passed briefly as my captor opened a closet exposing the janitor's mops and pails.

"Here," said Shatraw. "You clean this cellblock with soap and water, and I'll forget all those tickets. If you get more of them, I might not be so easy on you."

I accepted the terms and spent the next twenty minutes serving my penance. Pushing the mop I had to think that perhaps the chief wasn't as slow-witted as we believed. Harold Manning, Red Condon and the boys on the beat never let me hear the end of that humiliation.

*　　*　　*　　*　　*

By this time I was having so much fun in Massena it was hard to tell which part of life I enjoyed most—the job or free time. Was there a difference?

The daily rounds of news sources provided pleasant socializing with many nice people. Town hall alone often took most of the morning, what with the mayor, village clerk, public works, town clerk, town supervisor and others, then downstairs to police headquarters where there were many fresh tales to tell, printable and otherwise.

The municipal parking lot was behind the police station, at the foot of the sloping alley between town hall and the Observer office. Wherever I was in the evening, chances were I had left my car in that lot, which made it not only easy but habitual to drop by the police station after the movies, bowling or a few beers at Mittiga's or the Silver Grill. A quick check of the newest blotter entries, some chit-chat with the night sergeant and home to bed.

On one such evening I had been working later than usual at the office three doors up the street, and strolled through the station on the way to my car in the lot. Harold Manning, as usual, was on the desk. Charlie Clement, a tall stringbean of an officer who had the longest service on the force except for white-haired Sergeant Tom O'Neal, was there, and so was Red Condon, Harold's buddy and a good friend of mine.

After some banter I was scanning the log book when Harold said to Red: "Hey, do we have Nat's prints in the file?"

"Geez, I don't think so," said Red. "Maybe we ought to get 'em now."

"Good idea," said Harold. " Let's go."

I was startled. "What do you guys want my prints for, overtime parking?" I asked.

Red and Charlie were moving toward me. "Grab him!" barked Harold, and my arms were pinned tightly behind my back by two strong cops. They marched me over to the fingerprint inkpad on the side table. A forward push, a quick slide of the prisoner's zipper and in seconds the deed was done. There was laughter all around as they passed around the ink-blotch on the form.

"Put it on file, Charlie," ordered Harold with a wink and a broad smile.

*   *   *   *   *

Between light moments there were times when tragedy intruded. For me the most touching came on a warm Sunday night in August less than an hour after I had returned from a speedy non-stop drive of 225 miles and a weekend with my family in Geneva. It was late, my eyes were tired from five hours on the two-lane highways of the era, and I was in the office hurriedly writing stories from the weekend carbons Fred Holliday had pushed under the door. I was trying to finish before midnight, run the batch out to the railroad station in a baggage letter for the morning train and get home to bed. Suddenly the phone rang.

It was a jolt to get a call at that hour. It was Charlie Clement, practically next door at the police station. "Nat, there's an accident out on the Malone road near the village line, head-on, could be pretty bad. Get your camera and I'll swing by on my way."

I reached the curb just as Charlie's patrol car arrived. In minutes we were at the scene, two badly smashed cars on the side of the two-lane concrete, flashing lights from a state police cruiser. There were only two or three people other than Walter Larkin.

I was a step behind Charlie when he approached an inert body on the pavement and switched on his flashlight. To my horror I recognized his eldest son.

An ambulance was arriving, but Charlie said nothing. Nor could I. He walked a few steps to the darkness at the side of the road, took off his visored hat, and stared downward at the grassy bank that sloped up from the roadside. I still couldn't say anything. I just put my hand on his shoulder.

"Dear God, it will kill his mother," was all he said.

I told Walter, the state trooper who was waving traffic through with his flashlight. He instructed me to take Charlie home and pick up Red or whoever was at the station. Charlie got into the passenger side of the patrol car and I drove. Neither of us said a word.

Back at the scene with Red fifteen minutes later a small crowd had gathered. Larkin gave me a flashlight and I was helping to keep traffic moving when a carload of high school kids stopped to inquire what had happened. I recognized the driver, a prominent athlete, and told him there were two dead and two injured. He asked if I knew the names, and when I gave them there was a gasp from the back seat. It was too dark to recognize others in the car, not even Irene Clement, Charlie's daughter.

7

Serpents in the Garden

In the euphoria enveloping a young reporter with a news beat that embraced the northern third of St. Lawrence County, the most spacious of New York State's sixty-two, it was perhaps natural that there would be some sour notes. No one would accuse Massena of being a beautiful town or a charming village, nor was the flat countryside that stretched some forty miles from the St. Lawrence River to the Adirondack foothills anything other than dull, but the inhabitants were, for the most part, hardy, genuine and friendly. As an outgoing, energetic fellow, I quickly found myself with many friends of all ages, types sizes and stations in this peninsula of civilization. In direct contrast to the shock I felt that gray April Sunday upon seeing for the first time a drab, weatherbeaten hodgepodge, I now was blissfully in love with the whole town.

With eleven thousand reasonably permanent residents Massena in 1940 was one of the most populous villages, municipally speaking, in New York State, larger than several small cities. It occupied (and still does) that corner of the state where the Canadian border of the USA leaves the middle of the St. Lawrence River and heads east on an uninterrupted line all the way to Maine. Ogdensburg, a city of some sixteen thousand, was thirty-three miles down Route 37—down because the highway runs southwest, but actually upstream. Malone, which also had a city government despite a population under nine thousand, was forty-three miles to the east across the barren flats of the St. Regis Indian Reservation.

Both these small cities, along with the elm-shaded college towns of Potsdam and Canton to the south, were prototype upstate municipalities. They had orderly and compact business sections and comfortable residential areas that separated the large Colonial and Victorian houses and spacious lawns of the aristocracy from the middle and lower echelons of the so-called working classes.

Not so Massena. Unlike its neighbors, Massena was a mill town, dominated by a huge fabricating plant of the Aluminum Company of America, where steaming potlines turned bauxite and other raw materials into cast ingots of a critical industrial alloy. In the late twenties the big plant had transformed a rural hamlet into a boom town; the village had grown too fast to develop any semblance of traditional aristocracy. No one had ever given a thought to municipal planning. The result was a mishmash. The business section, consisting of several rows of stores crowded along a narrow main street, spilled over onto several side streets without noticeable pattern. Sprawling residential sections accommodating blocks of modest frame houses on small, orderly lots displayed a mix of architectural styles notable only as examples of mediocrity. It was hard to find more than three or four dwellings that might bespeak wealth or a link with aristocracy rooted in the early nineteenth century.

Down near the Grasse River, which bisected the village, there were rows of mill housing and tenements along the road to the Alcoa plant on the outskirts. Across the river to the north was the Pine Grove section with more jumbled residential areas and a few oases of business structures clustered to the west of the big Alcoa plant.

But in all those dwellings, from the modest houses in the older or "nicer" parts of town, to the newer low-cost residential developments there was a community spirit that far over-shadowed the obvious shortcomings in visual or traditional

54

attributes. It was a prosperous town; thanks to "the Alco" it had never known the Great Depression. Everybody worked at the plant or in local businesses. There was no social class distinction, no dividing line between millworker and jurist, merchant or clerk, doctor or cop, plant executive or plumber, bank president or schoolteacher. The county judge, stopping on the way home from his law office for a couple of shots of bourbon at the Silver Grill, socialized on even terms and first-name status with the owner of the elbow next to him at the bar, potline worker or shoe salesman. A prominent dentist was on the same bowling team as a day-shift worker, an electrician, a mail carrier and a bartender, and in the next alley a plant supervisor was bowling with a banker, a meatcutter, a store owner and a janitor. On weekday afternoons in the fall day-shift workers on the way home, lawyers, sales clerks, insurance agents and cops getting off duty would stop by the high school athletic field to watch fifteen or twenty minutes of football practice and exchange chit-chat of the day before heading home.

Massena had no hospital, no hotel, no airport. What purported to be a country club looked more like a farmhouse in a meadow waiting to be mown. There was only one movie theater, two undertaking parlors, one department store, one drug store and two men's clothing stores. Thanks to the plant, the population had an active Armenian community, which worshipped at the Episcopal church, and a far larger French-Canadian population, which contributed heavily to the village's two large Catholic parishes. The largest Protestant church was the Emmanuel Congregational Church on West Orvis Street. Here young conservatives enjoyed the spectacle of prominent husbands from teetotaling households absent-mindedly hoisting and belting in their pew seats the tiny communion vials of Welch's grapejuice in the manner of downing a shot glass of Four Roses at John Pialoglous's varnished bar at the Silver Grill.

All these people were my newfound friends. On my news-gathering rounds I criss-crossed Main Street a dozen times a day, chatted with people entering or leaving town hall offices or the police station, taking a coffee break at the Sweet Shoppe or a coke break at Kinney's drug store. Each morning I looked in on the two banks, fire house and Saul Rosenbaum's department store. All that was part of the news beat; if anything was happening, or about to happen, in town, one of these people would say something to tip me off to a story.

As the days got warmer and the town began to take on a more spruced-up appearance after the long North Country winter, it was inevitable that I would run into some roadblocks on the job. I was only a rookie on the news beat, but I also was aware that there were people in this world who tried to keep stories out of the papers, or who tried to hide or cover important facts, but in Watertown and in the first few weeks in Massena I had not enountered any such circumstance. That is, until I came head-to-head with a corporate giant, the mighty Aluminum Company of America.

The huge fabricating plant that dominated Massena's social, political and economic life from the outskirts was, in my view, a veritable mother-lode of news stories. I introduced myself and my function to the local plant management through a Mr. Volz, who I learned was the man to contact for any and all information.

Volz was a pleasant enough fellow whose main function was to see that no information of any kind ever got out of the plant and into the papers. He was the gatekeeper and guardian who insulated the plant manager, Raymond Whitzel, from any public exposure.

The plant derived most of its power from hydroelectric generators in a canal that diverted water from the churning rapids of the St. Lawrence, emptying the flow into the Grasse River and thence back to the St. Lawrence. When I learned from one of my friends that a problem had developed in the powerhouse, I called Volz for details. To my astonishment, he said he knew nothing about it. When I pressed him, he conceded that there were a few minor changes being made, all routine.

That evening I went back to my powerhouse buddies, one of whom was a young engineer on the management training program, and got the full details. Another call to Volz and another polite brushoff. I felt the story was accurate and factual, so I ran it, mentioning that plant officials said the work was routine maintenance and declined to give details.

Massena officials at a ceremony marking the transformation of a nearby meadow into an airfield of sorts. Mayor Newton is in left center, Supervisor Allan P. Sill second from left, and Raymond T. Whitzel, Alcoa plant superintendent, second from right.

A day later I had a call from Whitzel himself. I had met him just once, at a Chamber of Commerce dinner at which he was the speaker, a pompous man with a face that showed too much nose and too many teeth and a waist measurement that showed too many pounds. He was less than impressive.

His call to the young reporter in the Watertown Times bureau was formal and direct with only a slight touch of paternalism. I should have it clearly understood, he told me, that nothing— repeat, nothing— about the aluminum plant should appear in my paper short of a wedding story or an obituary. With a major war in Europe, he explained, it was imperative in the interest of national security that no information of any kind concerning the plant be released. When I told him I was a patriot as well as a reporter and had high professional ethics in the performance of my job with the Times, he didn't appear to get my message, to wit, that I would continue to report what I felt was important and legitimate.

During the remainder of my two-year tenure in Massena Whitzel and I observed a fragile truce. He was the baronial lord of the manor, I the undisciplined maverick among the serfs— a renegade beyond the ken of his control. Although several of my later stories displeased him, we did not have another clash.

* * * * *

The Whitzel flap was one of several that underlined the precept that in the function of a newspaper reporter strained relations often came with the franchise. The arrival of spring brought the baseball season to the North Country and I had done a preview story on the Massena Alcos team in the upcoming Northern League semi-pro baseball season. I had also done a feature piece on George Miner, the new manager, who had at one time managed one of the Yankees' minor league clubs and was being imported from Binghamton to run the Alcos.

The president and business manager of the community team was Tom Fay, Massena postmaster. Two days before the opening game I mentioned during a regular news-beat call on Fay at the postoffice that I would be needing press credentials to cover the games. To my amazement Tom informed me that I would have to buy a ticket like everybody else.

I pointed out that it was customary to provide reporters covering sports events not only with courtesy passes, but also with access to the clubhouse, manager and players at appropriate times before and after a game. Fay said he couldn't do any of those things. He explained that the baseball enterprise depended on public support, and that if I wanted to see the games I could get in line at the boxoffice.

Would he have any objection, under those circumstances, if I were to find I didn't have time to cover the games personally? Not at all, he said, I could always find someone, he was certain, to give me the scores. Fine, I replied. Since the Times policy did not

58

require coverage of Massena bowling and softball leagues other than on a voluntary basis, I explained, I now saw no reason to write about Northern League baseball. However, I assured him that I would attend a few games if I could. We left it at that.

The no-ticket-no-coverage theorem, however, bothered me greatly, not only as a passionate baseball fan, but as a newsman. It was one thing to bypass bowling and softball, especially with space limitations in the Massena edition, but quite another to boycott a baseball team playing such arch rivals as Malone, Plattsburgh, Ogdensburg and Saranac Lake. I didn't want to have my problem sound like a threat, but Fay was dead wrong, and something had to be done.

A word to Miner and another to a bank vice president who was a prime booster and investor, and a pass was delivered to my office. My subsequent relations with Tom Fay were fairly cool, but when we did have commerce the dialogues were efficient and we were able to co-exist without further conflict.

*   *   *   *   *

Having fast semipro baseball at Alco Field was a special bonus. I enjoyed covering the games, and several of the players, all of whom were imported from elsewhere, became good friends of mine. With the exception of the manager, only one of the players was married. The team played twilight ball, which meant they had to idle away most of the day. They were my age or slightly younger, and five or six of them fell into the habit of dropping into the Times bureau.

They would drift in about 1 p.m., and since that was past my deadline, I enjoyed batting the breeze with them. I thought they enjoyed hanging around the office, too, until I realized the chief attraction was not so much talking with a sportswriter as perching on the window sill of the front windows, which were always open on warm afternoons, and peering down on low-cut blouses of pretty girls passing below or, better yet, girls entering the Niagara Mohawk office directly underneath.

One of the most faithful devotees of this birds-eye view was a strapping six-foot-three outfielder from Syracuse University named Jim Konstanty. Like many of the players Konstanty was striving to pick up "expense money" in the summer to help with fall tuition. He was a handsome fellow with a broad smile who had been with the rival Malone Maroons the previous season, but had been dropped when Pappy Smith, his manager, had to cut down because of low gate receipts. Konstanty had deeply resented Pappy's attempt to comfort him by saying, "I gotta keep my pitchers, Jim, and play 'em in the outfield between starts." I knew Pappy, whose regular employment was as manager of a bowling emporium in Massena, and it was easy to picture him doing this.

Konstanty said he tried to convince Pappy that he was indeed a pitcher and a good one, but to no avail. With that background information, I got a huge chuckle the day those two bitter Route 37 rivals, Malone and Massena, played a Sunday doubleheader before an overflow crowd at Alco Field. Konstanty went to George Miner, who was unaware of this item of history, and begged him to let him pitch one of the games. The teams were tied for first place, and Miner, knowing the emotion in the stands, was skeptical, but when he heard the anecdote he agreed to give Jim the second game if Massena won the first game.

The Alcos came through, and when the second game got underway the crowd was surprised to see an outfielder go to the pitching mound. Their doubts quickly turned to joy as big Jim began firing fastballs and sharp curves. He struck out two in the first inning, and two more swinging at third strikes in the next inning. At the end of each inning he would stride off the mound, glaring over his shoulder at Pappy Smith on the Malone bench. "Gotta keep my pitchers, Jim," he would taunt his former manager. In this emotional fervor he shut out the Maroons on one hit on a day Pappy Smith wished there had been a tunnel under the bench big enough to hide in.

Ten years later I was privileged to have a press ticket to the 1950 World Series in Philadelphia. The surprise choice as the Phillies starting pitcher in the opening game was Jim Konstanty, who had set a major league record for relief appearances and relief victories and had been voted the National League's Most Valuable Player that season. The series start was his reward. I had a moment to chat with him before the game, thanks to my press pass, and reminded him of the Pappy Smith incident. He remembered it well, and laughed at the recollection of those lovely Massena cleavages as viewed from the window sill of the Times office. Moments later his concentration reverted to the New York Yankees, and when the game got underway, he lost a brilliant six-hitter to Vic Raschi and the Yankees, 1-0.

8

Conning the Cops

Apart from moments of levity and tragedy, things were quiet on the police beat in the northernmost corner of St. Lawrence County that first summer, and I found myself enjoying every facet of life in Massena. It had taken only a few months for me to realize that I had the best newspaper job in New York State, and even the foreboding and often devastating news of the war in Europe failed to dent enthusiasm that seemed boundless.

There was no end of story possibilities. Life was so abundant in this spirited town with so many friends that I found it difficult to separate the fun on the job from recreational fun during free time. The fighting in Europe seemed far distant despite the prospect that Congress had set a date for a military draft registration of U.S. males aged 18-29.

Perhaps that summer was the lull before the storm. One of the first of several imbroglios involved no less a character than Darwin Shatraw, chief of police in Massena and the often-insulated boss of my friends on the force. When Shatraw embarked on a venture that was far from humorous, it caused repercussions all over town, and this Times reporter found himself in the middle of it.

It started with a fast-talking promoter who came to town to sell a sure-fire fund-raising scheme to whatever community agency would listen to his pitch. He quickly found an eager prospect in Chief Shatraw.

The visiting artist identified himself as Scoop Kennedy, and presented a long list of credentials and triumphs. As a professional promoter Kennedy would put on a gala dance, for which ticket sales and patronage of local businesses would generate substantial revenue that could be applied for community benefit.

Shatraw saw immediately that this was the perfect vehicle for realizing his fondest dream, a radio system for his small-department. In 1940 only large and sophisticated municipal and state police units had the fiscal clout to install radio communication in patrol cars. Now such a luxury seemed within reach of little Massena. Why not a festive Policemen's Ball?

Shatraw had an equally enthusiastic ally in the mayor. No resident of this remote outpost spent more time and energy boosting the Incorporated Village of Massena than Mayor Rollin A. Newton. In short order Kennedy sold Shatraw, Shatraw sold the mayor, the mayor sold the village board, and the fund drive was official.

Despite Shatraw's passion for promenading, no one in Massena had more frequent or higher visibility than Mayor Newton. He had lived in Massena all his life. He was in his sixties, a dentist by profession whose residence, appropriately, was next door to the town hall. This resemblance to a church-rectory configuration, however, was coincidental— the house had been in his wife's family a generation before Rollie became mayor.

In this bulky frame dwelling only a few feet from the sidewalk on Main Street's primary commercial block Dr. Newton lived with his wife and, in facilities on the first floor, administered to his patients. A spacious veranda extended the width of the front, protected by a spindled railing. In comfortable weather an occupant of the porch, installed in a rocking chair overlooking the low wooden railing that separated the porch from the sidewalk, had a fifty-yard-line seat for the

This photo of a war bond rally in 1942 shows Mayor Newton's house on Main Street between town hall and the Niagara Mohawk building, which housed the Times bureau. Note the full veranda.

passing scene. No pedestrian hurrying on errands to the town hall, Niagara Mohawk office or nearby stores could escape even a brief dialogue with the ebullient mayor.

Rollie's advanced years had left him with bent shoulders, a slow gait, and a weatherbeaten face that featured bushy gray eyebrows. When he talked, which was most of his waking hours, his lips hardly moved, with the result that his words and sentences were mumbled rather than spoken. Even when he raised his voice for emphasis his consonants were slurred, emerging as softly and as unintelligible as the vowels.

An overwhelming percentage of the mayor's utterances, whether in public or private discourse, was devoted to his life-consuming dedication to bringing the St. Lawrence Seaway and Power Project to reality. The river, practically in his back yard, poured millions of gallons of fresh water into the flying spray and churning whitecaps of the Long Sault (pronounced Soo) Rapids just beyond the village limits. For many years the St. Lawrence had been viewed, not only locally but in Washington

In later years the north end of Dr. Newton's veranda was usurped to provide more room for his dental practice.

and major Great Lakes ports, as the logical route for a waterway that would bring ocean freighters deep inland. At the same time the volume and force of its flow, matched on this continent only by the Columbia River, provided a potential source of hydroelectric power that rivalled the Grand Coulee in the State of Washington. The project had been an obsession with Mayor Newton, and now that the U.S. Corps of Engineers had, in early 1940, established a field office for an authoritative three-year engineering survey of the site, culmination of his hopes and dreams seemed near.

Chief Shatraw's full espousal of Scoop Kennedy's scheme was one of the rare items that was able to divert the mayoral mind from the Seaway. Rollie endorsed the venture with delight and set up a formal presentation to the village board. Approval

was automatic. Almost overnight Kennedy was given office space in the town hall and provided with secretarial help.

In the weeks that followed the newspaper announcements and the first community-wide promotional mailing, the upcoming Policemen's Ball was the hottest conversational item in town. Patients entrapped in Dr. Newton's chair reported that even the practitioner himself, whose non-stop vocal ramblings regularly extended a normal one-hour appointment to an hour and a half, had permitted the dance project to get nearly equal time with the Seaway.

But the flamboyant Kennedy, putting the arm on local businesses and citizens with big-city tactics, found it wasn't all smooth sailing. The Big Band Era was still in full swing. Teenagers and young adults regularly and willingly paid a full dollar for tickets to dances in the large ballroom upstairs in the town hall featuring North Country bands playing hit tunes popularized by Tommy Dorsey, Benny Goodman, Artie Shaw, Glenn Miller and Bunny Berrigan. They had even splurged two dollars a couple when Ina Ray Hutton, a sexy blonde in a strapless gown of shimmering silver, led her touring all-girl swing band into Massena for a one-night stand that packed the hall.

Kennedy had set the price for his extravaganza at two dollars. To Massena's grass-root populace that was steep enough for the nationally known and provocative Ina Ray, let alone some band from nearby Potsdam or Canton. But the Kennedy formula also included a high-powered mailing to a selected list of prominent merchants and businessmen, professional people, political and civic leaders, and plant executives. Enclosed in each envelope was a pair of five-dollar patron tickets. The letter, signed by Chief Shatraw, asked for a ten-dollar check made out to the Massena Police Benevolent Association. Additional tickets were also available.

The turbulent Long Sault Rapids of the St. Lawrence were unharnessed during my Massena tenure, but later became the site of the St. Lawrence Seaway and Robert Moses Power Project.

67

The intrepid promoter had picked the wrong town for this sort of badger. Reaction from the targeted elite ranged from guarded grumbling to open outrage. A good number of people on the list sent checks, whether or not they were going to the ball, grudgingly conceding the merit of the cause or accepting it as a gouge that was easier to submit to than protest.

None in the sponsoring triumvirate of Shatraw, Newton and Kennedy or the volunteers on the citizen committee bothered to anticipate how the uniformed men on the force, who comprised the membership of the local Police Benevolent Association (PBA), would take all this. It soon became apparent the cops didn't want any part of it. The uniforms apparently had gone along with Shatraw's scheme in the beginning, mainly because they saw no alternative, but they had second thoughts when they found themselves subjected to jesting remarks on Main Street every time they stood beside a parked car writing out a ticket for an overtime violation. There was always a pedestrian or two on the sidewalk who would offer an observation such as "Hey, Harold, whazza matter? Didn't he buy any tickets to the ball?" followed by raucous laughter. It was all in fun, but to the cops it was not amusing. After a week of this there was action.

I was covering a regular meeting of the Massena Village Board one Wednesday evening, seated in a corner of the board room taking notes of the proceedings and discussion. It was a well-established routine, and proceeded in the dull, familiar pattern until a cadre of seven Massena police officers entered the small chamber in full uniform. Since the board table occupied most of the room, there was space only for four or five straight wooden chairs along one wall, forcing the visitors to stand shoulder-to-shoulder behind the seats of board members on the near side. As they took their places in front of me, I found myself peering through a narrow opening between the bulky hips of Harold Manning and Red Condon, two large men wearing sidearms in holsters. With this wall of blue-clad humanity blocking my view, I had to hunch forward to observe.

Sergeant Manning, my good friend who had taken me bass fishing in the St. Lawrence several times, was the spokesman. He apologized to the mayor and board for the unscheduled intrusion, and explained the reason. The membership of the Massena PBA, he announced, had voted to disassociate themselves and the organization from any connection or alliance with the upcoming Policemen's Ball. Further, the PBA was no longer to be listed as a sponsoring organization. The sergeant was careful to explain that the PBA was unanimously in favor of a police radio system, but did not approve the current method of fund-raising, implying that selling tickets was one thing, Kennedy's tactics another.

Manning's words hit the board like an exploding grenade. The mayor was thunderstruck. For a moment it seemed everyone at the table wanted to speak. Suddenly one of the trustees in the far corner panicked in the hubbub. "Are there any reporters here?" he shouted, knowing very well I was in my usual chair near the wall.

"Yes," he was told as Harold and Red moved apart to reveal the countenance of the Times chronicler. "In that case," the trustee continued, "I move that the board declare this a closed meeting, retroactive to the beginning of the agenda, and that the village clerk be authorized to issue a statement to the press tomorrow morning."

In a trice the motion was passed by unanimous vote. All eyes turned to me. My friend Walter Clark, village engineer who doubled as clerk of the board, opened the door to the hallway, looking somewhat uncomfortable. I made a prompt exit, but not before catching a wink from Harold Manning, as if to say, I'll-fill-you-in-later.

Outside in the hall my mind was racing. How could a board do this? Was it legal procedure to declare an open meeting closed retroactively? What is the ground rule that enables a public governmental body to hold an executive session? Here I was, with a pocketful of notes and quotes, sitting on the hottest local story since the Central Building fire, probably even hotter. Was it privileged material? My instinct told me to write the story regardless, but what kind of legal trouble would I get into, and get my paper into, if I did? This was a new experience, and in my first newspaper job a hundred miles from my nearest colleague, I was in a quandary.

I walked half a block to Andrews Street and ordered a beer to sort things out in my mind. It was still early in the evening, just a few minutes after 8. I reluctantly decided that this was serious enough to do what I had hoped I'd never have to do, call Gordon Bryant for counsel. After all, I had been in Massena all spring and summer, writing stories every day on my own without ever having to ask for anything from my mentor, that gruff old bear city editor. The last thing I wanted was to admit I didn't know how to handle a delicate situation. But then, suppose I got the paper into a sensitive legal situation?

I played one game on the pinball machine while finishing the beer, and decided to risk a call to Bryant. I knew he would still be in the city room on Arcade Street tapping out his regurgitated copy for the Herald-Journal. I had not spoken to him since leaving Watertown six months earlier.

"Gordon, this is Nat Boynton in Massena. I've got— "

"Bucko! How are you?"

"Fine, Gordon. Listen, I have— "

"You got a story?"

"Yeh, but— "

"Then write it. Say, how you getting along up there? Got a girlfriend?"

"Gordon, listen, on this story— "

"Write it. You going out with anybody up there?"

"Well, yeah, but— "

"That's good. You're doing fine, Bucko."

"Gordon, please— "

"See you. Write the story for tomorrow. We'll probably need it."

And he was gone. Typical Bryant. If you have a story, write it. If somebody gives you trouble, the hell with them. The story comes first. He didn't want to hear anything about my problem. Write the story.

Did I really expect him to say anything different? I hiked back to the Times bureau, unlocked the door, switched on the lights, scanned the scribbled notes from the board meeting, and wrote the lead. I called the police dispatcher and left a call for Harold Manning. He called back before I had finished, so I included a few more quotes, put the story in a baggage master envelope, took it out to the railroad station and went home.

The story was self-explanatory, but I half expected Bryant or Homer or some deskman in Watertown to call me. No one did. They played the story in a top spot in the Massena edition, and the next day it was a hot conversation piece on Main Street.

It also brought personal and professional repercussions. On my morning rounds the day after the story broke I got an earful of flack from both Mayor Newton and Chief Shatraw. Shatraw took a degree of pleasure in showing me a memo he had just typed for the department, signed by the mayor, notifying all police personnel that henceforth access to the police blotter and other police information was being denied the Watertown Times and its reporter until further notice.

Banned from the police station! A miscreant should be that lucky, never a newspaper reporter. But Harold Manning and the boys loved every printed word. They gleefully suggested I drop by between 10 and 11 each night, and if the blotter just happened to be lying on the counter, well, they were just too busy to put it in a safe place. Accordingly, the flow of police news to the Times was uninterrupted. Sergeant Manning confided a few days later that when Shatraw asked him how these items were getting into the Times, he told the chief he guessed Boynton was picking them up from the Post-Standard. Anyone comparing the two papers could easily see through that fabrication, but not Shatraw. He just shook his head and let it go, said my informant.

The mayor's anger lasted only a few days, if that. By the weekend my villainy had been crowded out of his mind by fresh municipal developments, some new Seaway gossip and other local items. The news embargo downstairs was never rescinded; it was so promptly and widely ignored it didn't have to be.

A few weeks later, on November 30, the gala ball played to a modest house, large enough to make a substantial profit. For a while I watched for an official financial statement, but it was delayed. Late in December Shatraw submitted his report to the village board, but there were many holes in it. The board not only rejected it, but pushed an investigation for a full accounting. It turned out that Kennedy had been promised a fee of three

Massena Board to Probe Police Dance Expenses; Report Is Not Accepted

Ohio Man Who Handled Benefit Affair May Be Summoned in Clearing Up Charges of Solicitations— Discrepancies in Expense Account Cited.

Massena Bureau
Watertown Daily Times

Massena, Jan. 10.—Detailed investigation into the expenses of the benefit dance staged by the Massena police department last Nov. 30 will be made by the village board following a special meeting in the town hall last night. The financial report of Police Chief Darwin D. Shatraw, submitted to the board two weeks

This story was the last of several on the controversial Police Ball. The first article, which caused the mayor and chief to react, could not be found in the Times's voluminous files, and I didn't keep any clippings personally.

hundred dollars by Shatraw, but apparently got out of town with a lot more than that.

In January the board neatly extricated itself from the mess. It issued a statement to the effect that the chief had "acted as an individual" in retaining a professional promoter whose campaign "aroused much comment." The board explained to the public that because the chief's records were incomplete, "it was necessary to render an accounting partially from memory." There was no contract with Kennedy, just a verbal agreement. The incident also attracted the attention of the St. Lawrence County district attorney, who started his own investigation. Some time later the DA dropped it because he was unable to find Kennedy.

As for the police radio, there were not enough funds to cover the cost, and the village had to wait a while longer before other methods were found to finance the inevitable system.

9

Chill From the Draft

A full year before the infamy at Pearl Harbor embroiled the nation in the European war I had a military altercation of my own in remote, peaceful Massena. My reportorial scrapes with R.T. Whitzel, the arrogant feudal baron who felt he could control what could or could not be written in the press, and with Tom Fay, the postmaster whose self-esteem was almost as great as Whitzel's, were mild compared with the fourteen-carat rift that developed between the Times and the chairman of the newly installed Massena draft board. That one was permanent; it was intact when I left Massena nearly a year and a half later, and I assume my protagonist, Philip H. Falter, bore it to his eternal resting place.

The first nationwide Selective Service registration since World War I was a momentous event. Some of the boys had already started to enlist, assuming that the expanding war would soon embrace the U.S. Along with several million of my American male contemporaries between the ages of 18 and 29, I dutifully complied with the nationwide draft registration on October 16, 1940.

A few weeks later there was excitement and apprehension as the first numbers were drawn from a highly publicized fishbowl in Washington, D.C. I had a low number, which meant an early call. As local boards set to the task of screening, poking, prodding and testing each registrant in the giant lottery, I was summoned for a physical exam. To the surprise of no one, especially Dr. Philip Mardon of Massena who discovered how myopic I was, I was classified 1-B, which meant single, the right age and eligible, but physically disqualified. At the time the war in Europe seemed far away, and like a vast majority of my generation, I tended to harbor isolationist sentiments. To me the military had no appeal whatsoever, and I was delighted when I realized the feeling was reciprocated.

Apart from personal politics there were reportorial responsibilities. Draft board appointments made news, as did policy announcements and procedural statements issued by state headquarters in Albany. My relations with the board's chairman, Philip H. Falter, during this time were friendly, at least as friendly as anyone's with a man who cloistered himself with the town's small circle of the proudest and most affluent families. What little aristocracy Massena had was concentrated in the Falters, Masons and one or two other households.

Falter had been a high-echelon Aluminum Company executive, and currently was president of the Massena Bank and Trust Company. He was aloof, cool, proud, polite when he had to be, and had minimal commerce with the rank-and-file. The accepted explanation was that he apparently felt he should be living in Scarsdale or Montclair rather than in relative exile in a place like Massena. His daughter, Phyllis, a quiet, extremely nice girl whom I had known slightly in my mid-teens when both of us lived in New Jersey, had been married in Massena that summer, and I had had a fine time at her wedding reception at what passed for a country club, happy to have been invited. That was, however, before the upstart reporter incurred the wrath of the elder statesman, father of the bride.

As the town's prime dignitary, Falter was tendered, and accepted, the chairmanship of the local draft board. He immediately devoted much of his bank time to the little office above Westcott's stationery store on Main Street that served as headquarters for Local Board 413. I established the somewhat gloomy but adequate little office as part of the daily news beat, and wrote routine stories for several months until the storm broke a week before Christmas.

I was brushing my teeth at 7:15 that Monday morning when Mrs. Warner, my ultra-conservative landlady, called to me from downstairs. I was stunned to have a phone call in the quiet rooming house on Clark Street, and anticipated some kind of crisis. I was relieved to find it was only Dominic Pepp, calling from the city room in Watertown.

He got right to the point. State headquarters in Albany, he said, had just released the quotas assigned each upstate local board for the first contingent of draftees. The early morning story on the AP wire, he explained, listed the number of men in each contingent, dates of departure and destination: the new induction center at Fort Niagara. Dominic said he was alerting each Times bureau to immediate action. Massena's quota was twelve, and my instructions were to get the names of Board 413's first dozen registrants with 1-A classifications and wire them by Western Union immediately.

Driving downtown I spotted Mr. Falter in his Brooks Brothers herringbone coat striding along the sidewalk on Andrews Street heading for his bank. I pulled over, rolled down the window, and offered him a ride. When he climbed in, I mentioned that I was coming to see him right after breakfast because the Times had asked for the list of names in the first draft quota. I was not prepared for his violent reaction.

"Twelve?" he exclaimed. "Twelve? Why, we only have six 1-A's so far!"

"That's all right," I said. "We can just list those names and I'll send them in with an explanation...."

"Absolutely not! We've had no word whatsoever from Albany. I strongly doubt what you're saying. The newspapers in their haste to print news are seldom accurate."

When I dropped him off downtown (in Massena it was called "downstreet") I mentioned that the notice from headquarters would probably be in the morning mail, and I would come around in another hour. He just grunted, and exited in a huff.

Breakfast at the Sweet Shoppe with the usual assemblage of bachelor friends, a quick check of police, troopers, fire station and trusty Fred Holliday for any overnight breaking news and obits, and it was time to get back to Falter.

His short temper was well known in the community, but I had never seen it. This time I did. He was adamant. Nothing in the mail. He was furious at me, or at the Times. No, he would not release the names. Again I suggested he give them out, if for no other reason than to avoid embarrassment alongside the lists from Canton, Ogdensburg and Gouverneur. That infuriated him. "This board," he declared emphatically, "has had no notification of the first quota. Until such time as we receive official orders from our regional headquarters, no names will be divulged."

That was a good enough quote for me, and I included it in the terse three-paragraph story I wired to Watertown. It appeared on the back page of the North Country edition that afternoon, along with the lists of names from neighboring boards. The next morning I had an angry call from Falter, accusing me of betraying a confidence and telling me that I was no longer welcome at the draft board office. He hung up before I could say a word.

A confidence! What confidence? Falter must have known he was speaking to a newspaperman, and there had been no mention of "off-the-record."

I passed that off as a misunderstanding that would disappear in the course of future developments. It was clear that Selective Service in Albany was the basic culprit, releasing the first quotas to the wire services before notifying local boards. It did not occur to them that whereas the mail took overnight, the AP and UP teletypes needed only a few minutes to flash the word across the state. Fortunately most of the boards did not react as vigorously as did the chairman of No. 413.

One afternoon a week later Fred Holliday, the Syracuse Post-Standard man and a fellow conspirator on the news beat, cruised into the Times bureau with his infectious good cheer and bouncy gait. The names of the twelve have been released, he announced, handing me a sheet of paper. "Here's yours."

It was Tuesday, publication day for the semi-weekly local paper. "Let's go down to the Observer first," I said. "I want to check something."

Sure enough, the Observer had the full story in print. Falter had given Leonard Prince the release and had held up the other papers until the Observer was on the street.

When we made separate calls to Falter, he honored Fred's complaint but refused to talk to me. I wrote a personal report to my superiors in Watertown, and it was Harold B. Johnson, editor and publisher of the Times, who took action by writing a restrained letter to Falter. That effort and subsequent correspondence seeking to restore friendly relations failed to budge the angered bull, and by mid-January Mr. Johnson, the personification of a general calm and unruffled under fire, had run out of patience. He went to the top in Albany.

Falter had rejected the publisher's premise that the draft board and the newspaper were public agencies committed to keeping the populace informed, but Brigadier General Ames T. Brown, Governor Lehman's choice to head Selective Service in New York State, did not. The general dispatched a peacemaker to Massena. His designated referee spent an hour with me and another at the draft board across the street. Falter got rid of him by agreeing to restore cooperation, and after a stopover at Watertown, the mediator returned to Albany confident the crisis had been resolved.

When the next draft contingent was announced, however, the discriminatory pattern prevailed unchanged. H.B. had done everything he could to support his beleaguered reporter, and it was obvious the next move should come from the Massena bureau. A few weeks later the opportunity for a new challenge presented itself.

Falter, for all his reputation for tantrums and arrogance, was a capable executive, and he had succeeded in getting the draft process at Local Board 413 rolling on schedule. When Albany decreed in March that the April quota would not be the usual ten, twelve or fifteen draftees but the astounding total of forty-eight, the news hit like a bomb. Every registrant who had taken a physical, and even those far down the list who hadn't yet been called, suddenly realized that this was it; his time had come. Who could escape such a huge conscription?

To me it was an opportunity to mount a fresh assault on Falter's fortress. I asked the ebullient Fred Holliday, whose acceptance of the favoritism shown the Observer kept him on good terms with Falter's operation, to tip me off the moment the board released the names of the selected forty-eight. Until that story broke, Massena would be living under the Sword of Damocles.

Fred, of course, complied in high glee. When the sword fell he rushed into the Times bureau through a heavy snowfall to announce that the list was out. I put on my hat, coat and galoshes and went across the street to address the guillotine.

When I pushed open the office door at the top of the dingy stairs, Corky McCullough, a personable girl we often saw at dances and parties, looked up from her desk and gasped. Corky was the typist for Harry Little, an insurance man who was clerk of the board. Both were well aware of the incendiary situation at hand. I asked to see Mr. Falter, but he had seen me from the inner office and came forward.

"What are you doing here?"

"I understand there's a news release, and I've come for the Watertown Times copy."

"There will be no release for the Watertown Times, and if that's your hat on the file cabinet, please take it with you when you leave."

He turned and went back to his office without another word as Corky, sympathetic to both her boss and her friend, looked on in nervous confusion. Harry, who had been standing there helplessly, gave me a mournful look that said, hey, I'd give you the release, but you know what would happen.

I returned to the Times bureau, typed out a report of the incident, and dictated the eviction story to the rewrite slot on Bryant's copydesk. It was Homer who took the dictation. I knew it would be shown to H.B. on the spot.

The final edition that afternoon had a 6-head on its lead story:

STATE TO PROBE
MASSENA BOARD

Immediate Investigation Will be Launched. Reporter Ordered From Office.

The city staff had done a complete job. H.B. had called General Brown. General Brown was quoted as stating that he

DAILY TIMES.

DRAFT QUOTA IS 12 IN MASSENA

Mssena, Dec. 19.—Only six of the January quota of twelve assigned to Massena local draft board, 413, have completed physical examinations for the selective service call, it was learned this morning. Reports from blood tests on a number of other eligible draftees classified in 1-A have not yet been received.

Philip H. Falter, chairman of the Massena draft board, refused to disclose the names of the six draftees that have already completed their physical examinations preparatory to being drafted in January. Falter said:

"This board has had no notification of the first quota. Until such time as we receive official orders from our regional headquarters regarding the quota, no names will be divulged."

STATE TO PROBE MASSENA BOARD

Immediate Investigation Will Be Launched by Selective Service Director

DRAFT OFFICIALS REFUSE TO GIVE OUT LIST OF TRAINEES

ONLY ONE OUT OF 540 IN STATE THAT REFUSES COOPERATION

REPORTER ORDERED FROM OFFICE

Action Taken by Philip H. Falter, Chairman of Board, Who Also Warns Reporter Not to Return —General Ames T. Brown Calls Refusal to Give Names Breach of Public Faith

By KENNETH R. FOBER

Brigadier General Ames T. Brown, state director of selective service, will begin an immediate investigation to determine why the Massena draft board, the only one out of 540 in the state, persists in its refusal to furnish all newspapers with the names of young men called into military service.

The Times has been unable to get any names from the Massena

This was the lead back-page story (with a 6-head) in Watertown the day I got thrown out of the draft office a hundred miles to the north. At left is the little piece that started all the trouble.

80

was getting tired of complaints about Massena. There were more than 450 local draft boards in the state, he told H.B., and the Massena board was the only one to "consistently and flagrantly" refuse to cooperate with the public press. I had earned several by-lines during my first year in Massena, but here was the first time my name had appeared in a Times news story.

The state investigator had enough clout to enforce a satisfactory compromise. Draft board releases were to be delivered to the Times bureau at the same time they were made available to the other papers. The clerk of the board would serve as spokesman to answer questions and provide information requested by reporters. This time the terms of the armistice were accepted and observed by both factions, Falter exempting himself from the channels of communication.

*   *   *   *   *

During the summer I was again called up for a draft physical as part of a routine procedure re-examining registrants previously classified 1-B. My classification was reaffirmed, freeing me to pursue my delightful employment with clean conscience.

On December 7 only one couple of the sixteen contemporaries who had gathered for a Sunday afternoon party at Tom and Pat Boak's apartment was married. We were celebrating Dick Gould's prize, a 24-pound turkey awarded to Johns Manville Corporation's Number One salesman in the Syracuse territory. Suddenly the festive spirit was dampened by the startling news that the United States had been attacked by Japan. The radio bulletins from Pearl Harbor were indelibly sobering. A full-scale war would change the lives of every American. Not one of us in the apartment that snowy evening was yet thirty years old, and each of us knew instantly that the impact would be most meaningful to our generation.

By 8 a.m. Monday, even before the U.S. Congress had formally declared war on Japan and Germany, more than a dozen young men were standing on the sidewalk in front of Westcott's store. When I got in line the draft board office upstairs hadn't yet opened. Soon Harry Little and Corky arrived to unlock the door, facing a busy day signing up registrants volunteering for immediate induction. Among them was a 24-year-old newsman, twice deferred on 1-B status, whose isolationist leanings had vanished overnight. The crowd in the draft board office that morning testified that a lot of others felt the same way.

10

Optical Delusion

For all its shortcomings Local Board 413 moved efficiently in handling the rush of registrants volunteering for induction in the days immediately following Pearl Harbor. Philip Falter, Harry Little and Corky McCullough didn't have to question whether the aspirants were motivated by patriotism or by recognition of the inevitable—the draft was going to get them sooner or later.

When it began to sink in, I realized that my impulsive decision to volunteer that fateful Monday morning was a combination of both, along with a smattering of pride and practicality. In any event, I soon found myself, after more than a year of gratitude for my 1-B exemption from a draft call, back in the center of Selective Service machinery.

I was twenty-four, single and otherwise in excellent condition when in January, 1942, barely a month after Pearl Harbor, the Massena draft board sent two busloads of registrants to Utica in chartered Greyhounds for physical exams. This was to be my third draft physical, the first conducted by the military itself and not by friendly local doctors. Dr. Mardon had told me only a few months before that my uncorrected vision was 20-600, and that the Army considered 20-800 officially blind. This time I wanted desperately to pass the exam, but the myopia was a problem.

On the 170-mile trip to the Utica Armory I rode with my good friend from the bowling league, Milt Landsman. Milt was thirty two years old and newly included in the registration process when the Army raised the draft age from twenty nine to thirty five. A meat-cutter by trade, Milt was facing his first draft physical. The second finger on his right hand had been sliced by an errant cleaver in the butcher shop years earlier, and the severed nerve had left him with a permanent ninety-degree crook in that digit. It did not prevent him from being one of Massena's top three bowlers and a nationally ranked rifle-shooting champion as well as several times St. Lawrence County champion. I had done a feature story on Milt's accomplishments and once covered a marksmanship demonstration in which he had excelled.

In the seat beside me on the long ride downstate (everything in New York State was "downstate" from Massena) Milt was uncharacteristically subdued. He kept picking nervously at his small dark moustache, and did not want to talk about the war or, as an unmarried man, the possibility of being drafted. He was unsympathetic to my determination to get into service.

In Utica the sleet stung our faces as we alighted in the National Guard parking lot. The lot was full of chartered buses from a wide area of Central New York. Inside, the Armory was crowded with potential draftees herded into large groups, handed forms on clipboards and ordered to disrobe. In the basement endless lines followed arrows like a life-size Uncle Wiggley board game, nude bodies shuffling along makeshift corridors from one testing booth to another— heart, blood, urine, teeth, knees, ears, eyes. Here I got the God-given break I had hoped for.

In a slow-moving line with scores of other naked males of all shapes and sizes in a corridor formed by sheets and blankets strung on overhead wires cordoning off the examining booths, I suddenly realized I was standing outside the eye test. Separated from it only by a thin bedsheet, I could hear every word of the litany inside: "Okay, sit here. Take off your glasses. Read the fourth line. Can you read the fifth line? Okay, put your glasses back on. Next."

It only took five or six such recitations for me to memorize not only the alleged fourth line but the fifth. When I came to bat, the chart, as expected, was an unreadable white blur, but I delivered the right answer for Line Four and put on a brief but effective act for Line Five, supplying a contrived hesitation partway through, then a nice little squint before finishing with what I knew was a perfect score. When the bored young technician pronounced the words, "Okay, next" without emotion, I knew the sting was a success.

By 4 p.m., back upstairs and fully clothed, we waited in line to hand completed forms to one of the five white-jacketed medical men handling final processing at a long table next to the exit. When my turn came, a doctor scanned my forms, stamped the four copies and signed his name without looking up. Was I his 200th of the day or the 400th? He gave me a methodical smile as he returned the sheaf. As I reached for the papers he suddenly jerked them back. "Hey, wait a minute. Let's see those glasses."

He tilted my horn-rims professionally, looked once again at the notations on the exam form, and shook his head. Of the five doctors at the table, I had drawn an ophthalmologist. "You got five lenses there," he said. "Go downstairs and get your eyes rechecked."

Back to the basement with its sheet-lined walkways, this time fully clad, I found the technician in the eye booth tidying up at the end of a long day. He was disgruntled to learn I needed a recheck. The liturgy was the same, however, and my memory was intact. Another squint with feigned hesitation on the fifth line and his annoyance was even plainer. "What the hell they sending you back for, anyway...." He signed the paper.

Upstairs the ophthalmologist stared at the signed note and looked at me in disbelief. "I don't get it. Do you want to be in the Army, son?"

"Sure," I said cheerfully.

"Alright, you're in. Far be it from me." And he signed the form and stamped it.

Outside the sleet had turned to wet snow and someone had already loaded a case of beer on the bus for the four-hour pull back north. In our seats Milt Landsman was feeling better. The

Army had unknowingly rejected one of New York State's champion marksmen for a permanently disabled finger on his right hand.

*   *   *   *   *

My subterfuge had worked. Seven weeks after the Utica junket the 7:05 morning train for Watertown and Syracuse—the same train that dependably carried my daily baggage letters to the Times—glided out of the New York Central station in Massena Springs. On a special coach on the rear of the train were twenty-six draftees from Board 413, soon to be joined by delegations from Potsdam, Canton, Gouverneur and other points along the line to Fort Niagara via Rochester and Buffalo.

Johnny Wilbur, a big pink-cheeked dairy farmer from North Lawrence, had been designated assistant leader of the Massena contingent. Nat Boynton, former Massena correspondent of the Watertown Times, was the appointed group leader. The chairman of the local board, one Mr. Falter, was not present at the ceremonial sendoff at the station. Harry Little, clerk of the board, did the honors.

II

The Military

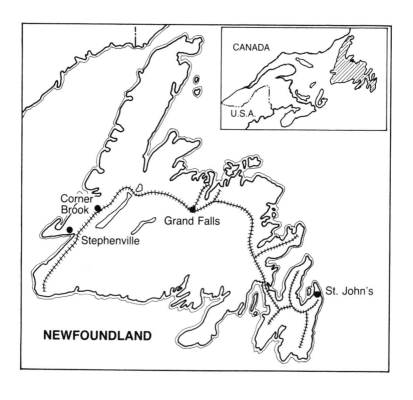

CANADA

U.S.A.

Corner
Brook

Grand Falls

Stephenville

St. John's

NEWFOUNDLAND

11

Stars in Stripes

Military bigwigs, historians, politicos and fiction writers have mined a rich vein in the gore and glory of major wars, but few have chronicled the unglamorous, mundane adventures of stalwarts in uniform serving far from combat zones.

In four years as a myopic draftee in a screwed-up U.S. Army during World War II, I never heard or saw a shot or shell fired anywhere other than a target range. The only time I was subjected to carbine instruction I managed only a few holes in my own target. When the drill instructor expressed surprise that Joe DiModica's target sheet on my immediate left had one too many punctures, I kept my mouth shut. If the Army had more marksmen like me they wouldn't put the target lanes so close to each other.

I entered the Army four months after the Pearl Harbor attack and was discharged four months after the war ended. Half of that duty was spent in continental USA, the other half on a remote North Atlantic airbase. There was little opportunity for valor or a show of courage, and no chance to be a hero under fire. The only time I saw an enemy soldier was when a group of captured German officers being flown to the U.S. for debriefing was permitted to leave the C-54 for a hot meal and a short walk on the tarmac during the brief refueling stop at our base in Newfoundland.

In my case the only real danger I encountered was as a flight engineer having to ride in planes for whose mechanical operation I was responsible while knowing little about such things as carburetion and manifold pressure.

En route to basic training in March, 1942 and awed by reports of American casualties in bloody fighting in distant theaters of war, I vowed to myself that if ever my substandard vision might pose a danger to my buddies or myself, such as sentry duty or night flying, I would turn myself in and confess the hoax. As it turned out, that was never necessary. The Army, unaware of being duped, could have sent me anywhere, but by divine gràce or pure luck, I completed my full service unscathed and relatively undetected, much of it on domestic flight status. I was honorably discharged with the rank of sergeant four months after V-J day following forty-six months of loyal, however undistinguished, service to my country.

The Army gave me a job for which I was totally unqualified; I performed it to the best of my ability, and it was not until the final few months of service that the powers of the militia permitted me to contribute in my chosen field, journalism. By that time the war was safely won. The fact that in my military career as an aircraft mechanic, flight engineer and aviation maintenance specialist I was advanced in rank three times shows how fouled-up the Army really was.

* * * * *

In those first few months of wartime USA the draft machinery was stepped up to high acceleration. At Army induction centers across the nation the classification of thousands of draftees a day became a giant lottery. At ancient and historic Fort Niagara the whirling carousel pulled in trainloads of American youth, ground them through a processing mill, loaded them back on long trains and spewed them in all directions to training bases in a dozen states.

I attributed the Army's decision to classify me as a mechanical technician to the fact that I was well rested and sober at 8 a.m. the day I took the mechanical aptitude test. Mechanical technician? I had rarely held a hammer, couldn't fix anything, could hardly check the oil in my car or change a tire. But at 8 a.m. I had had a good night's sleep following sixteen hours on a beer-splashed New York Central daycoach from Massena, and relaxed after a hearty government-issue breakfast. Furthermore, the Army's mechanical aptitude test would have been simple for the average fourth grader.

I attributed the fact that I was assigned to the Army Air Corps to the fact that I emerged from the induction mill on a Tuesday. Another day or another week this human lottery might have dispatched me to the infantry, artillery, anti-aircraft or tanks. For me it was the first of several occasions where the military's roulette-wheel procedure dictated where I went and what I did as an individual in the war effort.

It can also be documented that on at least three occasions my military destiny was shaped alphabetically. During basic training at Keesler Field, Mississippi, the Air Corps saw a promising technical career in a draftee who had passed a juvenile aptitude test but who actually had difficulty distinguishing a paintbrush from a screwdriver. Accordingly, and since it was a Thursday, I was given a choice of two vital military occupations— aircraft mechanic or aircraft radio operator. I flipped a coin mentally, wondering if any experienced mechanics were being drafted into public relations or assigned to Army newspapers.

I signed for aircraft mechanics despite the distasteful realization that the AM training school was here in steaming, humid Biloxi while radio school represented an escape to the more temperate and more civilized environment of Scott Field, Illinois. Imagine my delight to find that another spin of the great Wheel of Fortune had favored me once more: the first hundred or so names on that day's alphabetical roster of several thousand, including many of our upstate New York contingent from Fort Niagara, were being shipped to the AM school at tiny Roosevelt Field in Mineola, Long Island. What a delicious rescue from that perspiring Gulf Coast swamp with summer coming! For the next twelve weeks my buddies, Bill Brill, Al Biagi, Caesar Boccino,

*Coke break at AM school
on Long Island*

George Beaton, Wayne Bell, other B's and a few C's offered daily thanks for a spectacular alphabetic and geographic rescue.

The next mass movement by first-initial surname was the most, fateful of my wartime career. The top half of the Roosevelt Field graduating class, alphabetically rather than academically, was consigned to the Air Transport Command and a small squadron at Bolling Field on the Potomac. We were now certified aviation mechanics, and while the bottom half of the Mineola roster went to a fighter squadron in California destined for Pacific combat, we saw nothing wrong with applying our newfound trade to maintaining small one- and two-engine aircraft that enabled high-ranking Pentagon brass to put in enough hours per month of recreational flying to collect flight pay.

I received my first promotion, from private to private first class, alphabetically rather than meritoriously. Bolling's November allotment of PFC stripes covered only from the A's to the mid-C's on the roster. A month later our colonel obtained a quota of corporal ratings, and with rare personnel insight he promoted the D's, E's and F's. That enabled my delightful bunkmate, Joe DiModica, to wear two stripes barely a week after he had inexcusably violated a mandatory maintenance procedure that resulted in the deactivation of a 14-cylinder Pratt & Whitney aircraft radial engine. Neither Joe nor the brass were bothered by his disregard on a sub-freezing morning of the order to all mechanics to cover engines and hook up gasoline-driven heater-compressors before starting up engines on the line.

Joe considered this a nuisance unworthy of freezing his fingers. He climbed into the cockpit of his assigned aircraft, turned the starter for routine morning warmup, and ground the $40,000 engine into a seized-up shamble. The corporal promotions, however, were already cut at headquarters.

In the barracks we all kidded Joe about screwing up, a crime he readily admitted, and all of his buddies rejoiced in his promotion. Joe, smiling and affable as befitting his warm personality, never showed a smidgeon of embarrassment for being promoted when he should have been penalized, and we were all happy for him. After all, this was the Army, it was wartime, officers had no feeling for what was going on beneath them, so what? As for Joe, he presumably went on to further advancements and greater contributions to the Allied victory.

*   *   *   *   *

Compared to hundreds of thousands of troops bearing arms in various parts of the world, life in the Air Transport Command was comfortable. Our squadron performed many functions, only a few of which could legitimately be called missions. We were running an air-freight line with domestic cargo linking major supply depots in continental USA, we did a lot of pilot training such as practicing stalls on twin-engined transports over Lake Michigan off Milwaukee (a maneuver I endured as flight engineer on dozens of stomach-turning flights that invariably ended with one-engine landings cross-wind), and we furnished air limousine service for congressmen, military brass and USO entertainers.

It was pure luck of the draw, with an occasional assist from the first letter of our last names, that led us to neo-civilian duty at domestic air stations. From the peaceful Potomac we moved to a friendly field in Cudahy, Wisconsin, which later became the Milwaukee County Airport, and thence to LaGuardia Field, New York City.

In these confines the main threats to health and safety came from the universally unabashed friendliness of Milwaukee people who made sure we swam in beer every time we ventured off the base at Cudahy, and from the congested perils of New York's subways, nightspots and ballparks. At LaGuardia we pursued our newfound profession in aircraft maintenance at two large hangars appropriated from TWA and American Airlines. We were billeted in a former aircraft mechanics school dormitory five blocks from the airfield and a short bus ride from the temptations of Jackson Heights with freedom to come and go as we pleased without having to ask for a pass each time we left military territory.

For me there were two other threats to security in such an environment. One was the requirement that, as flight engineer assigned to a particular twin-engined transport plane (we had a flock of Lockheed Lodestars called C-60s), I not only was solely responsible for the maintenance and mechanical performance of my aircraft and its 14-cylinder radial engines, but I had to fly in it each time it went aloft. The second was a succession of periodic pushes from squadron officers, noting that I possessed an Ivy League diploma, urging me to apply for Officers Candidate School (OCS). I was able to reject all such overtures, explaining that I was happy to serve in my assigned capacity instead of giving the real reasons— one, that I had a lot of good buddies in the squadron and, two, that once commissioned I risked being given some dreary assignment like an infantry supply officer or armored personnel officer in some tropical swamp or desert. All I was asking, I realized, was to be permitted to pursue my current career without interruption for the duration of the war.

12

Allergic to Combat

After two years of domestic duty in such habitable urban centers as Washington, Milwaukee and Jackson Heights, N. Y., no one in our squadron had cause to complain when word came that many of us were being shipped out of the country. It meant the end of a stint that would have been the envy of a million GI's had they known where we were and what we were doing, living and working like civilians in uniform.

At least a dozen of us B's, C's and a few D's who had gone to aircraft mechanics training school in Mineola, Long Island were still together in our ATC squadron when it was broken up. We had been billeted at Fort Totten in Bayside, Queens and working in and out of the hangars at LaGuardia Field when orders came through assigning many of us to the North Atlantic airlift, the armed forces' most vital supply line to the fighting in Europe, Africa and the Middle East.

Our destination was an air base we had never heard of in Newfoundland, which could have been a lot worse. For many of us it meant the end of flight pay, a modest bonus in the monthly pay envelope for crew chiefs and flight engineers who had been on flight status. Our new mission was strictly ground crew. That didn't bother me a whit, especially since a young

Maintenance crew in action on the flight line at Harmon Field during a routine 60-minute refueling stop on the hopscotch North Atlantic airlift. We averaged thirty C-54s every twenty-four hours.

lieutenant, freshly out of medical school assigned to giving physical exams to soldiers shipping overseas, discovered the true level of my myopia. There was nò opportunity here for a scam akin to the Utica Armory, so I accepted my lot, amused at the shavetail's shock at my inability to read beyond the oversized black E at the top of the chart without prescription lenses.

As it was, most of us spent the rest of the war at remote Harmon Field near Stephenville, a tiny fishing hamlet on the thinly-settled western coast of Newfoundland, then a British crown colony. The base was small, unreachable from the rest of the world except by air and by a single narrow-gauge railroad track. There was no highway link to the nearest civilization, Corner Brook, at that time.

For personnel on the isolated base, the major problem was boredom. The field was used exclusively as a refueling base and repair shop for the heavily loaded C-54 cargo planes short-hopping from Presque Isle, Maine, to Newfoundland to BW-1 (Greenland) to Iceland to Britain. The big birds swooped in from both directions, and the ground crews were allotted sixty minutes to refuel, inspect and perform routine maintenance while the flight crews were having an hour's break at the food bar. A few remained overnight, especially crews of smaller aircraft crossing to or from Europe on short hops. My assignment was as a flight-line inspector, which called for boarding each plane on arrival and performing a full checklist in the cockpit and on the engines and control assemblies. It wasn't rigorous, but it often was uncomfortable in cold weather, especially when winds loaded with icy salt spray stung our faces.

The duty routines were unchanging, 7-to-7 in the hangars and on the windswept flight line, twelve hours on, twenty-four off. That translated to all day Monday, all night Tuesday, all day Thursday, all night Friday, all day Sunday, and so on. We reported for work regardless of whether the big birds were landing and taking off every few minutes, or whether the base was socked in for several days in a Newfoundland fogbank.

Off-duty there was little to do and nowhere to go on a pass other than Corner Brook, fifty miles away by rail only, and weekend passes were strictly rationed.

For entertainment on the base we had only a small movie theater with wooden benches, a canteen with soda bar in the PX, a miniscule library and the NCO club, the non-commissioned officers' counterpart to the exclusive Officers Club. For recreation we had athletic facilities in a converted barn called the Rec Hall. We had occasional access to three-day or weekend passes to Corner Brook, a somewhat picturesque paper-mill town on the Humber Arm where there was a USO and several dozen eligible girls. The USO was the best I ever encountered; it served civilian meals and had a dormitory along with dances, ski equipment and a comfortable atmosphere.

Our only access to Corner Brook was by an odd doodle-bug vehicle called the GI Trolley. The trolley, an ingenious creation credited to a former base commander, Colonel Maxwell, was a cross between a box car and a bus. Its wooden frame body was rectangular and ungainly, mounted on railroad wheels and powered by an 8-cylinder Buick gasoline engine with a standard gearshift. On its trips on the Newfoundland Railway's narrow-gauge track it could accommodate about eighteen passengers. The railroad's regular three-times-a-week trans-insular passen-

The GI Trolley, powered by a Buick automotive engine, was a cross between a railcar and a bus. It had a standard gearshift and a capacity of eighteen soldiers on the fifty-mile trip to Corner Brook.

ger train was neither convenient nor reliable, and I never knew any soldier to consider taking it.

In barracks life we found warm fellowship. We were drawn together by a common adversity— torn from our homes and families by a national emergency, forced into servitude in an isolated outpost for an indefinite duration— and by a compulsion to make the most of it with a minimum of complaint. In this close confinement I developed many good friends.

There was also the opportunity to do a lot of reading and writing without distraction and to play many hours of bridge and cribbage. In the dead of winter the nights were long— 3:30 p.m. to 10 a.m.— but in summer we could play baseball or softball until nearly 11 at night (unless you had to go to bat against the pitching of one Bucky Buchanan, in which case the games were over quickly). In winter there were basketball leagues, bowling and a home-made outdoor hockey rink, plus the standard ping-pong and pool tables in the Rec Hall.

There was unlimited beer on draft at the NCO Club for ten cents a tall glass. Canadian ale was available for fifteen cents a bottle, but no bottled liquor was permitted. That embargo, however, was easily circumvented. Officers could get Seagram's VO and Canadian Club for a dollar fifteen a fifth, and on a small isolated base that dispensed with saluting and other military formalities of rank, there were many accommodating officers. I was content with beer and ale, but kept a cache of Seagram's in my foot locker as trade bait for transient air crews outbound from the States who discovered they could trade a quart carton of fresh milk for a fifth of VO. Although I made several such deals, I never had to trade more than one fifth of whiskey for a treasured quart of fresh Borden's. As a non-coffee drinker depending on milk and cereal for breakfast, I was unable to stomach canned or powdered milk on Corn Flakes, and would have gladly parted with three bottles of VO for one carton of fresh milk. Such are values when whiskey is cheap and milk unobtainable.

Small wonder Bob Hope had once cracked: "Take down your service flag, Mother, your son's in the ATC." We were also known as the Asiatic Taxicab Company and/or Allergic to Combat. In the North Atlantic Division NAD/ATC stood for Never A Decision, Always Too Confused.

*   *   *   *   *

In GI parlance there are three ways to do things— the right way, the wrong way and the Army way. Midway through my first year in Newfoundland I was hospitalized for the first and only time in my military career, a distraction that provided a classic example of this traditional axiom. My confinement was a triumph of Army regulatory procedure for its four million troops deployed across the globe, snarled in paperwork and counter-logistics, because I wasn't sick at all. Furthermore, once confined, I was fortunate to escape without contracting at least one highly contagious disease.

For several days I had been bothered by four or five spots on my left hand that my right had scratched raw enough to draw blood. I paid little attention, nor did it occur to me there were no mosquitos in Newfoundland in February.

At 9 a.m. I was in line in the corridor of our pint-sized hospital, a modest frame building that looked more like a CCC barracks than a medical center. When my turn came the doctor grunted, scribbled a prescription for the base pharmacist and dismissed me with the only words I heard him utter: "Next man."

For the next several days I applied the yellow salve from the small flat tin the pharmacist had given me. Several of the spots dried up promptly, the remaining two all but vanished. That would have been the end of it, but here I outsmarted myself by seizing the now-depleted vial of salve as a goof-off gambit.

For a GI with a hangover the standard duty dodge is "going on Sick Call." The only qualification is some sort of symptom or malady that might be deemed acceptable to the medic on the desk. Being a conscientious type whose late-night or bacchanalian excesses were reasonably few and far between, I rarely had occasion to resort to such frauds, but when a new and lavish NCO Club was opened at Harmon Field, the celebrations lasted for several weeks. On one such sortie what normally would have been a standard seance of three or four drafts turned into a debauch of modest proportion, making it more difficult than usual to confront the morrow's tour of duty on the flight line, starting at 7 a.m. on a dark February dawn where the sun didn't come up until 10. I elected to skip breakfast and report to Sick Call at 9 a.m. The medical excuse was simply to ask for a refill of the prescription.

Nor did my conscience trouble me. The field had been socked in with a typical Newfoundland fog; not a plane had landed in three days. Under these conditions the twelve-hour shift at the hangar seemed eternal. With no planes there were no two-day-old Philadelphia or New York newspapers and no new magazines. Even worse: Captain Montgomery had banned card-playing during duty hours, even when we had run out of hangar housekeeping chores in a fogbank. I felt my sick call ploy would not impede the Allied war effort.

Fortified by two and a half extra hours of delicious sleep, I returned to the lineup at the hospital. Once again the doctor greeted me with a bored grunt, but this time he examined my hand more closely. Instead of granting me the prescription refill, he turned to the medic standing by with his clipboard and said in an offhand manner: "Corporal, admit this man."

I was stunned. The doctor turned back to me. "Get your pajamas, robe and writing paper, whatever, and report to the corporal here in thirty minutes. You're in the hospital."

"Could I ask what for, sir?" I chirped, meekly. "All I've got here is two little bites, and they're coming along nicely."

"You've got scabies, sergeant. There's been a growing incidence of scabies, and the Surgeon General has issued orders to put every case in isolation."

"Isolation? My gosh, sir, is this recent?" I was thinking of the bloody sores I had exhibited several days earlier.

"We got the order yesterday. Okay, sergeant, isolation. Next!"

I had never heard of the malady. But the military medicos knew all about a highly contagious skin disease common in India and Africa, spread by invisible insects. I had apparently picked up a mite from the door handle of a plane on the regular run to Karachi or Rangoon. I was caught—literally—red-handed.

The base hospital was a two-story frame building that would have looked like a rectangular storage shed if it hadn't been for some windows and an exterior painted white. It had one main ward at the end of its only wing, optimistically called Ward A, and only half a dozen smaller rooms. When I presented myself for admission to isolation, it caused a bit of a fuss. There was no isolation facility, and apparently the small rooms were reserved for or occupied by officers.

The flap was solved by moving a bed to the near corner of the ward, and walling it off by a louvered portable screen. Thus the isolation mandate was met, however informally, and it bothered no one that my dangerously infectious Asian scourge was separated from other patients by ten feet of floor space and a thin screen.

This barrier shrank alarmingly the next day. I was enjoying the peace and rest of sick bay with a stack of library books when a burst of activity by medics and orderlies caused my screened partition to be moved further out. To my horror another bed was

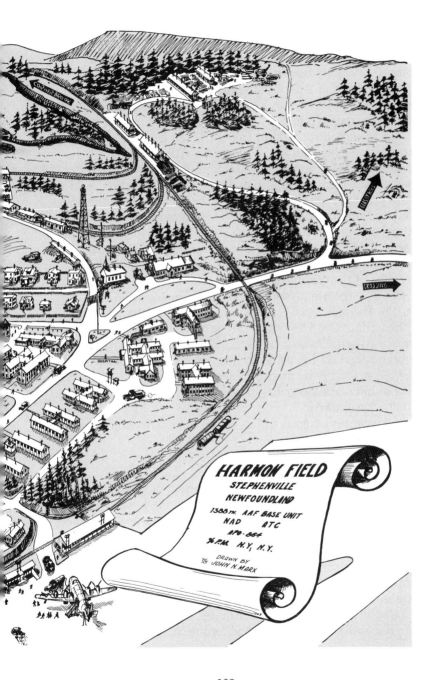

HARMON FIELD
STEPHENVILLE
NEWFOUNDLAND
1388TH. AAF BASE UNIT
NAD   ATC
APO-864
% P.M. N.Y., N.Y.
DRAWN BY
T/5 JOHN N. MARX

103

rolled in beside mine, barely six inches distant. Would this be a guy with the real scabies, or something worse requiring isolation? I held my breath.

Moments later a dark-haired fellow in a hospital robe was escorted to the fresh bed by a medic. His left cheek was covered by a bulging gauze compress, so weighty he had to hold it with his hand to keep it from sliding free of the bandages. Oozing from the top was a yellowish goo. He looked awful.

Once settled in our expanded isolation ward, we introduced ourselves and identified our maladies. His was empetigo, a skin disease perhaps even more contagious than scabies, and our first of many laughs together was the somewhat foreboding realization that the Army's routine inefficiency had given us the opportunity to infect each other with our respective cruds.

"I don't see why we're laughing," my newfound buddy said. "It really isn't very funny."

My new roommate's name was Bob Hurlbut and he came from the Poconos near Stroudsburg, Pennsylvania. He was a first lieutenant and a navigator on one of the C-54 crews making the trans-Atlantic freight runs out of New Castle, Delaware. He had been taken off his plane at Harmon when his malady had advanced so swiftly he needed immediate treatment.

"I didn't see a silver bar on your pajamas or I would have saluted," I remarked.

"I'll wear my insignia when you put some stripes on yours," he replied, grinning.

We spent four days in this ridiculous warren, writing letters, reading, chatting, always making sure to avoid contact despite the fact our beds were no more than six inches apart. Bob Hurlbut became one of the best friends I had in the service, and for many months on flights to and from Europe and the Mediterranean theater he never missed an opportunity to stop off for a brief visit, several times overnight. He regularly served as a courier delivering VO to my sister in New York City, one of the many commodities civilians found difficult or impossible to obtain in wartime.

I also have a vivid recollection of the first time I conspired to sneak Bob into the new and splendiferous NCO Club. Since the early days of Harmon the Officers Club, a fairly attractive building on the main street of the base, had a sign at the entrance that declared For Officers Only. The enlisted men, consigned to a crowded shack on a side street for an NCO Club, grudgingly accepted this discrimination as the Army way, but when they obtained authorization to allocate several hundred thousand dollars in the NCO club profits for construction of a new club, they did it up brown. The new edifice was a palatial showplace that made the Officers Club seedy by comparison. When the commanding officer and selected staff officers, invited for a brief dedication ceremony, were ushered out as the band and the girls were arriving, they passed in the entrance foyer a sign, elaborately carved and painted in keeping with the neo-gangster decor, announcing "No Officers Allowed."

My squadron buddies knew Bob well enough to dispense with formalities and saluting when he would stroll into our barracks looking for me, hence it was a simple matter to fit him into Whitey Makiowiec's OD shirt bedecked in corporal's stripes and take him down to the club for an evening. Bob enjoyed several such outings with the blessings of friendly corporals and sergeants, undaunted by the knowledge he was violating Army codes by impersonating an enlisted man.

13

How the War Was Won

Apart from the double-decked bunks in the drab and weatherbeaten barracks at Harmon Field, I spent most of my off-duty hours in the Rec Hall, a barnlike wooden structure that housed a basketball court, three bowling alleys, a lounge that served as a reading room, game room and card room, and several small offices. Outside was a baseball diamond and a field for soccer or touch football, which in winter gave way to a crudely constructed outdoor hockey rink. Little did I realize that these unimpressive facilities in the trackless wilderness of a remote British crown colony would produce for me an unexpected break, a form of journalism that meant welcome liberation from the aviation industry.

The Rec Hall complex was the domain of a genial first lieutenant named Stubby Struble, whose given name, John, appeared only on official papers. Stubby was barely 5-foot-6, built low to the ground and in civilian life had been a playground director and professional softball umpire in Washington, D.C.

As Base Special Services Officer he was in charge of all athletic, recreational and educational facilities and activities. His mental and intellectual capacity was modest indeed, hence he struggled daily to keep abreast of what for him was an administrative overload that constantly threatened to overwhelm him.

Stubby was not only likeable; he was fortunate. He had a mature, experienced staff sergeant, Eddie Field, efficiently running a full athletic and recreational program. Stubby could understand all those things, but making a man with a limited academic background responsible for overseeing the base newspaper, the base radio station and the facility the Army called I&E, Information and Education, was as cruel as making a Watertown Times news reporter a flight engineer responsible for safe operation of military aircraft.

Stubby's luck went beyond Field. In the enlisted ranks the Army blessed him with Corporal Bob Shryock to put out the base newspaper, Sergeant Hank Marquit to be the disc jockey, program director and voice of the base radio station, and Sergeant Howard Scherin to administer the correspondence courses and reading clinics in I&E. All were college graduates.

All these stalwarts were close friends of mine, and I often dropped in on Shryock while he was putting together the two-page mimeographed sheet called The Harmon Flash that passed for the base's daily newspaper. Skyrocket, as everyone called him, was a young articulate corporal who had graduated from Gettysburg College in his hometown in Pennsylvania before being drafted. He assembled the little newspaper each evening from local items, a weather report from the other side of the island, and a terse summary of one-paragraph items from Washington, various world capitals, the war fronts and baseball scores supplied by a teletyped Armed Forces News Service. Although I didn't know it at the time, my big break came when Skyrocket took a furlough.

Unlike the poor devils in faraway bases and combat zones, Harmon personnel had periodic access to home and family via routine seventeen-day furloughs activated by hitching rides on the C-54s that regularly and frequently touched down en route to or from the American mainland. It was rare that a GI on furlough had to wait more than twenty-four hours to hitch a ride to some air base in eastern USA and a return ride, squeezing into a loaded cargo plane headed out on the short-hop route across the North Atlantic.

Bob Shryock
at work on the Flash.

The day that marked a turning point in my military life came in early 1945 while Allied troops were pushing slowly but surely across France toward what the Free World hoped would wrap up Berlin and victory. I was playing gin rummy with Ed Field in the Rec Hall when Skyrocket came in to say goodbye. He was in full uniform with visored hat, unusual dress for a base where everyone wore fatigues. His barracks bag was slung over his shoulder, and there was a happy grin on his face. He was heading home on furlough.

His appearance got an instant rise from Struble, wrestling with paperwork at his desk in a far corner of the large room. "Where you goin'?" asked Stubby, coming over toward Corporal Shryock standing at our card game.

"Home," said Skyrocket cheerily, unable to contain his elation.

"Home?" cried Stubby incredulously. "Home? Jesus Christ! Who's gonna put out the Flash?"

"I dunno," said Bob, showing zero concern. "You got anybody yet?"

The pudgy lieutenant was overwhelmed by the sudden crisis and a bit perturbed by the disinterest shown by the enlisted men within earshot. In the relaxed fellowship of a small, intimate and isolated airbase such as ours, strict military discipline was relatively unknown, and salutes were rare except when the colonel was around. "Your play," said Field over the rummy hands. "I picked up your seven."

Struble's mental gyrations ground to a climax. He looked at me as inspiration burst inside his cranial cavity. He knew me well, and suddenly remembered I had often helped Shryock with the Flash and currently was working with Corporal Steve Vento, a photographer on the hangar crew, in trying to organize a base magazine. "Say, Nat, could you put out the Flash while Skyrocket is gone?"

"Sure," I said, knowing exactly what was coming.

"Gin," said Field, laying down his hand.

"Can you do tomorrow's paper?" persisted Struble.

"Not unless you can get me off the hangar shift tonight," I said. "I go on at 7."

"Chrissakes, deal the cards," said Field impatiently, paying no attention to the officer who was his boss. Stubby turned and hurried to his desk to call Captain Montgomery, base maintenance officer in charge of the flight line.

"Hey, Stubby," Skyrocket called after him. "You signed the furlough, remember?"

Struble ignored that. He obviously had forgotten, or had not connected the fact that approving a furlough for the Flash editor meant there would be no Flash editor for seventeen days.

A few minutes later he was back. "I talked to Captain Montgomery," he said. "I asked him if he could lend me Sergeant Boynton for the next two or three weeks 'til Skyrocket gets back. He said I could have you for the duration."

He laughed, and so did Field. I should have felt hurt, because I had worked conscientiously at a trade at which I was adequate if not particularly competent, but I was too happy at the thought of being liberated from a job I didn't especially care for. The new opportunity meant easy hours, good duty, weekends off and no more climbing around big planes in rain and sleet. I'd have to work a few hours each night, but not 7 p.m. to 7 a.m. I was elated. "I guess he figures the war's already won," I said.

"Can you start tonight and get out the paper?" asked Struble, still somewhat apprehensive because Field was dealing another hand and Stubby wasn't sure he was getting proper attention.

"Sure, Stubby," I said. "Just be sure I have a weekend pass on the Trolley this Friday."

"Consider it done," he said, obviously relieved.

And thus it came about that, with the end of the war in sight, a year at the most, I went back to my first love and true profession, of sorts. I joyfully reported to the Rec Hall each evening after mess, picked up the Armed Forces News wire copy from Hank Marquit's radio room, checked the established sources for home-base items and notices, and became editor-publisher of a two-page mimeographed daily (except Sunday) news sheet. It only took a few hours per issue. I'd been on the new duty only a few days when Stubby told me he had noticed a new professional touch in the Flash. The colonel must have said something about it, because just before Skyrocket was due back Struble asked me if I'd like to stay on and work with Shryock and expand the paper as a two-man staff. I said it was fine with me, and reminded him that Captain Montgomery had said I could stay for the duration of the war, for all he cared.

In an unrelated action Germany surrendered a few months later, in May, 1945, and Japan followed in August. The end of the war did not bring instant liberation from the commitments of several million draftees and volunteers in uniform, but it did bring a major change in the spirit and routines at Harmon Field and presumably at U.S. military installations around the globe. Now it was just a matter of time, perhaps only a few months for some of us, before the dream of our lifetime— discharge from the service— would come true.

*   *   *   *   *

In the confinement of a long, dark winter closer to the Arctic Circle than we'd ever been, it was natural for soldiers to while

Stubby Struble

*Hank Marquit,
Harmon's deejay*

away time by talking of their civilian pursuits. One such conversation at the NCO Club spawned an off-duty project— the birth of a magazine by and for Harmon Field base personnel.

The chief conspirators were Corporal Steve Vento, a bright-eyed product of Brooklyn, New York, whose official function was base photographer, and Sergeant Nat Boynton, a fugitive newsman late of Massena, New York, masquerading as an aircraft maintenance specialist. We slapped together a rough layout of proposed articles and photos, and made a presentation through channels (starting with Stubby Struble) to the base commander. Our request for modest funding was quickly granted by Colonel Edson, who, it turned out, considered it a way to go one-up on his counterpart at the other major U.S. airbase in Newfoundland, Gander. (It also turned out that when he proudly

The main drag of Harmon Field as viewed from headquarters. Two-story buildings on right are barracks. In the distance is St. George's Bay.

112

sent the first issue to the base commander at Gander, his rival sent back a copy of the third issue of their glossy magazine, already well established. Such was military intelligence of the era.)

Vento and I enthusiastically threw ourselves into the production chores with the blessing and support of officers and enlisted men alike. It was the first time since my days in dice baseball that I was an editor-in-chief in full control of a publication, let alone one that was actually set in type and printed.

The first two issues of twenty-four pages each were so well received that the base commander gave us a virtual blank check on a budget for Number Three. Partially because we were already seeing wholesale reductions of U.S. armed forces and partially because his ego was driving him to outdo his Gander rival, he made it clear he wanted the biggest and best Harmoneer ever. This time we could go to four-color plates and include a special section of squadron photos in the format of a typical school yearbook that would serve as a souvenir keepsake for each member of each squadron based at Harmon Field. By the end of summer this project had become a full-time job, and I relished it.

In keeping with the yearbook charter I wanted the lead feature article to be a comprehensive profile of the Crown Colony of Newfoundland itself, a land the GIs automatically detested only because it was so isolated and far from home. Being an independent soul always drawn to woods, streams and lakes, I liked what I had seen and wished I could see more than just the bleak vista of Stephenville and the rail line to Corner Brook. This was my big chance.

The story would be an illustrated travelogue. Naturally the editor would do the story himself. When I mentioned in the barracks one night that I was planning to take an "island furlough" and explore the interior and the Avalon Peninsula on the Atlantic side, the boys hooted and jeered, certain that I was kidding. Who ever heard of taking an "island furlough?" Who would ever want to see any more of this crummy rock?

To my surprise and delight, there was one taker in their midst. Vincent Tye, a tall, quiet fellow from Vermont, said he'd

The author doing page layout for the Harmoneer.

entertained the same thoughts for some time, and if I was serious he'd go along.

Stateside furloughs had become next to impossible to get since V-J Day, but island furloughs were easy, mainly because no self-respecting GI would ever want one charged against accumulated leave-time. By the same token the Army's new discharge program based on a point-system (one point for every month served, an additional point for each month of service outside the USA) had resulted in long-service personnel being detained at stateside embarkation points when they checked in to hitch a ride back to Harmon from a furlough at home.

Tye and I made plans to hitch a ride on a plane to Fort Pepperell on the Atlantic side, spend a few days at St. John's,

Newfoundland's capital and only city, then take the Newfoundland Railway across the interior to Corner Brook. We planned a two-day stopover at Grand Falls, and to finish out our allotted leave at the attractive and popular USO at Corner Brook. A few days later we went down to Base Operations and sat on our barracks bags to await a passing plane headed for the Army's permanent base at Pepperell or the Navy base at Argentia.

Neither of us will ever forget that hitchhike. We caught a ride on a "fat cat," the GI term for a whiskey-and-beer supply plane for the Officers Club at Fort Pepperell. The lumbering old C-47 (Douglas DC-3) was making the run from a U.S. depot in short hops, and had landed at Harmon for refueling (gas and oil, that is) en route from the air base at Presque Isle, Maine. There was hardly room in the cargo bay for two bodies, so tightly were the cases packed. We squeezed in behind the two-man crew in the cockpit.

It was a clear night with a full moon. The flight path was a direct line across the trackless uninhabited interior of Newfoundland, densely wooded with no roads and dotted with hundreds of small lakes and ponds. The moon was ahead of us, and I will carry forever the thrill of being aloft on a cloudless star-studded night, the blackness of the vast wilderness below broken only by the shimmering reflection of moonlight bouncing off a thousand lakes and ponds as if the landscape were dotted with sparkling torches.

In St. John's we installed ourselves comfortably in the USO dormitory, enjoyed the almost-forgotten sight of city traffic and even a red-green traffic signal, and relaxed in a civilian atmosphere. When I went to Newfoundland government offices to research my article, they were so eager to get publicity they immediately placed a car and driver at our disposal. For two days we toured the picturesque Avalon Peninsula in the southeast corner of the island, where the bulk of Newfoundland's population resides in a myriad of colorful fishing villages. We had only to tell the driver where we wanted to go or ask him where to find photogenic or typical coves and settlements. The war and its after-effects seemed a world away, and indeed they were.

We had been enjoying life in this luxury for only two days when we were surprised to be joined by Hank Marquit, the sergeant who operated Harmon's base radio station. Hank was a favorite of mine, a highly intelligent and fun-loving fellow. He had inveigled a pass from his lieutenant— our friend Stubby— for the professed purpose of going to the well-stocked supply depot at Fort Pepperell to obtain a new batch of phonograph records. He contended that was legitimate, in that they were needed to update the radio station's collection and to play at the Saturday night dances Hank ran at the Rec Hall for Newfoundland civilian employees on the base.

We complimented Hank for his resourceful ploy, and for two more days we lived a carefree vacation-type life, with late breakfasts, relaxing afternoons and enjoyable evenings with beer and USO girls. Hank's effervescent presence made it all the more fun. He had acquired two cartons of new recordings within a few hours of his arrival, and seemed in no hurry to return to Harmon.

"When do you have to be back?" Tye asked after another day of casual revelry.

"Actually I was supposed to be back by now," replied Hank. "They're sending a plane over for me tomorrow, but I think I'd rather go with you guys on the train. How long you gonna stay here?"

"We're going on the train tomorrow night," I said. "But we're stopping over at Grand Falls to see what the interior is like before we go on to Corner Brook."

"Well, then that's what I'll do," said Hank, lighting another of his favorite cigars. "I'll go with you on the train."

"What about the plane?" asked Tye, true to his Vermont discipline.

"Hell with it," said Hank. "I'm with you guys on the train."

"Won't you get in trouble if you stay so long?" pursued Tye.

"Naw, they don't have anybody else to run the station and the dances. Don't worry about it. Anyway, what can they do to me?"

The next day we packed leisurely for our departure for the railroad station, astonished at the number of bags and cartons,

NEWFOUNDLAND COMES OF AGE

Stories of the Island's Bleakness and Backwardness Are More Fiction Than Fact

By Sgt. Nat Boynton

In the viewpoint of the average American soldier countries other than the U. S. A. take an awful beating in comparison to the forty-eight States. Newfoundland, where several thousand changing vista of mountains, trees and water for months on end, to think of Newfoundland as a colorless land. It is easy to forget a lot of good fishing trips in unspoiled virgin country abounding in vince the traveller that there's something here.

Further than that, you'll be hearing from Newfoundland. It is a "natural" for tourists. In the years ahead don't be

The lead story in the final issue of the base magazine would have been a travelogue for anyone other than a Harmon Field GI.

including a case of "Newfie lager" we would be carrying aboard the train. Waiting for the taxi we realized we had a minor problem: would all these barracks bags, carry cartons, the case of beer, Marquit's two cartons of records and other goodies fit into the taxi and onto the train?

Marquit gazed at the stack of baggage piled in the USO lobby moments before the taxi was due. He took immediate action. Tye and I gasped in amazement as our stalwart buddy strode across the lobby to the desk occupied by the Grey Lady volunteer on duty that afternoon and said quite audibly: "Madam, would you accept on behalf of the Harmon Field Special Services Officer fifty of the latest swing-band recordings as a gift to the St. John's USO?"

Tye looked at me, his jaw agape as the lady at the desk said, "Why, thank you, sergeant, thank you very, very much. We'd be most pleased." Whereupon Henry Marquit, sergeant, United States Army Air Corps, deposited the two cartons of phonograph

117

Two extremes for a Harmon GI: work on the flight line, play at the USO in Corner Brook.

118

records he had acquired on his mission to Fort Pepperell on the lady's desk, offered his most gracious smile, reinstalled the inevitable cigar to his beaming visage, and returned to his seat beside us.

The taxi arrived. Tye, Vermont righteousness personified, remained in shock as we loaded our impedimenta into the unsuspecting cab, and we were off to the railroad depot. All I could do was laugh inwardly at my intrepid friend, conjuring up a flimsy excuse for a one-overnight (at best) boondoggle he stretched to three days, then jettisoning the items he had come for.

As the train slowly moved out of the station along the single narrow-gauge track that traversed the forested thinly settled interior to the rugged east coast and thence down to Port Aux Basques, Sergeant Marquit showed no remorse. "You think you can get away with this?" said the incredulous Tye, opening a beer to start the long overnight journey.

"Sure," said our Henry. "Hey, are you guys gonna be in Corner Brook this weekend?"

The USO at Corner Brook was the only recreation spot available to Harmon GIs. Weekend and three-day passes were rationed.

119

We assured him that was our plan.

"I'll be up Friday night on the Trolley," said Hank. "We'll have some more fun."

"Stubby will never give you a pass after this," observed Tye.

"Don't bet on it," said Hank.

Tye and I left the train at Grand Falls, which we appreciated on a brief visit despite its isolation in the Newfoundland wilderness that surrounded it. Marquit went on to Stephenville.

Three days later, soaking up the luxury of a relaxed life at the USO in Corner Brook, we were on hand when the Harmon GI Trolley deposited a full contingent. Among the embarkees was Marquit, a stogie in his beaming countenance.

Tye was impressed. "Stubby give you a weekend pass?" he asked in disbelief.

"Sure," said Hank. "Why not?"

*   *   *   *   *

In December I hitched a flight to LaGuardia Field and thence to Grenier Field, Manchester, New Hampshire, to oversee the printing of Colonel Edson's pride, a 68-page four-color magazine, third and last issue of a slick-paper periodical that flourished on a relatively inaccesible airbase on the remote western coast of Newfoundland. In dusty drawers, basement boxes and attic trunk there may still exist rare copies of this memento, a yearbook of World War II military squadrons, technically under arms in the nation's most historic wartime emergency. Mine is in semi-tatters, but the squadron photos are intact, the eight-page feature article on Newfoundland's potential as a peacetime tourist attraction still readable.

The press run in Manchester completed, my orders called for proceeding to Rome Air Depot in upstate New York to be discharged. My military commitment ended on December 20, 1945, approximately 200 miles and 46 months from its beginning at Fort Niagara. The myopic draftee who began as a trainee in aircraft mechanics finished, unheralded but grateful, as an editor, eager once again to return to the journalistic ranks as a reporter, copyreader or whatever.

Welcome back, peacetime.

III

The Finger Lakes

14

Wedding of the Decade

The blue stars on the service flag alongside Old Glory were still waving above narrow Arcade Street from the Times building in Watertown that first Monday in January when I returned to civilian pursuits. Each star represented a Times employee serving in the armed forces during the Late Unpleasantness. One of them was mine. I was glad to see there were no gold stars on the proud banner.

Upstairs on the second floor I found double happiness in post-war employment— back with old friends in the city room and an exciting new assignment. Not only was I back under the wing of my old city editor, Gordon Bryant, but I was stationed "on the rim"—i.e. the copydesk. My new title was Assistant State Editor, a fancy name for copy reader, headline writer and practicing assistant for Bob Wells, the state editor responsible for putting together the North Country pages and the Jefferson-Lewis county pages. It was on the state desk that all those baggage letters from the bureaus up the line in St. Lawrence County landed, along with the bulging envelopes that came in each morning from the bureau correspondents in Carthage and Lowville.

Up to now my career in journalism had been exclusively as a reporter and news writer. Apart from a brief foray in Newfoundland as editor of a mimeographed sheet that attempted to simulate a newspaper and a stint as editor of a concocted base magazine (we had put out three issues of The Harmoneer), I had had zero experience as a copy editor on a bonafide newspaper. I was elated by the new opportunity.

But before I could get a proper introduction to an assigned slot on the semicircular copydesk half a level beneath Bryant's esteemed chair, the Times had a surprise bonus for me. A new reporter who had been groomed in the Times tradition—on the old federal building beat—was being sent to Massena, and my first assignment was to accompany him to my old stamping ground and show him the ropes.

Seldom has a returning gladiator been given such a delightful reward, for I loved Massena and was happy to have a week in my old haunts—and on the Times payroll to boot. Joe Kelly, my young ward, was so charged up with energy and enthusiasm I found it hard to realize that in a similar circumstance six years earlier I had probably been just as unbridled. Joe's eagerness and overflowing zeal almost wore me out, but after a delightful reunion with many friends in town and on the news beat, I made it back unscathed to start baptismal routines on the copydesk.

It was natural for Bryant and Wells to make sure that in that mountain of copy arriving each morning from all those bureaus and other correspondents, the baggage letter from Massena always fell on my desk. Here I found myself trying to keep Kelly's vigor within bounds and to restrict his effervescent writing style to straightforward factual reporting. I spent the summer editing out a sizeable percentage of adjectives and adverbs from the Massena copy, telling myself that I couldn't have been as carbonated as Joe. My old friend Homer Baker, who had been on the copydesk editing my daily baggage letters in 1940-41 and was now helping Howard Lennon on the telegraph desk, assured me that Joe was indeed unusually hyper and that I had not caused any such waves during my Massena tenure.

A returning veteran, formerly of the Massena bureau, is assigned to the copydesk upon his return from service.

Meanwhile it was enjoyable to have a daily pipeline to everything that was transpiring in my old bailiwick. In this scenario it came as only a mild surprise when one of Massena's best-known and highly respected families put on a wedding that few witnesses will ever forget. The nuptials that joined young Connie Cappione, youngest of seven children of Amadeo (Sam) Cappione and the apple of her father's eye, and John McAloon, son of a prominent local physician, featured an eight-hour gastronomic extravaganza for eight or nine hundred people in the town hall auditorium, which also served as the local dance emporium.

The populace took for granted that the beer and liquor distribution operation Sam Cappione headed was clearly the most prosperous in the North Country. Sam was everybody's friend, a stalwart pillar of the community, who never let his economic success change his lifestyle. He and his wife brought up their large family in the same unostentatious frame dwelling in the Pine Grove section where he had always lived.

The story goes that when his youngest child, beautiful dark-haired Constance, told her father she wanted everybody in town to come to her wedding, Sam made arrangements to hold the reception in the largest public indoor arena north of the Clarkson Tech hockey rink in Potsdam, the second-floor ballroom in the Massena town hall. A few weeks before the big day Sam let the betrothed couple pass the word around that the invitation was open to everyone and anyone.

As the wedding date drew nearer, Massena worked itself into a municipal party mood, and the contagion was felt in the city room on Arcade Street a hundred miles to the south. Clarence Webster, an editorial writer, and Homer were interested in going to Massena with me on the big day, and we made plans for a quick breakaway. The final edition went down at 12:15 on Saturdays, and we figured on getting on the road by noon at the latest. There was no way we would miss this one. The marriage ceremony itself was in the early morning, but given the parameters we were confident the bash would still have plenty of life by mid-afternoon.

On Saturday morning the bundle of North Country bureau letters arrived on schedule, and I dived into the thick Massena envelope as usual. Among the routine police stories, obits, school football and the day's stories from the beat was the Cappione wedding story, and this was vintage Joe Kelly.

The lead literally vibrated with the excitement that had enraptured our energetic man in Massena. It was quickly apparent that of the scores of weddings he had written up since his January debut, this one had to be special. No routine cliches this time, not even an "exchanged vows" or "united in marriage" stuff. With adrenalin flowing, Joe reached for the ultimate:

> The marriage of Miss Constance Cappione, daughter of Mr. and Mrs. Amadeo Cappione of 77 Beach Street, Massena, and John B. McAloon, son of Dr. and Mrs. R. F. McAloon, 166 Allen St., Massena, was consummated before a floral-banked altar at St. Mary's Roman Catholic Church, Pine Grove, today. The Rev. John M. Bellamy, pastor and former chaplain of the 46th Division, New York National Guard, celebrated the high nuptial Mass.

Bryant was working in his elevated slot above the rim of the copydesk chewing on his 7:30 White Owl when I tossed him the sheet with Kelly's lead. "You gotta read this lead, Gordon," I said. "Better get a photographer up there right away."

Bryant took one look at the story, threw it back to my slot and growled, "That goddam fool." He strode out to the composing room in his nervous, energy-charged gait, not even a chuckle, let alone a smile. When I passed it to the boys on the rim they all howled with laughter. Webby came over from his desk to see what was causing such hilarity so early on a day when everybody had to hustle copy for the early Saturday deadline. I rewrote the lead, realizing that poor Joe, trying to outdo himself, didn't know the true definition of the fanciest word he could think of.

When the rumble of the big presses started downstairs Homer and Webby and I raced for the parking lot and drove north. When we got to Massena shortly after 3 the tribal rites had been in full swing for several hours. Hurrying up Main Street I encountered one of my favorite girlfriends, Ruth Garvey, standing in front of the theater across from town hall with a glass of beer in her hand. Her speech was a bit slurred, her posture not entirely steady, but the greeting was warm. "Oh, God, you gotta get up there," she said, swaying slightly. "You won't believe it."

One of Sam's big trucks was in the side alley unloading cases. Upstairs the dance floor was jammed and the music blaring from the bandstand. Along the front of the hall was a long table heaped with whole hams, chickens and roasts, surrounded by platters of basic foodstuffs. There was a bar setup at each end of the hall, and for me it was Old Home Week.

In the years since, I have witnessed many a wedding, but never one like that one, and I look back on it with unbounded admiration for all Cappiones in the North Country.

*   *   *   *   *

In the midst of the new and exciting function of editing, along with the experience of writing all kinds of headlines, I occasionally had a chance to learn page layout, which I found especially appealing. All this made for a delightful spring and summer, the first in nearly eight years without a global war or the threat of one. I was also enjoying the relative proximity to my adopted hometown of Geneva, where my two sisters, my hospitable aunt and uncle and several cousins lived—a mere 125 miles away instead of the 225 I had had to cover in those pre-draft Massena days.

I had been so busy in my new environment in Watertown that I had paid little attention to a number of startling changes in the Geneva newspaper scene. Once or twice on domestic leaves from the Army I had dropped into the Geneva Times to pay respects to that venerable city editor, E.T. Emmons, who in 1939 had declined my offer to work without pay just to get a foot in the door of a newspaper. It also was a chance to soak up a bit of nostalgia with staffers in the news room. Now it was 1946, and on a July visit with my family I took a few moments to look in on the Geneva Times, say hello to Emmons, and get the word on a shakeup at the top. Old W.A. Gracey, the longtime editor, had died the previous year, and Emmons introduced me to the new managing editor, Al Learned, who had come several months earlier from the Oneonta Star.

In September I took a week's vacation after Labor Day to get in some good Seneca Lake sailing before the season ended. One rainy afternoon I went around to the Times for a little socializing with friends in the city room—Bob Prentice, the telegraph editor, and Vern English, the oldtime city hall reporter who still wore his battered fedora while pecking out routine stuff in his colorless prose. There may have been another reason for dropping in: perhaps just to be in a news room when the building starts to shake with the rumble of the presses downstairs.

I was chatting with Prentice when Learned, who had been in the composing room overseeing the final pages before press time, burst through the door to the city room. He greeted me in his hurried stride through the room and moments later, to my surprise, called me into his office.

I had met Al Learned only once, and briefly, hence I was unprepared for the conversation that followed. Closing the door to shut out the noise of the typewriters, he came right to the point. "I know more about you than you think I do," he said. "I need you on this paper. How much are you making in Watertown?"

I answered instinctively rather than prudently. "Forty-six," I said, taken aback by the abruptness of his approach. Furthermore, it was the first time in my life anyone had ever spontaneously offered me a job.

"I don't think I can get you quite that, but if I can get you forty-four, would you be interested?"

I loved Geneva, where my mother had grown up and where I had many close friends from many summers on the lake, not to mention my delightful cousins. The more Learned explained his plans for restructuring the staid old paper, the more attractive the deal became. He wanted to do more managing and less copy editing; he wanted his young friend Charlie Bennett to be a key assistant despite his lack of experience, and he wanted me to be the catalyst on the precept that any newsman trained in Watertown would have a lot to offer any staff. Specifically he wanted me to teach Charlie the art of head-writing and copy editing, after which, presumably, he and I would be his lieutenants.

I took the job.

15

Changing Times

It was hard to leave the Watertown Times, where I had so many good friends and great experiences, but the chance to be a key participant in a major newspaper renovation project was exciting. In the five years that followed it turned out to be just that, and through all the staff turnover and the near-total facelifting that resulted in doubling the circulation, we rarely had commerce with the publisher downstairs. G. B. Williams was the personification of the editor's ideal publisher, the hands-off owner who leaves the professionals alone as long as they do their jobs and commit no visible journalistic felonies.

Thus I found myself working for a publisher who was the direct antithesis of the revered Harold B. Johnson. Both dedicated themselves to the pursuit of journalistic excellence as each defined it. H.B. was the chief executive and legendary editor, delegating business management and profitability to others. G.B. was the chief executive and business manager, delegating the specialized skill function to a professional editor. Each of these two men, poles apart in personality, background and precept, was successful in achieving his career objective along with directing a highly profitable corporate entity.

Geneva, billing itself as the Queen City of the Finger Lakes, was (and still is) an aristocratic, unprogressive and salubrious center on the main traverse of New York State midway between Syracuse and Rochester. The city, maintaining a fairly steady population of seventeen thousand, has the beauty and charm of a college town, enhanced by Seneca Lake, longest and deepest of the Finger Lakes. The surrounding country is relatively flat, but its rich soil provides verdant fields, orderly fruit orchards and miles of vineyards. It is farm country, fruit country and wine country.

When I accepted a new job offer and returned to my late mother's birthplace in the fall of 1946, Genevans were still recovering from the shock of discovering that the family they thought had been publishing their hometown newspaper for a generation did not have controlling interest, and had been ousted by the majority stockholder. William A. Gracey had been editor-publisher of the Geneva Daily Times and various forerunners since 1898. Gracey and the survivor of several early partners, George B. Williams, consolidated several local newspapers at the turn of the century, and in 1907 formed the Geneva Printing Company to publish the Times. For the next thirty-eight years the partnership remained intact, Gracey as president and editor, Williams as secretary, treasurer and business manager.

In the eyes of the populace the Times was Gracey's paper. The soft-spoken Williams, known as G.B., was noted more for his distinguished VanDyke beard and unpretentious manner than for any personal or professional achievement. For most of his nearly forty years in residence in Geneva he had been content to live modestly in the shadow of his partner, the editor, quietly unobtrusive at a rolltop desk in a rear cubicle of the first-floor business office.

During the Gracey regime the Geneva Times had reflected the character of the city it served, which is to say casual and self-subsisting, comfortable in its inherent resistance to change, and secure in an unruffled lifestyle. The population had remained stable for several decades, content to draw its economic sustenance from several small industries and two

E.T. Emmons

small private colleges, Hobart for men and William Smith for women. Even the wartime stimulus of the U.S. Navy's burgeoning training base on the other side of Seneca Lake twelve miles distant failed to dislodge Geneva's economy from its slumber.

While the quiet charm of Geneva was protecting it from many incursions of modern civilization, its newspaper maintained the same restful insulation from the problems of the world. It would be hard to find any upstate paper sleepier, less aggressive or duller. The community demanded little from the Times, and the Times made sure it did nothing to interrupt its civic passivity. It would be safe, and certainly charitable, to describe the newspaper as a frontispiece of mediocrity.

As post-war Geneva resumed the delightful nineteenth-century dormancy it treasured, few people were aware of intrigue in the staid old Times, still using in 1946 the same typefaces and headline styles it had presented in 1907. When W. A. Gracey died in 1945, no one lifted an eyebrow as his son, Lawrence, who had been a member of the news staff for some twenty years, moved into his late father's office and took over as editor. With Lawrence Gracey, a likeable enough fellow, in the editor's chair and E. Thayles Emmons continuing as city editor, a post he had occupied since 1906, the old order was preserved. Times readers could still find stories leading the local news page under verbless headlines such as:

HOSPITAL REPORT
FOR OCTOBER

This and other antique classics came from the white-haired Emmons, a gentle teetotaling Vermont Presbyterian who also was the town's unofficial historian. In 1946 he was still writing his headlines in pencil on yellow pad paper, as he had done for four decades.

But behind the scenes all was not harmony. If Lawrence Gracey had never seen eye-to-eye with his father's partner, the friction was a closely kept secret. Even after W. A.'s death it was still, outwardly, the Gracey paper.

Whatever the truce between Lawrence and G. B. it was a fragile one, and when it exploded shock waves raced through the community. The news that Lawrence had been fired was secondary to the astonishing revelation that it was meek G. B. Williams who had ownership control and not the Gracey heirs.

The drama on that fateful day has been reconstructed by witnesses and persons within earshot. G. B., wearying of a succession of clashes with Lawrence, went down to Seneca Street early one morning, climbed the stairs on one of his rare visits to the second floor, and locked the door to the editor's office. Lawrence, habitually casual in his work and working hours, arrived shortly after 9, a good hour after the rest of the staff. Finding the door to his office resisting a vigorous shaking, he stormed downstairs to confront his suspected antagonist.

Typical Geneva Times headlines during the Gracey-Emmons regime. Note subject matter of the stories that led the news pages. "The" should never appear in a head (nor the fact that football is played in the fall).

Several staffers in the city room on the second floor and in the business office on the first floor confirmed the account of that historic dialogue. G. B. reportedly waited for Lawrence's angry discourse to wind down before telling him that he could have the keys to his domain on condition that he clean out his desk and personal effects by the end of the day.

Thus began the transformation of the Geneva Times from a sleepy Victorian journal to a modern-day newspaper. The G. B. Williams Geneva had known as an almost mousey introvert was now unmasked as a man of action, a newspaper publisher in his own right, determined to brighten and sharpen a dreary product.

At the time of his emergence he was 73 years old. His own background was as a mining engineer in Arizona and as an accountant in neighboring Rochester prior to his move in 1907 to become secretary of the Geneva Printing Company. Experience told him that Gracey's replacement should be a field professional. In short order he hired an experienced editor and gave him unfettered rein to make whatever changes were needed.

Within a year the Times was offering a complete new format, modern typography and expanded news coverage. The circulation, which had remained constant at around six thousand for more than twenty-five years, doubled in the five years following G.B.'s decision to give the paper a new life.

*   *   *   *   *

On the Geneva Times most of the changes on the news side were choreographed by Al Learned, a gregarious fellow who had been news editor of the Oneonta Star, a small morning daily in Central New York. No one would accuse the Star of being a top-flight paper, but it was lively enough to be a clear cut above what Genevans liked to call "The Geneva Deadly Times" or "The G. D. Times" or, for short, just "The Deadly."

Unlike Gracey, Learned was a flamboyant newspaperman. His effusive energy compensated for whatever shortcomings he had as a writer or stylist, and he was instantly and permanently likeable, a valuable trait for an incoming executive. His enthusiasm had a motivating effect, and it didn't take long to get the feeling he not only demanded good work from a staff member, but recognized and appreciated it when he got it.

His presence in Gracey's old enclosure quickened the pace on the second floor of the drab Seneca Street landmark, much to the displeasure of the Gracey-Emmons holdovers in the city room. Learned enhanced their discomfort by bringing in a young friend from Oneonta with virtually no previous newspaper experience, and by hiring a 29-year-old from the Watertown Times recently back from war service on the North Atlantic airlift with a mere nine months' experience on a copydesk. When he gave both newcomers important editorial positions, the incumbents knew it was time to move elsewhere.

16

World on a Wire

If the rules of journalism mandate that a reporter, whether covering a breaking story or writing a feature, observe accuracy and objectivity, the copydesk can add a bit of pizazz by way of a catchy head— a play on words, a provocative phrase or some innovative gimmick. The New York City tabloids of my youth, the Daily News and the Daily Mirror, were masters of this art, quick to pull out a double meaning or a daring piece of slang to lure readers into a story, the dull ones as well as the lurid or sensational. Among scores of clever heads, the one I recall most vividly was a Daily News banner in the early thirties that told the whole story of a grueling pitcher's duel at Yankee Stadium in nine units of space: RUTH, 1-0.

On a conservative paper like the Watertown Times in the thirties and forties, most of the stories that got into print were straight news and we gave them format heads. Humorous pieces and human-interest stories were relatively rare. One of the few exceptions I can recall was a daring one by Clarence Webster. Editing the items from the Times correspondent in the rural outpost of Pikeville, Webby realized that all the social notes that week involved visits made to nearby towns and villages by various natives named Pike, so he topped the column with a head that said, "Pike Run is On."

In my relatively brief but intense stint on the copydesk in Watertown under the lovable but tyrannical Gordon Bryant I had never been tempted to be daring. In switching to the Geneva Times, I quickly saw that Al Learned, my new boss, was committed to brightening the visage of what had been a dowdy, humdrum newspaper, which promised a new dimension of freedom in head-writing and page layout.

One of my first assignments in Geneva was to polish the art of head-writing in the person of Charlie Bennett, the young friend Learned had retrieved from Oneonta a short time before my arrival. Charlie had been working in a bank, but being a bright fellow was adapting easily to newspaper life. He had a natural aptitude that compensated for his lack of experience, and he had the talent to become a competent copyreader and head-writer. His rapid development enabled Learned to implement his plan to install Bennett and Boynton as his key editorial assistants, and thus advance the staff transition from the dull mediocrity of the former administration.

That changeover got a significant boost the day Learned called Charlie and me into his cubicle and shut the door, the same door that G.B. Williams had locked against Lawrence Gracey less than seven months earlier. The conference lasted only a few minutes.

As one of several dozen dailies serving the smaller one-newspaper cities scattered across New York State, the Geneva Times had no copydesk as such. There were four editing posts moving the copy. The city editor put out the local pages, the so-called state editor was responsible for the pages covering the rest of the circulation area embracing Ontario, Seneca and Yates counties, the sports editor generated the sports pages and the telegraph editor handled all the teletype copy coming over the wire from the AP in Albany. We all were aware of the time cycle in getting out the paper— county pages and sports went early, keeping open as late as possible Page One and the lead Geneva page. At the Times in 1946, two editors could handle the four "desks" by splitting their working day.

When Al summoned Charlie and me to a closed-door conclave to divide the four plums in the pie two ways, we looked at each other and smiled. We had a pretty good inkling of what

Al Learned

might be coming, and were prepared. We knew that because of early deadlines for sports and county copy, one of us couldn't choose to be city editor and wire editor simultaneously, and we knew each other well enough to suspect that our respective preferences would fit like a glove.

"I'd like sports on the first trick," I said, having had a good dose of correspondents' copy on the desk in Watertown. Charlie grinned, because he had ideas about beefing up the coverage in Waterloo, Seneca Falls, Penn Yan and the outlying towns. That took care of half the pie.

"How about city editor?" Charlie ventured.

"All yours," I said, welcoming a chance to design Page One the way I thought it ought to look.

"Great!" enthused Al happily from the mediator's seat. "That's the way I figured it would go. Okay, we start tomorrow." End of conference.

From that joyous beginning, our triumvirate worked in close harmony for five years, overseeing changes of personnel on the city room staff that saw only two holdovers, not counting the venerable E.T. Emmons, survive. Mildred Jennings handled

Postcard views of Seneca Street, Geneva, above, and beautiful tree-lined South Main Street, probably in late thirties.

View on South Main Street,
Geneva, N. Y.

society news and women's activities until her retirement many years later. Rita Rickey, a facile young writer, did general assignments, wrote features and helped Mildred on the club beat.

Jim Campbell, a reporter who had been on the staff for the last several years of the Gracey regime and had resented Learned's demands for better production, told me shortly before he left that he felt I had made a big mistake in not taking the city desk.

"Isn't it obvious that Charlie is 'Al's boy' and he wants him to be in the key job, city editor," Jim observed. I replied that Charlie had more patience than I, and anyone willing to wade through all that county copy each morning deserved to have the city desk. I enjoy sports, I said, and I'm more interested in typography and page layout than either Al or Charlie, and now I have that with Page One and all the top AP stories of the day. Jim just shrugged. Several months later he was gone.

*   *   *   *   *

It's one thing to like your work, quite another to love it. In Massena it was clear that I had the best possible newspaper job a young fellow could have— covering a busy beat on a quality paper in a wide area with the freedom that comes with being a hundred miles from the main office. The added bonus was having a lot of good friends in a large circle of single contemporaries and living in an active recreational environment.

Now the scene had shifted to Geneva and what perhaps was an even more ideal job— total command of two full sports pages, and an open license to do anything I wanted with any and every news story in the rest of the world outside the counties of Ontario, Seneca and Yates. There was enough daily pressure in both locations to make a seemingly repetitive routine more like an ever-changing kaleidoscope. All this on a paper congenial colleagues were striving to make even better, and in a beautiful college town on a lake in magnificent upstate New York. Could anyone want a better life?

In Geneva the day started at 7:30 in the city room, got into high gear at 7:35 and ran at cruise speed, except for a half-hour

Cool or Warm
It's good form
to use Times ads

GENEVA DAILY TIMES

Home Daily for Ontario, Seneca and Yates Counties—Heart of the Finger Lakes Region

Vol. 56, No. 43 — GENEVA, N. Y., WEDNESDAY, JULY 19, 1950 — Member of Associated Press — Price Five Cents

Truman Asks $10 Billion for Korea

Yanks Hurl Fresh Troops in New Landing--Reds Shell Taejon

24th Division Holding City Despite Barrage; First Cavalry Landed

Today only 18 — Red artillery shells screamed into Taejon today in a resumption of the western battle as thousands of fresh U. N. reinforcements plunged into the Korean war on other fronts.

U. N. Warning:
Reds Plotting
Greek Thrust

U N troops in South Korea region at a harrowing point to consolidate their positions against North Korean spearheads. Drawn back from the Taejon area, defending forces in retreat are trying to set up new positions on a high ridge of the Kum River.

Bridge Game

A Line On Korea

Tax Boost, Controls Near, President's Message Warns; Preliminary Blueprint Set

Washington, July 19—(A)—President Truman asked Congress today to vote all the men and armed strength needed to turn back the Communist armies in Korea and to block armed aggression elsewhere in the world.

He put the starting cost of building up the military power of the United States and the free world at $10,000,000,000.

He said a sharp tax increase together with other economic controls are necessary to curb inflation and help beat the military bills. The tax recommendations will come later.

For the present, Mr. Truman asked power to curb time installment buying, establish priorities, allocate materials, control inventories and requisition needed supplies and machinery.

He reserved for the future more drastic measures such as price control and rationing, and called upon all Americans to avail them through voluntary restraint.

The president made clear that he proposes that only the building. He itemized the early need of more billions to reinforce the military strength of the nation. Almost another one billion dollars bordering Soviet Cuba. He called for further defense spending would in the future.

And the future? Mr. Truman might emphasize an United Nations action, a force with a strong against further aggression that costs at least in Marshall means of Moscow the reports.

"The free world has made it clear through the United Nations, the nations agreement, will be met with force. This is significant of Korea—and it is a significance whose importance cannot be over estimated.

Mr. Truman said at least twice on the size of the armed forces as cited to permit increasing them substantially.

Johnson Given Power to Call Reserves

The president was reported to given in a little-word message to Congress he has empowered Secretary Johnson to call reserves that present rate of Johnson. Johnson is increased and he said in detail as what has had ceiling privacy for many National in Korea and said that the United States the service of the reserve of major force home.

Forces of the Army, Navy and Air The attack upon the inventories

Draft Call Okayed in 'First Step' to Bolster Forces

Move Viewed as 'Prod' To Recruits, Reserves; 500,000 May Be Asked

Washington, July 8—(A)—President Truman dangled the draft law over the heads of reservists and prospective recruits today in an appeal effort to build up military manpower for the demands of the hot war in Korea.

The president gave the Pentagon power to draft men in a general order late yesterday. It is designed to lift economy limits imposed on the Army, Navy, Marines and Air Force.

That let Defense department hoped to get by at least suitably without actually using the draft authority was evident in the comment of selective service officials who were very happy.

PERHAPS 587,583 MEN
No official would say how many men were wanted Wednesday—a resumption of the inevitable that by the appeal the present strength of the armed forces indicates that the figure could run as high as 587,583.

LAWMAKERS AGREE
Lawmakers generally commended the decision to call up on top of the 10,000,000 figures.

GENEVA DAILY TIMES

Home Daily for Ontario, Seneca and Yates Counties—Heart of the Finger Lakes Region

Vol. 56, No. 34 — GENEVA, N. Y., SATURDAY, JULY 8, 1950 — Member of Associated Press — Price Five Cents

Reds Aim New Punches

Draft 'Proves'
U.S. Determined
To Save Koreans

By JOHN M. HIGHTOWER
Washington, July 8—(A)—President Truman's decision to summon American armed forces furnished the world anew proof that the United States intends to carry through in Korea.

While Russia was expected to assail the action as further evidence of American "aggression," there was some confidence here that the Soviets do not perceive a world war.

Responsible authorities believe, therefore, that the draft announcement will not be viewed upon by the Kremlin as a "provocative" act by the United States, regardless of what propaganda line the Russians make of it.

Two issues the president did not meet in his call on the draft boards will start drafting men now, and if he did not say how many members of the reserves will be called for duty.

What he did say, in effect, was that the armed forces need a lot more men, marine as much as more reserves—and he wants them now to fill these men by the employment method, if possible.

If enough volunteers don't come forward, then the draft will again be forced, although he made no mention of the draft in order to make up the difference.

-How Will the Draft Affect Me?-

Men 25-26 Would Be Called First; But Many 'Ifs' Cloud Next Moves

By JAMES MARLOW
Washington, July 8—(A)—Wait but not till then. Just what happened of reluctance are simplified?

This is an attempt to explain what President Truman said to the draft yesterday and how it may affect families because a lot of men and their families may be uncertain about it.

Of course, since the world whatever is changing, what is true today may not be true next week.

1—you can predict what changes a new week will bring and what the government will do then.

When the call—when?
The rules are answer: the age law starts now—later, as present the law itself to be specific as an emergency, but there's no talk about it. Is it necessary?

Under present law there are many who realize it might respond with the local draft board although he can't be drafted until he's 18. An 18-year-old should volunteer he could a month before.

Reenlistment is the youngest age for volunteering the soldiers, for his personal amount. Assume his personal amount.

If drafting becomes necessary, men must serve 21 months. Not anyone who already in service who takes the law in the reserve gets rebellion. Not so the volunteer, but what of reservists and recruits?

Korea Vets Sweat It Out

The news from Korea, which U. S. military men all over the world are watching with keen interest, isn't good.

Chonan Captured; Pusan, Key Point Faces Next Threat

Tokyo, Sunday, July 9—(A)—Fall of the south Korean town of Chonan and a renewed American retreat before the north Korean invaders were reported today by field dispatches.

This news by telephone from correspondents in the field came shortly after a Tokyo headquarters communique said the Red drive had been "curtailed" but that the invasion were massing troops, armor and artillery for a renewal of their offensive.

There still has been no public word of unmatched, however, a spokesman of American forward headquarters in Korea declared.

In a communique issued from the front AP correspondent O. H. P. King said angry and smoke American forward troops had re-treated upon Saturday King said the Reds had regained their Chonan, a large town 26 miles south of Seoul for deeper penetration of unknown yet.

FORCES SMALL
King's report of the American retreat gave no inkling of the numbers of men involved, the earlier dispatches had told of perhaps several hundred.

King said American equipment had arrived and that troops had reached the present area, further indications of the movement.

A decisive battle apparently had not yet taken shape in south Korea for there had been no Red firing heard only in a little.

Here's Our Draft Setup At a Glance

Washington, July 8—(A)—Here is a brief summary of the draft action taken by President Truman yesterday using with major personnel:

1. From the start of the Korean incident two weeks ago in peacetime, many with major personnel ability has existed that it was a government's move to the Korean situation.

Armed forces strength may be increased by draft, if voluntary enlistment fall short to level allowed in law. ...

I tried to use 8-column and extra-bold heads sparingly, but the Korean War was exciting. Lower page is an example of "floating the flag." Note new typefaces, as contrasted with those on page 134.

142

lunch break, until the paper went to press at 2:20. That left an hour to set up stories and columns for tomorrow's race. At 3:30 or thereabouts we were on Seneca Street in the sunshine, the day's travail behind us, ready for the tennis courts or a couple of blissful hours of sailing in Thirty Dash, my sixteen-foot Comet waiting at mooring ten minutes away. In contrast to the strung-out working day in Massena, the Geneva day was compact, ending in mid-afternoon unless there was a baseball or basketball game to cover at night.

The tempo on the desk in Geneva was intense and steady. I was sports editor from 7:30 to 10:30 or 11, depending on the volume of copy to be written or edited; then I was telegraph editor until Page One "went down" at 2:20. The first shift involved local sportswriting as well as processing the overnight scores, standings and roundup stories from the AP, plus page layout. I was always glad I was one of those unique persons who didn't drink coffee; there was no time to look up from the desk or typewriter before the sports deadline. The last sports story was hardly on its way to the composing room before I was cutting up the accumulation of four hours of stories rolling out of the AP teletype, sorting the day's budget of state, national and international stories for Page One.

Like Watertown, Geneva kept Page One inviolate for wire stories, but unlike Watertown, played the top local stories on a segregated inside spread rather than on the back page. To further emphasize his break with the old regime, G.B. Williams had given Learned authority to replace the archaic typefaces with new, modern fonts. Learned, in turn, gave me a free hand to redesign Page One, including carte blanche to "float the flag."

In newspaper jargon "flag" is the term applied to the title logo atop Page One, proclaiming in our case GENEVA DAILY TIMES. Permission to "float" was license to put a story or a banner head across the full eight columns atop the flag, tighten the flag to six columns and run the story down one side, then put a second lead story in a bold headline beneath the flag.

There were many other variations, and with a full, clean page the opportunity for trick heads, boxes and experimental measures was almost limitless. I could hardly wait for the next day to do something different.

Nowadays newspaper graphics, especially in the computer age, have made all these things old hat, but in the late forties Charlie, Al and I attracted a modest degree of attention and notoriety for being graphically daring while still avoiding the kind of sensationalism that alienates conservatives and moderates. Our readers apparently liked what we were doing; the circulation, mired for several decades at a modest six thousand, doubled by 1950.

17

No Bathtub in the Park

In laying out the sports pages in the days that followed the little seance in Al's office I became increasingly haunted by the realization that I was now the designated sports chronicler for a town that I suspected was the least baseball-minded precinct in the vast spread of upstate New York.

Geneva was overwhelmingly a lacrosse town, thanks to the prominence of Hobart College as a perennial power in the structure of that ancient Iroquois game. Teams from the little institution at the head of Seneca Lake held their own not only among small colleges like itself, but regularly administered lacrosse lessons to Cornell, Syracuse, Penn State and other proud campuses far larger and more prestigious.

The architect of this dynasty was a giant of a man, both in physique and professional technique if not in vocabulary. Few people outside of Geneva knew of Francis L. Kraus, a modest, unassuming man, but everybody in the entire lacrosse world knew who Babe Kraus was—Hobart lacrosse coach and the accepted dean of college lacrosse coaches.

In bodily dimension he was large enough to eclipse the sun as he strolled across the campus between his house on St. Clair

Street and his office in the gym. He stood about six-foot-five and weighed perhaps 285 in stocking feet. He had a generous thatch of wavy grayish-white hair. His voice was soft and his speech as deliberate as his gait. I never saw him without a pipe, either in his mouth or in one of his great paws. He took everything as it came, rarely showed emotion even in the waning seconds of a tie game, and offered basic home-spun philosophy from his ample armchair in his favorite corner of the living room to any or all listeners, be they friend, foe or family. He was also my next-door neighbor.

It was a tribute to Babe Kraus that a large segment of the Finger Lakes region was wild about the game of lacrosse and his team year after year. But it was not his fault that in the late thirties and during the war years neither Hobart nor Geneva High School had a baseball team. The reason for this—a genuine phenomenon in twentieth-century America—was that there weren't enough baseball players on the campus, in the city or in the county to field a team.

The only exception was a direct result of the war. During a brief period in 1943-45 the U.S. Navy had a V-12 officer training program at Hobart, and the cadets, being normal red-blooded

Francis L. (Babe) Kraus in younger days.

Americans, forced the college to allocate a baseball diamond and set up a schedule of sorts. Few of them had ever heard of lacrosse or had seen a stick. However, in a typical Geneva household with teenagers it would be hard to find a baseball bat lying around, but in the front-hall closet there was always a cluster of lacrosse sticks.

I became aware of this strange environment when, as a ballplaying youth from New Jersey visiting my cousins in Geneva, I noticed that their friends would often pick up lacrosse sticks each time someone offered the suggestion—at least once a day—that we walk downtown to Isenman's for ice cream. Moseying down Castle Street we would take to the sidewalks on both sides, flinging the lacrosse ball from one sidewalk to the other, the ball zipping between tree branches, flying across the Rochester & Eastern trolley track in the center of the faded brick pavement. In New Jersey we did the same thing en route to ice cream or the railroad station to watch the big engines roar through on the Lackawanna Limited or the Phoebe Snow, but we threw a scuffed baseball, if we had one in those Depression years, or at least a beat-up tennis ball.

*   *   *   *   *

Sports editor in a town without a baseball team? Intolerable! Unacceptable! Unforgiveable! The challenge was clear. All right, Nat, go out and get one.

In that bleak winter of 1946-47 there were rays of hope. In such places as the Seneca Hotel bar and Walgreen's lunch counter there were, I discovered, people who liked baseball in addition to lacrosse. There were even people in this oasis who like baseball *better than* lacrosse. One of these, a hustling man-about-town salesman named Bill Beattie, was willing to help me launch a campaign to bring in a minor league franchise. Our thrust was that Auburn had one, perhaps not on the level of a Triple A Rochester Red Wings and Syracuse Chiefs, but still a bona-fide professional team of its own. It was quickly agreed that if Auburn, only twenty-five miles down U.S. Route 20 and a hated rival since the founding of the republic, could have such an asset, so could Geneva.

147

I knew where a franchise was available, but getting it for Geneva was a far bigger question. In Watertown the previous summer I had spent many an evening watching the Watertown Athletics play in the first season of a newly organized minor league. The Class C Border League had three upstate cities and three Canadian cities. Many of the players were experienced professionals, and the brand of baseball was good. Watertown was a charter member, and as a ballpark regular I had occasionally enjoyed a few post-game beers with several players on visiting teams as well as the home team.

Now I was in Geneva, as perhaps the only local resident who had ever seen or heard of the infant Border League. I called Barney Hearn, a veteran minor league outfielder who lived in Auburn. Barney, one of the most personable fellows on the planet, had spent that summer as playing manager of the Auburn Cayugas in the new league, and between his strategic skill and sharp batting eye—and despite his aging legs—had won the league's first pennant.

Barney, well aware of the long-standing rivalry between Route 20 neighbors, was enthusiastic about the prospect of Geneva joining Auburn, Watertown and Ogdensburg on this side of the St. Lawrence. He confirmed what I had heard—that the league was shopping for places to move two Quebec franchises, Granby and Sherbrooke, in order to increase attendance and cut down travel costs. The Sherbrooke team had disintegrated, but the Granby enterprise was relatively viable while looking for a new home.

Somehow the push for a baseball team in lacrosse-minded Geneva got underway that winter and gained momentum. Beattie and I persuaded several Geneva businessmen to begin tentative negotiations with the Granby owner, and by January the transaction looked promising. Leon Curry, a strong political figure who operated the Finger Lakes Laundry in downtown Geneva, became the moving spirit, with a major assist from Mit Harman, an optometrist and prominent sportsman who owned the city's most popular sporting goods store. Neither of these civic benefactors were baseball experts, least of all in the business end, but to their everlasting credit they pursued the quest.

There were many angles to consider in such an undertaking, and as the project slowly developed it encountered a formidable and surprising roadblock. The Geneva Kiwanis Club, a national service organization of local civic leaders, announced its opposition, explaining that its sponsorship of a youth baseball program in three age-group levels would not permit it to share Geneva's only playable baseball field with a professional team.

This setback was enormous. Curry, Harman and an emerging number of fans realized that the life of a professional team in a small town depends on night games in a good ball park. In Geneva that meant using Shuron Park, a site adjacent to the Shuron Optical plant that the company had deeded to the city for recreational purposes, and on getting lights. Furthermore, the ball club had to count on the city financing the lighting installation, erecting fences and a small clubhouse, and providing additional bleachers.

The Times sports editor explained in his column that a professional team was a community resource that would provide healthy family entertainment. It would play only at night, leaving daylight hours free to conduct baseball clinics at which professional players would instruct aspiring youngsters in the fine points of the game. The team would also give a major boost to Geneva businesses by drawing spectators from nearby towns to Shuron Park as well as providing recreational amusement for local households.

Barney Hearn came over from Auburn several times, and on an icy night in February brought in Eddie Sawyer, manager of the Utica Blue Sox in the Class A Eastern League, to address the Geneva Common Council during a city hall rally on behalf of the growing group of fans. Eddie, a popular upstate sports figure who lived in Mount Morris near Batavia, made a favorable impression, but he was no match for Ase (for Asa) Brooks, the highly regarded president of the Kiwanis Club who led the opposition. It was Brooks who persuaded city councilmen that it would be political suicide to give aid and comfort to people who would undermine a program that made the national pastime accessible to the youth of America.

Yet the struggle continued. The Times kept hammering away. More and more voices joined the chorus of fans, including fathers of Kiwanis ballplayers and even Kiwanians themselves. Joe Jenkins, the extremely popular director of the Geneva YMCA who was state commissioner of the Kiwanis baseball program, came out with an endorsement of the proposed professional team. Babe Kraus, in his younger days a ballplayer of note who reputedly had hit the longest home run ever witnessed in his hometown of Fulton, N.Y. (it landed in an empty hopper on a passing freight train and came to rest somewhere between Syracuse and West Virginia), spread the word he felt Geneva needed baseball. Even Ase Brooks began to see the light: the pros would hold clinics for the youngsters.

Six weeks before the scheduled opening of the 1947 league season the city agreed to put up lights and renovate the park, Curry and Harman signed papers to purchase the Granby franchise, and Border League officials hurriedly revised a schedule that included Geneva and Ottawa along with holdover teams in Auburn, Watertown, Ogdensburg and Kingston, Ontario. The miracle had become reality: one of upstate's lacrosse capitals was now a member of Organized Baseball's minor league network.

*   *   *   *   *

The new entrepreneurs of the Geneva Baseball Club found they had to begin virtually from scratch. The only items they had purchased along with the franchise were a small roster of holdover players and a trunk of well-worn uniforms and assorted baseball equipment. There were, however, several dozen serviceable pairs of baseball socks, which were bright red.

"The team colors will be red," announced Curry after the discovery.

"We can be the Cardinals," said Harman, the sportsman-naturalist.

"Too close to a major league team," I counseled. "Better call 'em the Redbirds."

"Done," said Curry. "But we'll need all new shirts, pants and caps."

The most valuable legacy in the package was an aging outfielder who had experience as a field manager. Charlie Small, an old-timer from Maine who had played briefly with the Boston Red Sox in the thirties, had spent nearly twenty years in the high minors. He had played in Organized Baseball's first night game (I think it was Omaha), and had won several batting championships and popular-player awards in half a dozen leagues. At 42 and trim, he could still hit rifle-shot line drives off breaking pitches. He was in such fine physical shape that he had played the outfield in Granby the previous summer for pure love of the game. Barney Hearn had played for him in the Eastern League and the Can-Am, and spoke highly of him as a master strategist. Charlie promptly agreed to manage the new Geneva team, but not to play, and set about contacting his many sources in the search for players.

By the end of April Charlie's letters and phone calls brought almost two dozen players straggling into Geneva by various

Manager
Charlie Small

transport. While other teams were assembling in warmer climes, Charlie had to conduct what passed for spring training on a makeshift diamond behind the Hobart football field. The backstop was barely twenty feet from the rear of the Humphrey Press printing plant on Pulteney Street. It was damp, it was chilly, the field was cramped and barely playable. Pop flies down the right field line thudded into a grassy embankment not much more than a hundred feet behind first base. Left field encroached on the end zone of the football field.

The first Redbirds were a nondescript flock at best, six or seven from the Granby roster, plus five or six friends of Charlie's from Maine, and a dozen or so players the new manager had rounded up or who had been recommended by various baseball contacts. Most were in their late or mid-20s, several 32 or better. The youngest—and smallest—was little Gerry Cabana, a nineteen-year-old alleged shortstop who was a nephew of the man who had owned the Granby franchise. The eldest was Phene Willette, a well-travelled left-handed hitting outfielder from Maine.

Charlie went about the business of screening this motley crew like a scoutmaster with cubs. He was thankful the Border League was too new and unproven to have affiliations with major league teams, for the players he had coaxed were either too old or too slow to be genuine prospects or too inexperienced to play at this level. There were, however, two or three pretty fair pitchers.

Only a few dozen townsmen came out to see what kind of people would play baseball for money in a city of seventeen thousand souls. At first the onlookers were merely curious, but the more they saw, the more they were impressed. "They may not be fast, but you ought to see them throw," they told their friends downtown the next day. The players looked smart in their new uniforms, and tales of the phenomenon began to filter through the populace.

When the sun came out on the fourth day Charlie let the pitchers throw harder in batting practice. The older players loved that, but when the lefthanded Willette whacked a modest fly ball that ruffled the highest branches of a tree atop the embankment in right field, there were gasps of astonishment from the dozen or so witnesses. Then they heard Charlie say, "Goddammit, Phene, I told you not to swing so hard. We can't afford to lose baseballs. Just meet the ball, don't pull it."

But then little Cabana, a righthanded hitter built like a barrel but hardly five-feet-seven in spikes, smote a fastball that rose in an arc over the goalposts at the near end of the football field. In the crisp windless air the ball soared the length of the empty gridiron, bounced in the end zone in front of the far goalposts and rolled to the fence in front of Smith Hall on the girls' campus. It was a titanic clout, and even Charlie smiled. "Bon," he said in his best Maine French to the youngster, a Quebecois who spoke very little English. At Geneva dinner tables and in the bars that night, Cabana's dinger was stretched to five hundred feet or more, and ticket sales for opening night took a sharp jump even though the lights weren't ready at Shuron Park and the fence hadn't arrived.

Little Gerry, whose fielding was obviously inadequate, was still with the team in mid-May when the Ottawa Nationals arrived for the momentous opening game. The little clubhouse had cinderblock walls and a roof but no interior as yet, the pitcher's mound hadn't been installed, and the outfield was ringed with deep postholes but no fenceposts from the left field corner to deep center. But there were bleachers— and lights. After one look at the park and the unfinished clubhouse, Cabana exclaimed to Clyt Theriault, a pitcher-third baseman from Maine: "Jesu! No fence, no mound, no bathtub!"

To make matters worse, it was a rainy weekend. The long-awaited home opener on Friday night was washed out. The rain stopped on Saturday, but the field was a quagmire under gray skies in the afternoon. At 6 p.m. Curry got permission to burn two thousand gallons of gasoline on the basepaths to accelerate the drying-out process, an extravagance he paid for out of his own pocket. By game time there were more than two thousand people in the stands, the largest gathering ever to witness a baseball game in the history of the staid old city.

The Redbirds, who had opened the league season by splitting a two-game series in Kingston, took the field to a tumultuous ovation, welcomed by the Winnek Post drum corps. The mayor threw out the first ball, and the mood was festive even when the Nationals took a 2-0 lead in the third inning. The crowd in its innocence cheered every strike and even the foul balls struck by Geneva batters. New local heroes were born, and in the third-base coaching box Manager Small was lustily jeered each time he held up a runner the eager fans felt should be rounding the base and digging full-speed for the plate.

Despite the marshy infield and the peril from open postholes in the shadowy fringes of the outfield, it was a well-played game. It was also appropriate that a hometown lad, Don Phelps from nearby Gorham, signed by Curry only twenty-four hours earlier, smote a two-bagger with two on in the fifth that gave Geneva a 3-2 lead. The Redbirds held on for a 4-2 triumph and a page of history was written.

*   *   *   *   *

It took this lovable, rag-tag crew less than a month to establish itself in sixth place in the six-team league. They maintained exclusive possession for the full 130-game season despite a September winning streak that fell one game short of overtaking the Kingston Ponies on the final day. But throughout that first summer the constituency took them into their hearts and homes. As enemy teams made their periodic visits the fans identified their favorite villains. The Auburn games filled the park, and there was a capacity audience on a memorable night when the Redbirds' ranking hero and slugging cleanup hitter was guilty of a modern-era Merkle Play.*

---

*Fred Merkle, a better-than-average first baseman for the New York Giants, committed baseball's classic "boner" that cost his team the National League pennant in 1908. In the ninth inning of a critical game with the Chicago Cubs at the Polo Grounds, the score was tied at 1-1, there were two out and the home team had runners on first and third. When the batter lined the game-winning single to right field, Merkle, the runner on first, ran directly to the clubhouse in center field as the exuberant fans poured onto the field. In the confusion Johnny Evers, Cub second baseman, got the attention of an umpire, stood on second base holding a baseball, and claimed that Merkle was out by reason of being forced at second before touching the base, thus ending the inning and nullifying the run. The historic controversy was not settled until several hours later when the league president upheld the protest, declared the game a tie and ordered it replayed. The Cubs won the replay and the pennant by the margin of a single game.'

154

This is what happens when the sports editor is also the wire editor putting out page one. We began "floating the flag" even before we got the new typefaces.

As fate would have it, the arch-enemy Auburn Cayugas were in town for a twi-night doubleheader that fateful evening. Geneva won the first game. The second game went into the bottom of the tenth inning. When Geneva loaded the bases with two out, Small sent up canny Phene Willette to pinch hit. The old veteran delivered the game-winner, a trolley-wire shot over the first baseman's head, ending the long evening. The crowd went wild, celebrating a two-game sweep over an arch foe.

As the weary players of both teams headed for the showers, the Auburn right fielder gloved the ball and tossed it in the general direction of the mound. The Geneva runner on first base, whose name shall be mercifully omitted from this translation, started for second with the crack of the bat. Seeing the winning drive skid on the outfield grass, he stopped and returned to the base to give Willette a congratulatory hug before they jogged joyously back toward the clubhouse.

155

In the elevated pressbox, where I had the job of official scorer as well as Times sportswriter, my mind flashed back to my beloved Giants and the historic Merkle Play. I mentioned to Bob Kieve, the young WGVA radio announcer in the chair next to me, that the runner could be called out for leaving the basepath or before touching second base. In either case the run would not count.

I gazed in horror as the ball came to rest on the basepath just east of second base. For a moment time stood still, the little white sphere lying peacefully in the smooth dirt as the field and grandstands emptied. I held my breath as Charlie Small left his third-base coaching box and sauntered across the infield, trying to act casual and glancing furtively toward the clubhouse to see if anyone else had noticed. He wanted that ball destroyed.

Len Zanke, Auburn catcher and a fiery pepperpot who was often a favorite target of Geneva fans, had also taken several steps toward the clubhouse to his right, mask and cap in hand, weary from a long evening of crouching behind the plate. Suddenly the situation dawned on Zanke, perhaps the best catcher in the league and certainly the brainiest. He turned back, saw Charlie Small crossing the infield to the right of the mound heading for the errant ball. Zanke broke into a dead run. So did Small, several strides closer to the scene of the crime. The Geneva manager pounced on the ball, straightened up, swung his arm in a windmill pivot and flung the white pill high over the right field bleachers. For a second it sparkled in the glare of the floodlights, then disappeared into the parking lot beyond the fence.

Zanke was furious. He yelled his frustration at the grinning Geneva manager, slammed his mask to the turf, and spun around to run for the clubhouse to get official help. Grabbing one of the dark-suited umpires, he quickly got his message through, and the umpires summoned the teams back to action. The PA system informed the milling spectators that the runner had been declared out because of interference, the run did not count, and the score remained tied. Play resumed, the eleventh inning began and the Cayugas scored five runs on the disheartened

Redbirds. The euphoric doubleheader triumph had vanished into an even split, adding yet another page of history.

The next night when I went to the dugout to get the lineups, the downcast base runner was sitting in quiet remorse at the far end. When Charlie tried to console him, the player said: "I'm sorry. I don't know what came over me. How can I make it up to you?"

"Forget it," said Charlie. "Just hit one out tonight."

The popular outfielder did that one better. He hit two picturesque shots over the fence, the first with the bases loaded, the second with two aboard. He finished the season with twenty-five home runs, tied for first, and led the league in runs-batted-in. For his momentary lapse the fans had already granted him instant forgiveness. It was, after all, a love affair.

18

No Place to Go But Up

Those pioneer Redbirds were heroes to the fans, even in adversity. Only their manager, the erudite Charles A. Small, was not beloved, primarily because of his habit, born of acute baseball instinct over many years, of holding up runners at third base. In their naivete the customers felt the boss was depriving them of a run. But this was professional baseball, and it took a while before the fans began to tender him a degree of reluctant acceptance. Some came to realize that there was a reason for holding up a runner at third—either the runner would be out by ten feet at the plate, or the most basic of baseball rules applied: when you're four runs behind, don't take chances. The 1947 Redbirds were often four or more runs behind.

Several weeks later Charlie's stock jumped many points when, in a game at Falcon Park in Auburn, he charged angrily from the dugout to protest an adverse decision at second base. The ensuing shouting match, as usual, failed to alter the verdict. Charlie ended his jaw-to-jaw tirade by whipping off his cap, and with the field lights reflecting brightly off his shiny pate, executed a perfect dropkick that sent his cap flying in a lofty orbit toward third base.

Baseball umpires do not take kindly to being shown up in this fashion. Small's antagonist was quick to give the signal for banishment. Two days later the league office in Ogdensburg announced that Manager Small was being suspended for five days for unbecoming conduct.

A sizeable contingent of Geneva fans who regularly drove the twenty-five miles to follow the team when it played in neighboring Auburn had delightedly spread the tale of Charlie's dramatic felony. The action by the league office outraged the fans. Leon Curry showed his mettle by hiring a local pilot and plane to transport himself and his beleaguered manager to Ogdensburg for a personal appeal to President John Ward. Ward, a banker by trade, gave the last-place team a measure of solace by reducing the suspension to three days, and the appellates returned to the Finger Lakes to cheers. The episode further solidified community support of the baseball venture and scored political points for Curry and Small.

*   *   *   *   *

All these shenannigans made me realize what fun I was having in my first year as a sports editor. I enjoyed every minute of every game, and poured my enthusiasm into the daily accounts of the joys and frustrations of the Redbirds along with Hobart teams and teams from several local high schools. Geneva High, which produced a succession of championship basketball teams, had no nickname, an ingredient sports editors desperately need for headline purposes as well as inserting color in the routine prose. The situation called for a contest to give the school's team a nickname, and impaneling three neutrals to do the judging. (The winner: "Panthers"—but don't ever ask why.) Yet my heart was always with the Redbirds, not only because of my passion for baseball, but because I felt a parental responsibility for originating the conspiracy that led to the birth of the team.

In the double capacity of maintaining the ball club's official scorebook and writing the games, I came to know most of the Geneva players very well, plus the managers of visiting teams. The league, a newcomer in the baseball establishment, had several well-known names. Bob Shawkey, the Yankees' top pitcher in the early twenties who pitched the dedicatory first game in the Yankee Stadium, was manager of the Watertown

159

Athletics. Paul (Daffy) Dean, younger brother of the famed Dizzy Dean, managed the Ottawa Nationals. Ben Lady, huge in popularity as well as girth, was the manager of the Kingston Ponies, but the big attraction when they came to town was Zeke (Bananas) Bonura, still hanging on after a colorful career with the Chicago White Sox. Big Bananas, more portly in his old age than he was as a legendary slugger in the big leagues, hit only singles and home runs—a normal triple to left center would get him safely to first base. The crowds loved him.

There were also two well-known hockey names in the league. Bob Dill, a star defenseman for the Rangers, was the playing manager in Ogdensburg, and Doug Harvey, a star with the Montreal Canadiens (who later made the Hockey Hall of Fame) played the outfield for Ottawa.

These established pros were always willing to meet the local sports editor for a few beers after the game, and provided colorful material for the sports column I had started writing for the Times. Visiting teams were housed in the Algonquin Hotel next door to the Times building on Seneca Street, a far cry from a first-class hostelry, but their proximity and free afternoons made them readily accessible. I loved those sessions, not because of the fame of my companions but for the wealth of baseball anecdotes and lore they had at hand.

A special favorite was Pepper Martin, legendary as the St. Louis Cardinal who practically wrecked the 1931 World Series. A dozen years later Pepper was touring the boondocks putting on baseball clinics for youngsters. He came through Geneva twice during my tenure, and after those sessions the columns virtually wrote themselves.

For pure baseball knowlege and mathematical strategy, however, none of these widely known idols had anything on our own Charlie Small. Charlie was a graduate of Bates College, a small but scholarly campus in Maine. He had been a lifetime student of the intricacies of the national game. He and I usually met after each home game for a beer or two, during the leisurely consumption of which he would restructure the key plays that had won or lost the game or explain the logic and timing of a particular move—steal vs. hit-and-run, positioning against certain hitters in certain situations, etcetera. For me these

160

The Algonquin Hotel, which served as headquarters for visiting Border League teams, was not even second-rate, but in those days it looked better than in this photo, taken just prior to demolition. In its threadbare lobby, next door to the Times on Seneca Street, I digested many an anecdote relaxing with visiting managers and players, among them Paul (Daffy) Dean, Bob Shawkey, Ben Lady, Zeke Bonura and Bob Dill.

dialogues opened an entirely new and deeper perspective in a fascinating game, offering an insight that has sharpened my interest ever since.

It was Charlie who pointed out the mathematical physics and anatomical philosophy in Abner Doubleday's invention, little things even players and die-hard fans wouldn't think about. Why ninety feet between bases? Because the consummate measure of the ability of homo sapiens to hurl a baseball from pitching slab to catcher's mitt and catcher's throw to second base is approximately equal to the time it takes a speedy baserunner to dash from first on an attempted steal. If the bases were 89 feet apart almost anyone could steal the base; if the distance were 91 feet hardly anyone would be successful.

In addition to his analytical mind and native intelligence, Charlie had a keen sense of humor. Basically he was a serious fellow, suffering in the frustration that comes with a last-place team and not having the players who would enable him to make the strategic moves he needed in game situations. He took his plight philosophically, enjoying close camaraderie with his players, always a diplomat in discussing their shortcomings and mistakes.

His boys worked hard in almost constant adversity, which made the occasional victories so much sweeter, especially in front of a home audience. One of his most diligent and dedicated employees was Ernie Craine, a solidly constructed catcher who came from Red Creek, N.Y., a hamlet in agricultural Wayne County only thirty-five miles or so from Geneva. Perspiration would pour from Ernie's brow as he gave his all from his stance behind the plate and hurled his bulky frame in front of runners charging down the line from third. Great patches of moisture appeared nightly on his uniform, which would start a game cleanly laundered and be covered with dust and grime by the third inning. At bat, to the delight of the parishioners, he would smite prodigious flies to distant reaches of the outfield, some of which would sail over the fence. The fans loved him, even when he struck out, which was frequently, and they cheered with unabashed affection at the sight of him trudging wearily back to the dugout after swinging at a third strike, as if to say, "That's

OK, Ernie, we will always love you." When he crashed into the backstop lumbering after a high foul the thudding impact could be heard in Penn Yan.

Ernie caught every game, including doubleheaders, despite bruises and aches from body-crunching collisions at home plate. With no backup catcher, Charlie was concerned that even Ernie's proven durability wouldn't last forever. One day in mid-season a slender young man came up to the Times sports desk and said he had been assigned to the Geneva ball club and told to report to the sports editor at the newspaper for further instructions. He looked to be about 16, and said he had ridden buses from his native Arkansas. He had never been east of the Mississippi or north of Joplin. His name was Omer Ehlers and his age was 18. I called Charlie to come down and pick up his latest ward.

Two nights later on my customary pre-game visit to the dugouts to get starting lineups for the scorebook, Charlie obliged with his usual recitation, so standard I often filled in the next spot before he named it. This night, when he got to the eighth spot in the order, I had started to write "Cra—" but Charlie in his usual deadpan expression, his eyes straight ahead watching the warm-ups, intoned, "Ehlers, catch. Theriault, pitch."

I was astonished, especially since Don Bryant, one of the best pitchers in the league, was starting for Ottawa. "Ehlers?" I said, shocked at what appeared to be perfidy, choosing a smooth-cheeked teenager over a workhorse veteran. "How come? You benching Ernie?"

Charlie turned to me, still deadpan. "It's because of Ernie's weakness," he explained with fatherly patience.

"Ernie's weakness?" I exclaimed, wondering what he knew that I didn't. "What weakness?"

"The pitched ball," he said soberly, watching Bryant spinning warm-up pitches like rifle shots in front of the Ottawa dugout.

The lithe little rookie caught the game and handled himself well. The next night Charlie gave Ernie back to the adoring fans, knowing now he could give the beloved catcher occasional rest and give the young relief catcher some valuable experience.

Those pioneer pros laid an unshakable foundation for Geneva baseball. They also had color. Two weeks after the end of the first season Curry and Harman purchased several established players from around the league. They brought in ex-villains Zanke, Moose Kromko, a happy-go-lucky slugger, and Bill Scally, a clutch-hitting outfielder, from Auburn, and Peanuts Klestinec from Watertown. Oldtime fans will also remember fondly such characters as Goose Gosselin, Pete Kousegan, Tony Romeo and Freddie Mularski.

The Redbirds had a good year on the field and at the gate in 1948, with help from the Brooklyn Dodgers, who sent Small and Curry some surplus players from their extensive minor league operations. In 1949, with a new flock of embryonic Dodgers on hand to support a solid nucleus of experienced veterans, the club showed its gratitude by changing its nickname to the Geneva Robins, a concession to a former Brooklyn manager, Wilbert Robinson.

The new Robins were younger and faster, stealing bases and providing exciting baseball while half a dozen older players were furnishing long-distance hitting and steady pitching. In 1949 this colorful mixture brought Geneva its first minor league pennant and completed a sweep by winning the playoffs. In 1950 a similar cast found out how hard it was to repeat, and finished a close second to Ottawa, but the support was still there.

It may have been coincidence that Geneva won the New York State Kiwanis senior league (ages 15-18) baseball championship in 1948, and in 1950 a bedraggled but enthusiastic group of teenage boys from a local Hi-Y club formed a Kiwanis team that went all the way to the state championship final at Ebbets Field in Brooklyn. In free hours before these Cherokees boarded a Manhattan subway for the trip to Brooklyn, Dewey Antinelli, the catcher, and Jon Kraus, an outfielder, ate four dozen steamed clams apiece, purchased from a sidewalk vendor on 23rd Street, then, with no money for an elevator, climbed the stairs to the top of the Empire State Building. They professed exhaustion and queasy stomachs at game-time, but the team played errorless ball and Al Antinelli pitched superbly in a 2-0 loss to Bayside, Long Island, a team that had won 36 straight games. So much for teenage baseball players in a town noted for lacrosse.

At the end of the 1950 season the Robins suffered several setbacks. They lost Charlie Small, who resigned at the end of the year for health reasons. By 1951 Geneva had the most solvent franchise in a league that was tottering from mismanagement and declining support in other cities. The slippage was nationwide; minor leagues were being devastated by the spreading popularity of television. The Dodgers cut back on their own organization, forcing Curry and Bev Chew, president of Shuron Optical who had played a major part in saving the franchise, to turn to Joe Cambria and the Washington Senators. With the color line broken by Jackie Robinson, Cambria had found a new source of talent in the Caribbean, and was mining Cubans, Puerto Ricans and Dominicans, a dozen of whom he sent to Geneva for orientation. He also insisted on sending up a bilingual manager.

In short order the league collapsed, Small fell terminally ill in his hometown of Lewiston, Maine, and the lights at Shuron were used only for high school football. But the foundation laid by Curry, Chew and the stalwarts in red baseball caps was solid, and Geneva soon was invited into the long-established New York-Penn League, an entrenched incubator of baseball talent with strong subsidies from major league organizations. Hungry for new heroes and imbued with love of baseball, the fans returned to the old ballpark in droves.

All through the sixties Geneva was a Cincinnati farm team in the NYP. Pete Rose and Tony Perez played their first professional seasons at Shuron Park. In the seventies the Chicago Cubs replaced the Reds as parents, and several dozen players from a steady stream of young hopefuls who started their careers in Geneva made it to the Big Leagues—Bill Madlock, Kent Tekulve, Mel Hall, Joe Collins to name a few.

And with the Mets, Astros, Red Sox, Pirates and others in nearby towns like Auburn, Elmira and Watertown, Geneva fans over the years have watched dozens of players now in the major

Three Redbirds who came to play baseball married Geneva girls and raised families there. From left, Fred Mularski, who took a job as mail carrier and rose to become Geneva postmaster, Clyt Theriault and Al Klestinec.

leagues or en route to baseball's pinnacle. Forgotten are the ghosts of Charlie Small, Don Phelps, Ernie Craine, Phene Willette, Moose Kromko, Len Zanke, Paul Dean, Barney Hearn and others, not to mention Fred Merkle, whose shadow, while it can't be seen in the glow of the field lights, still lurks on the basepath between first and second.

Barney still lives in Auburn with lasting memories, and three old Redbirds—Clyt Theriault, Peanuts Klestinec and Freddie Mularski—married Geneva girls and settled down to raise families in that charming little college town on the banks of Seneca Lake. The ball park occupies the same acreage at the end of Lyceum Street, but it has a new name now. Not Curry Park or Curry-Chew Park or any association with the pioneers who brought baseball to Geneva, putting up funds they knew they'd never get back, working their heads off to promote, improve, compete, build and preserve.

Nowadays the Geneva Cubs play home games at McDonough Park. It has a covered grandstand now, a larger clubhouse, an orthodox refreshment stand and a roomier pressbox, but the attendance is disappointing despite several first-place finishes in a strong league.

166

I knew Joe McDonough well during my stint on the Times. He was a friendly, likeable police sergeant and a familiar sight around town in his three-wheeled motorcycle with a sidecar seat. In those fun-filled days of Redbird baseball and happy crowds Joe McDonough must have been one of those hundreds of loyal fans. I'm sure I must have seen him at the games, but it's hard to remember details after all these years. He also must have been a good contributor to the Reds and Cubs who came later.

Today the new generation of Geneva baseball people who changed the name from Shuron Park aren't the only sports fans with short memories. From 1980 to 1987 Hobart lacrosse teams won eight consecutive Division III national championships, the most by any collegiate team in any sport at any level. Those teams didn't play home games on Babe Kraus Memorial Field. Maybe they will some day.

Meanwhile, with each passing year, it becomes less likely McDonough Park will ever become Curry Park in tribute to the man who brought baseball to Geneva and who once dipped into his own pocket to buy two thousand gallons of gasoline so the fans could see the first pro game ever played in Geneva, on an evening when there was only half a fence—and the uncompleted clubhouse had "no bathtub."

19

But Not Forever

In five blissful years in Geneva, rivaling in pure journalistic joy those exciting pre-war years in Massena, there were different blends of colorful experiences. No Bryants, Shatraws or Falters to provide humor or drama, but a free rein in putting out Page One and an abundance of warm stories from the Geneva High basketball court, Hobart football field and Shuron Park, the ancient ballpark that still houses, under a new name, a major league farm team. Not to mention Seneca Lake, where we swam, fished and raced sailboats, and Art Kenney's bootblack shop on South Exchange Street, at that time the upstate capital of four-part harmony that in 1947 spawned the first official barbershop quartet chapter in New York State.

In this paradise journalism continued to be great fun amid hard work and deadline pressures. If there was a low point, it would be the time one of my wire-copy headlines turned to ashes, and that was more humorous than faulty. If there was a high point, professionally speaking, it was a job offer, repeated semiannually by the AP bureau chief in Albany, who insisted that of the 25-odd small dailies that subscribed to his single-wire news service, the Geneva Times had the brightest and most selectively sophisticated front page.

That errant headline is etched forever in my cranium. The wire copy deadline was 1:35, always a tense race with composing room people demanding strict adherence to their production schedule. The Korean war was a running story on Page One, and that day's story from the front was already in type, three-quarters of a column of shiny lead linotype slugs in place in the deep dish of the page form, awaiting the remaining trays·of type that would fill the page before lockup. At 1:32 the bell on the AP machine in the newsroom sounded, our signal that an important bulletin was breaking. Sure enough: the U.S. Congress had at that moment approved extending the military draft to married men in the applicable age group, but exempting those with children. It was a momentous story, for the Korean crisis up to that time had mandated only single men.

I had three minutes to write a new head and find a place on Page One for two or three paragraphs at best. In several years on the job I no longer needed to count units for headlines, I could sense word lengths by "feel" and could balance line lengths in two-column heads by instinct. In the new crisis I quickly rolled a half piece of paper into my trusty typewriter and wrote

CHILDLESS FATHERS
TO FACE DRAFT

attached it to the wire copy and ran it out to the back room.

Moments later little Betty Oughterson, the "printer's devil" handling the copy bank, was back at my desk, throwing back the sheet with the headline. This was routine procedure, for even the finest instincts can be off at times, and I assumed it was another case of a head that didn't quite fit. I took Betty's offering and shortened it by pencil to read

CHILDLESS DADS
TO FACE DRAFT

"That'll do it," I said, but instead of rushing back to the composing room, Betty didn't budge.

"G'wan, git," I said, urging her on her way with the clock ticking away valuable seconds.

169

"Read it," she said, shoving it back at me.

"Dammit, that'll fit, I know it will," I insisted. "Now, get going."

She still refused to move, flashing me a big grin beneath her silver-rimmed glasses. "Read it again."

Only then did it sink in. I no longer can remember the replacement head that got me out of that jam, but you can treat the incident as an exercise. Write your own head, 16 units per line, two lines. Lower-case thin letters (i,j,l) count half, caps one and a half, space one. Have fun.

The job offer from Albany carried more wallop. I was immensely flattered, and got a huge dose of professional satisfaction each time Norris Paxton, the bureau chief, made the approach on his periodic visits to AP clients around the state. He found it difficult to understand my reluctance to accept what he saw as a major advance in status, experience and career opportunity. But I was so happy in my role at the Times, and felt so lucky to be able to live in a place like Geneva, that I was unable to even consider a change.

One afternoon Paxton and I were discussing the subject after Page One had been put to bed. I invited him to come for a short ride around town. He accepted, and I took him first to the yacht club and showed him the *Thirty Dash*, bobbing invitingly at her mooring in the bright sun and light breeze, forty miles of beautiful lake stretching behind her to the skyline. Then I drove him around Geneva, along South Main with its stately old houses and big elms, past the college, and poured him a coke in the attractive little bungalow on St. Clair Street I shared with my two sisters. Then along White Springs Road where beautiful orchards overlooked the lake. Next we drove past the expansive plantings at the state Agricultural Experiment Station, then down the red-brick pavement of Castle Street, and back downtown to the Times. The message was simple: I may be guilty of career myopia, but how can Albany top all this?

Paxton, whom I liked and respected, had no choice but to concede my point, the while believing this young editor, single and just past 30, was wearing blinders, and certainly had his priorities mixed. But even Paradise can begin to wear after five years, and Paxton won in the end. I eventually accepted the job in Albany and on St. Patrick's Day, 1951, packed my Ford for new adventures and a new life two hundred miles to the east.

IV

The Capital District

20

Follies in the Fast Lane

Few observers other than ambitious politicians would classify Albany as the big league, but for a young (33) newspaperman the move to the Empire State's capital city had all the earmarks of a giant step upward. Actually it turned out to be the same old industry, but in a starkly different geographical, social, political and professional orbit. Whether it was a loftier level of journalism was questionable.

In the Albany bureau of the Associated Press the focus was statewide rather than local or regional. The bureau's primary function was operation of a selective news network that gathered "wireworthy" stories from every corner of New York State for immediate distribution to every AP member paper in the state via teletype. Stories of national significance or those of interest to nearby states or regions were transmitted to adjoining networks in the AP grid for selective distribution.

The whole environment in the capital was intensely competitive. AP's chief rival, United Press, was ever present. So were the New York Times, Herald-Tribune, Post, Buffalo Evening News and a host of other major dailies with statewide or regional focus. The challenge was to get exclusive stories, write better stuff than the other guy covering the same story and, in the case of the AP-UP rivalry, get it out faster—even if only by a minute or two. There was a third wire service at the time, International News Service (INS) operated by the Hearst Corporation, but as a competitor it was negligible, and eventually was absorbed by the UP to form the present-day UPI (United Press International).

Unlike a conventional newspaper, a wire service is a round-the-clock operation. The AP "day" opened at 2 a.m and served afternoon newspapers, called PM's, until most of the final editions had "gone to bed." At 4 p.m. the day wire became the night wire and morning papers became the beneficiaries. That cycle ran its course until 2 a.m., the cutoff for the switch back to PM's.

*   *   *   *   *

A change of venue can do wonders for perspective and motivation, not to mention a whole new routine, socially, professionally and, to some degree, economically. In Albany, a part of the state I knew almost nothing about despite many trips through it by road and rail, I found myself in the late winter of 1951 beholden to the third employer and the fourth locale of my legitimate career, apart from the military.

Life in the express lane wasn't that much faster; it just seemed that way at first. For me it was simply a matter of adjusting to a new system and a new cast of characters. Perhaps a little tougher, a little more demanding, a bit more pressured, and certainly more competitive.

By any measure, a wire service like the AP was a breed apart from a newspaper. No presses rumbling in the basement or the back room. No city room. No country correspondents from Ovid or Oswegatchie, no church notices, no local paragraphs. No reporters out on beats in the city. Every member paper in the state did the beat legwork for AP in their respective bailiwicks. In Albany we had access to local stories in the Knickerbocker News and the Times-Union as they were being written.

We did develop an occasional local story when appropriate, but for the routine stuff we monitored "dupes"— carbons of stories reporters on the Albany papers were required to make as they wrote. Even then we had only to skim the cream. By the same token, each AP member newspaper had a staffer serving as an AP "stringer" responsible for calling in wireworthy stories from that paper's coverage area. The Albany AP bureau, serving as the command center for the state, took calls from eastern New York stringers, our man in Syracuse handled stringers from central New York, and our one-man AP outpost in Buffalo handled the western section. In Rockefeller Center, Manhattan, the New York bureau covered everything south of Poughkeepsie, but Albany controlled the state wire and directed transmission traffic from Montauk to Niagara.

The closest we came to the old-fashioned news beat was in the bureau's satellite office at the Capitol, where a three-man staff of AP legislative correspondents was assigned to the Senate, the Assembly, the governor, legislative leaders and major issues. They occupied a cubicle attached to quarters consigned to the news media on the third floor of the Capitol. The AP office was connected to headquarters downtown by a direct intercom phone.

In the fifties the bureau's main office was housed in a dusty, messy, crowded and noisy one-room garret on the third floor of the Knickerbocker News building on lower Beaver Street, a sliver of an alleyway in downtown Albany barely a hundred yards from the Hudson River. To make poor conditions worse in this airless attic, most of the occupants in that era were smokers. Instead of the single teletype at the Geneva Times or three at the Watertown Times, there were nine, several with keyboards for sending.

Ten people worked in that stifling little rectangle. Instead of a city room with a cadre of reporters, the average daytime staff on the AP had two editors, a rewrite man, two bosses and a secretary, two teletype operators called punchers, a mechanical specialist who had the inexplicable job title of Traffic Chief, and a photographer. The bank of rattling teletypes ran half the length of one wall. Tiers of partitioned shelves bulging with files of wire copy stuffed to overflowing occupied the opposite wall. The bureau chief's desk was wedged in a far corner, the desk of his male secretary abutting it. The desks and typewriters of the state editor and the rewrite man were jammed back-to-back in the middle of the crowded room, leaving narrow aisles along the wall with the overstuffed files and the wall with the teletypes.

That left barely enough area for the "day desk," the key station that directed the flow of copy to the state wire, and the relay desk, occupied by the editor who fed the single wire to the smaller upstate papers (including the Geneva Times). There were two punchers on duty during the day cycle, one machine at the day desk editor's elbow, the other punching out copy for the relay wire. The traffic chief, who was responsible for the operation and preservation of the teletype circuits, was crammed into a corner near the only access door. The AP staff photographer had a closet off the front of the room for a darkroom, and thus was spared the forced intimacy of the central ghetto, but he had to squeeze his shoulder bags and cameras through the alleged aisles on each traverse between his cubicle and the door to the outside hallway.

The teletype machines raised an incessant clatter. Occasionally one would sound its high-pitched bell above the cacaphony, calling attention to an important news break. The bell was the signal for what was known in the trade as a "bulletin," in which case the telegraph editor on a client newspaper would leave his desk and rush to the machine. Phones rang frequently, either the outside lines or the intercom link with the Capitol office six blocks away.

When I asked one of my new colleagues why AP brass forced such miserable Seventh-Avenue-sweatshop conditions on their minions, I was told it was not their immediate fault. Member papers in cities where AP bureaus or correspondents were located, it was explained, were required by their membership contract to provide working space for the AP. The loophole was that the contract language didn't specify what kind of space, hence the Gannett people, who had the Knickerbocker News as the chain's capital outlet, could get away with giving their wire-service tenants a small, third-floor attic without having to provide as much as a shoehorn, let alone heat or air conditioning.

It seemed like a madhouse, a whole new system to learn, a side of the newspaper world I had never known or thought about. Compared to Massena, Watertown and Geneva, it had the earmarks of mainline journalism, at a breakneck pace that never let up. For a bureau that covered the full expanse of New York State north of Poughkeepsie and west of the Hudson for papers and radio stations in every section of the state, and connected with a national grid serving every time zone in North America, there was literally a dozen news deadlines every hour.

The bureau routine in Albany was honed to such a tailored format that my feeling of being a novice among professionals vanished in the span of a few days, so much so that by Friday night of my first week I was en route to Stowe with three skiers I had met at the Albany Ski Club meeting the previous evening. It was just another weekend adventure, but to me it was a private celebration of my entrance into the five-day work week.

Six days and two hundred miles after leaving the place where I had thought I would always want to live, Geneva seemed a continent away. I knew almost nothing of Albany and had had only a glimpse of the AP, but I was certain I was going to like both.

21

Never Assume Anything

Being part of a small newspaper staff provides a sense of camaraderie that tends to unify a mix of personalities under a common purpose—getting a paper out every day. Working under one roof, reporters and editors learn respect for the people in the back room who set type, lay out pages, make the cuts or halftones for photos and do the make-ready for the presses. They also appreciate the people out front who sell ads, take classifieds, keep the books and handle the payroll, and the people downstairs who run the presses and bundle papers into the trucks. You pass these people in the hallways, see them at the lunch counter in Walgreen's and have a drink with them at office parties. You know them by their first names and know what they do. They are friends in a closely knit organization, united in dependency on the faith and wisdom of an employer.

In the Albany bureau Norris Paxton had only fifteen people under his command. In normal circumstances in such a small group working intimately under the constant pressure of a wire service, it was inevitable that each member would know the whims and quirks of each personality intimately, but here such was not the case.

I had been on the AP for several months before I met two of the three staffers in the Capitol office, and almost a year before a

Christmas party that enabled me to have an introductory handshake with Paxton's three staffers who operated the radio wire serving upstate broadcasting stations. There was, after all, little occasion for the Capitol staffers to come down to the bureau and none for the radio people, who were based across the river in Troy. It even took several weeks before I was able to meet the two fellows who worked the third shift in the wee hours of the night.

There were widely divergent personalities on the staff, and as is often the case with talented professionals who are artists in their own right, there were sensitivities that at times clashed. Paxton was a remote administrator who had to work at being warm. Henry Leader, the state editor, was a brilliant news-paperman with a volatile temper. The two key staff positions, day desk and night desk, were held by experienced women, each exercising strong authority on the full cycle of the wire operation. In that era, a full decade and a half before the women's movement had made even a small impact on the nation's lifestyle, Paxton's two female editors were often resented by the rest of the staff, all males. Both women were thoroughly professional and were accepted as such. The occasional friction arose not so much because of their gender, but because their personalities and modi operandi tended to ruffle feathers, especially on the occasions when they became dictatorial. They were cool and competent under fire, and they were excellent writers, masters of the AP stylebook. They also had that treasured commodity—seniority.

They had been hired from member papers early in World War II when there was an acute shortage of durable males, especially in jobs the draft machinery considered non-essential. Accordingly, Toni Adams had been a fixture at the day desk, which ranked her only a small administrative step behind Henry Leader, the state editor and number two in the bureau pecking order. Kay Parker had the night desk, which was, in effect, an eight-hour continuation of the day desk. When I came on the AP the two women had been there eight or ten years. They also had privileges that went with longevity and permanency, one of which seemed to be that of exercising dominance from the wire desk and antagonizing, no matter how unintentionally, their associates.

Paxton was a fastidious fellow who sported a gray moustache in an era when 99 of 100 U.S. adult males were smooth-
shaven. He also wore spats on occasion, and smoked a cigar when
appropriate to the image of the suave executive he was striving
to project. He was proud of his status as AP bureau chief with
access to Capitol bigwigs—politicians and heavyweight
newsmen—but most of them accepted him as a vain, somewhat
stuffy colleague who put on a casual air in an effort to show he
was really a good fellow.

Although he wrote an occasional piece for the wire, one or
two a year, I never knew how good a writer Paxton was, but he
did have keen insight into the wheeling and dealing of capitol
pols and could be critical if one of his legislative correspondents
failed to project the real inside stuff or portray the political
intrigue of a particular issue.

He had been Albany bureau chief for twelve years or more, a
tenure that was in itself a private embarrassment because it
meant he had reached his career pinnacle before age 40. Albany
was considered one of the key bureaus in the AP hierarchy,
mainly because New York State governors were automatically
presidential candidates, actual or potential. That phenomenon
made the Albany job a coveted step on the ladder to even more
important bureaus such as New York or Washington. The fact
that the AP brass had hung poor Pax out to dry on the Albany
threshold at an early age was frustration enough, but what
understandably gnawed him even more was that several of his
Albany staffers had vaulted into those jobs themselves or gone
on to higher acclaim in the AP power structure.

But Pax, as he liked to be called, was a capable administrator, as witnessed by his deep pride in the fact that of all the
bureaus in the AP national network, Dallas and Albany were the
only ones that had not been unionized by the Newspaper Guild.

*   *   *   *   *

The number two man in the bureau was Henry Leader,
whose title as state editor licensed him to oversee virtually
every sentence that went on the wire from Albany. While Paxton

was projecting a somewhat stiff paternalistic image or that of a remote executive, Leader had an intensity that tended to intimidate junior members of the staff. He possessed an incendiary temper when angered or crossed. In an argument he could bore into the deepest sensitivity of his antagonist, but once the dialogue had finished, he reverted to his likeable self without malice. Everyone in the bureau had felt the full sting of Henry's Hibernian wrath at one time or several, but no matter how deeply he had humiliated a foe in battle, it was impossible not to admire and respect him.

Henry had grown up in the school of hard knocks, which rendered him fearless of anyone in his path, whether it was a governor, senior senator, corporation head or AP executive. He had a mind like a steel trap and a thousand questions that covered every conceivable angle of the story he was working on. Seeing Henry operate made me realize I could have made all my stories better by asking more questions at the sources, and I came to recognize that all of us who worked with him became better writers and newsmen by subconsciously emulating him.

In my first few weeks in Albany I was on day rewrite, taking stories over the phone and culling the dupes from the Knick city room downstairs. In that capacity it didn't take long for me to feel the wrath of Henry's temper. On his periodic review of the copy files he would look up, stare me in the eyes across our desks, and inquire whether I had asked so-and-so about such-and-such, and, knowing I hadn't, immediately ask why I hadn't. Or, why hadn't I called so-and-so to check on this or that instead of just taking the information as given? Or, whom did I call to confirm a certain fact? Did I know this for sure? When I once made the defensive mistake of telling Henry that I assumed a particular statement was indeed factual he virtually exploded. His voice rose to a pane-shattering pitch. "NEVER ASSUME ANYTHING! DO YOU UNDERSTAND THAT?" he bellowed. Before I could answer Yessir, he repeated with only a slight drop in decibels: "I said, do you understand that?"

The rewrite station abutted Henry's, and I recall being awed the first time I saw his vocal pugnacity. He had put on his overcoat and hat to go out, and paused to ask Toni Adams on the

Henry Leader (in bow tie) at the AP day desk in the third-floor garret at the Knick. Note phone with headset for taking bulletin dictation. Rewrite man in foreground is unidentified in this photo from Dorothy Leader's collection, dated May 22, 1946 in Henry's handwriting. Standing is Paxton. Herman Smith, traffic chief, is in shirtsleeves at far left.

day desk if our Schenectady stringer had come through with a story on the strike situation at the big Alco locomotive plant. Toni said yes, but pointed out that there were several gaps in the story. When she called the plant direct, she said, the Alco PR man dodged her questions. That was all Henry had to hear. He turned back to his desk, grabbed the phone and barked at Toni: "What's his number?"

In the dialogue that followed I couldn't help overhearing Henry's end. He began gently, identifying himself and the information he was seeking from the giant corporation. Apparently denied the information, he tried a new approach, still in a polite tone. When that didn't work, he increased the volume several notches and made it clear the PR man's explanation was not acceptable. As the argument developed, Henry's pitch rose with his ire and the veins in his neck began to expand under the lapel of his overcoat. I was entranced by the performance, and I noticed Toni was also listening.

"No, goddammit, I don't want to talk to your plant manager," we heard him shout into the mouthpiece. "I want to talk to the president of the company. What? You won't put me through?" Whereupon Henry laid the poor lackey out in spades, ending with: "All right. You can't let me talk to him, but you can give me the proper spelling of his name."

With that Henry dialed the plant a second time and we heard him ask the switchboard operator, in a voice that dripped honey and syrup, for the president by name. Then to the president's secretary, the same. She must have needed further identification as to the caller and nature of his mission, for we heard him say in a voice he was struggling to keep calm: "This is Henry Leader of the Associated Press in Albany. We are on a press deadline and I have an important question. No, I have already spoken with Mr. Samuels. No, I do not want to leave a message. It is imperative that I talk to him. Yes, I will hold."

The president, perhaps impressed with the outrageous gall of an intruder who had penetrated the walls protecting the fortress, came on the phone. Henry began in the epitome of calm propriety, but that didn't last long. In moments the veins were protruding once more, the vocal pitch was approaching a high tenor, and our fearless Leader was reading a riot act to Executive Suite that left the poor inhabitant no escape. Presumably Henry wrung from him what he needed for the story.

Henry was adamant on grammatical construction and proper word usage in wire copy produced or edited by the Albany staff. Bureau procedure dictated that each page of each story typed by each staffer be filed each day, one file for the PM cycle, another for the AM wire. Several days a week Henry examined the copy files as a means of scrutinizing each sentence his people had put on the wire. In this guise he would mark up each piece like an English teacher grading a classroom essay, scrawling comments on the margins or scribbling a scathing denunciation across the top of the sheet. Usually it was the night shift that bore the brunt of his angry pencil, but the day people would also find critical remarks when they arrived for work the next day and picked up the file, as required, to familiarize themselves with everything current or pending that had transpired since their previous duty.

In addition to fierce insistence on rhetorical purity, Henry demanded disciplined judgement from editors on the desk who were controlling the flow and timing of the dispatches to member papers. Minutes counted, so did the clean, crisp language of the story, in strict adherence to the highest of AP standards, which he believed were superior to any and all newspapers subscribing to this world-renowned news service. Bart Bardossi, an extremely intelligent staffer doing night rewrites, sometimes had difficulty controlling a combative reaction when the tone of the familiar handwriting he found on copy he had toiled over diligently the night before was particularly grating.

Although the picture of Henry in his hat and coat shouting into the defenseless phone remains vivid, I also find clearly etched in memory the spectacle of Bardossi almost choking with emotion over Henry's scrawled comments on the pages of the previous night's travail. I will never forget one explosion when I was filling in on the night desk. Henry had written in large looping characters across the top of one of Bart's nightside rewrites, "Too long. The Second Coming can be written in 800 words."

In these vigilant stints of auditing the reportorial and rhetorical content of the Albany production, our Leader did not spare the day desk or the night desk people, whose performances were expected to be sacrosanct. If the offender was at work in the bureau at the time, Henry would put on his most benign countenance, complete with kindly smile, and address the miscreant with an inflection that carried only a slight edge of irony. If the felon was on the night shift Henry would call from his home in the evening. Such a discourse invariably began politely, giving the poor wretch time to brace for the inevitable. The patented lead-in was invariably: "Please explain, if you can, why you. . ."

Henry Leader was clearly the best newspaperman I ever knew. He came from Worcester via Syracuse University, and had been telegraph editor of the Little Falls Times and Rome correspondent for the Utica papers. On the AP he became one of Albany's most respected legislative correspondents and political columnists before taking over as state editor. With that background and accomplishment, it was small wonder that experienced journalists on our small but select bureau staff could accept these periodic lashings without lasting rancor, and that Henry could chew us out in spades without diminishing our admiration for him.

*   *   *   *   *

Number three in the bureau organization structure was the permanent occupant of the day desk, who had, in effect, jurisdiction over the night desk and the Early as well. Toni Adams, whose Christian names, June Aretha, were never used, had an equally volatile personality. She had come to the bureau from the Binghamton Sun during the war, and was several years older than I. She wore her hair in an English page-boy cut, and was of slight build. Her mouth was thin, and her complexion pale. Her cheeks were pockmarked, and she wore heavy makeup. She spoke in a quiet, measured tone that dripped confidence, but she could raise hob when aroused. Her chain-smoking seemed to belie the calm assurance she projected as she handled the pressurized routines of the day desk, but in bulletin crises she was a real pro, steady and efficient, instinctively making the right decisions.

At forty Toni was still single, carrying a heavy torch for Bob Tuckman, a swashbuckling AP legislative correspondent at the capitol who had picked off a job as an AP war correspondent on the Korean front. Tuckman's departure for the war zone not only fractured her heart, but created the staff opening for me to join the Albany bureau.

Kay Parker, like Toni a product of the Binghamton papers, was more businesslike and less passionate about changing copy written by fellow staffers. I got along quite well with both women, especially Toni, whom I occasionally joined for drinks at Eddie's Bar on Sheridan Avenue a block from the Times-Union, a watering hole frequented by newspaper people. Toni's heartsickness for Tuckman left her vulnerable to partying, but I saw little of Kay after hours. Both were friendly to me, and during my second or third week in Albany they teamed up to give me a welcoming dinner party at Kay's apartment on Hamilton Street. Also invited was the AP's other bachelor, Bob Jensen. I had never met Bob by reason of his being on the early desk, midnight to 8. It was an interesting introduction, for after several rounds of martinis, a well-prepared dinner, wine and a few nightcaps, a near-immobilized Toni had to be carried up three flights to her apartment on Eagle Street.

In that period it was unusual to have women in such jobs, let alone in the bubbling cauldron of a competitive wire service, but Toni and Kay held their own in a man's world. Paxton was intensely proud of them. In one of his warmer moments, with Scotch in hand, he told me of the time several years earlier when Toni was sent out to cover a bizarre and highly dramatic crime story. Competing with the other wire services and aggressive New York City tabloids, it was her beautifully written lead that swept the board.

A man who had committed a murder in New York by rigging a portrait camera in a studio had been a hunted fugitive for several weeks, providing the Manhattan tabloids with garish headlines and stories. On a cold February day state police had cornered him in an isolated farmhouse deep in the Catskill mountains. Toni was one of a horde of reporters kept at a distance while troopers circled the barricaded house. By the time they flushed the fugitive it was late in a chilly evening. When Toni got to a rural phone, quite probably not the first reporter to do so, she dictated a lead that few editors on the morning dailies could resist. It went something like this:

"The trail of the Camera Killer came to an end this moonlit night on a remote farm amid snow-covered fields in Patchpocket Hollow in the Catskills..." It wasn't so much the moon and the snow that melted the editors down the line, it was Patchpocket Hollow. None of the other by-line stars had bothered to ask where that rutty little road in the boonies led to.

But on the throne of the day desk, Toni was allergic to letting more than a few lines of copy escape her ever-present pencil. Albany copy filed on the state wire on dayside was dotted with editing changes in her neat little handwriting. One night I mentioned to my fellow staffer Harvey Travis, a special favorite, that I found it remarkable that Toni Adams could not let a one-sentence "fatal" written by an experienced newsman pass through her desk without making at least one editing change. Harvey's response was classic. "That broad would rewrite The Lord's Prayer if she had the chance."

During my tenure on the AP Kay became somewhat more mellow—"almost human," Harvey conceded—after getting married. Her husband was Johnny Jones, a golf writer on the Times-Union, a romance obviously born of coffee breaks on the night shift, inasmuch as Johnny worked roughly the same hours in the sports department and on the same floor in the T-U building as did Kay on the AP night desk.

*   *   *   *   *

The two most volatile members of the staff, Henry Leader and Toni Adams, co-existed in a reasonable state of harmony, presumably through a mutual respect for each other's professional expertise. It was natural and understandable that there would be periodic explosions ignited by the clash of two incendiary personalities, working side-by-side in a cramped office on the same shift day after day, each noted for an unyielding adherence to his or her side of the controversy. Paxton always enjoyed telling a listener about the time he returned from his weekly Rotary luncheon one afternoon to find neither Henry nor Toni in the bureau. The day rewrite man was sitting at the day desk, the only staffer on duty in early afternoon with the home edition of PM papers going to press across the state. Paxton might have thought little of it until he found on his desk in the corner two hastily typed messages on regular copy paper. The wording on each was roughly similar: a one-sentence notice of resignation, one signed by Henry, the other by Toni.

Knowing both personalities, Paxton recognized the situation immediately, correctly assuming there had been a fiery clash over some small point, perhaps even the definition of a single word or the placement of a participial phrase. He called Dorothy Leader and told her to tell Henry he was coming up to their apartment later in the afternoon, then went downstairs to Beaver Street and walked thirty yards to the side door of the Plaza Grill on the corner of Broadway. There he found exactly what he knew he would find, Toni Adams on her fourth martini, an ashtray overflowing with cigarette stubs at her elbow.

He had mediated similar collisions in the past, but not on the double-resignation level. This one, he would relate, took a while, in separate interviews at the Plaza Grill and in the Leader duplex on Southern Boulevard, but both belligerents showed up for duty the next morning, and it was business as usual—until the next eruption.

22

Drowning Can be Fatal

The AP operation in Albany translated to three eight-hour shifts seven days. The state wire, known simply as the S-wire, was the bureau's prime responsibility, providing statewide news coverage for New York State papers. Stories and bulletins of national or east coast interest were relayed directly on the A-wire, the AP's elite express circuit. We also fed appropriate stories to two separate circuits, the financial wire and sports wire, the latter having a supplementary circuit devoted exclusively to the horse racing industry called the race wire, or simply, the R-wire.

The dayside office was in the Knickerbocker News building because the Knick was an afternoon paper and its staff worked days. The nightside AP staff had working space at the Times-Union, a seven-day morning paper whose staff theoretically worked at night. Reporters on both papers were required to make carbons of their stories as they wrote. By checking the "dupes" every half-hour or so, the AP had a window into everything on the Albany news beats.

At 4:30 each afternoon the night desk editor, rewrite man and second-shift puncher would pack the necessary files and other vital impedimenta into a battered black suitcase and move by taxicab eight downtown blocks to the T-U building on Sheridan Avenue, to carry on the function of the bureau. At 2:20 a.m. there would be another cab waiting, the bulky suitcase would be repacked, and the ritual reversed. Back at the Knick the first two floors were dark, and would be for several hours until 6, but in the attic there was light—and the clacking litany of the teletypes.

I got to know these routines well. My introductory assignment, day rewrite, was 9:30 to 6, which bridged the transition from day desk to night desk. That gave me several hours working with the second-shift editor and the privilege of lugging the suitcase on the taxicab shuttle to the Times-Union.

The three staffers who moved each afternoon to the nightside office had ample room and comparatively less noise than in the notorious closet at the Knick. There were, however, other discomforts. The T-U had excessive heat in cold weather and no air conditioning in hot weather. Opening windows in June to get fresh air invited every winged insect in Albany to join us in the glare of our fluorescents.

The relative peace and quiet of nightside travail stemmed from the Hearst Corporation's incredible neglect of the newsgathering function in its Albany property during that period of the fifties. After 7:30 p.m., when "The Metro" edition went to press, only three staffers, exclusive of the sports department, remained on the job in the city room, and one of them went home at 9. By then they were down to two, the night editor and one rewrite, thus leaving the paper's unsuspecting subscribers virtually unprotected for the four hours before the presses were scheduled to roll out the final edition at 1:30 a.m.

What was even more astonishing was that once the Metro had gone down at 7:30, there apparently was no need to keep a wire editor on to update the 4 p.m. summaries of the day's major world and national stories. This phenomenon effectively deprived readers of Albany's morning paper of access to fresh news or breaking stories on the wire, providing instead warmed-over rewrites of yesterday's stories barely four or five hours after the rival evening paper's Home Edition had rolled off the presses. It was hard to believe that any newspaper in a metropolitan area, let alone the capital city of the nation's most populous state, would be so irresponsible or show such indifference to anything other than token coverage.

*　　*　　*　　*　　*

The enclosure that housed the AP night office at the Times-Union was separated from the city room by a half-wall and a glass partition. As the rewrite man entrusted with keeping an eye on the dupes, I often had a chance to chat briefly with Ray O'Connor, the T-U night editor. Ray was a remarkable newspaperman. He was a lot older, of indeterminable age and unusually slight stature. He couldn't have weighed much more than ninety pounds before breakfast. He was a friendly fellow, and when he smiled he revealed two widely separated upper teeth and one lower.

I recall having once been told that Ray had had little formal education, and that his grammatical grasp was limited, but Bill Lowenberg, a scarred veteran of the Times-Union reportorial staff, contends that Ray had firm command of what Bill called "thirties newspaper English." Whatever the case, Ray O'Connor had had a long and colorful career by the time I arrived on the Albany scene.

His true value lay in his reputation as the best "street man" in Albany journalism—for knowing every cop, fireman, cab driver, pimp, hooker, wino, bookie, bartender, numbers runner, dock worker, precinct captain, ward heeler and machine politician in Albany. His years on the police beat and his intimate familiarity with virtually every bar and corner tavern in the city (he was unmarried) enabled him to find any of these people on short notice when he needed them. He not only knew every back alley and riverfront hideout, but he knew the location and code of every fire alarm box.

His colleagues marvelled at Ray's instant response whenever the fire bell sounded in the city room, as it did in both the T-U and the Knick as well as in the firehouses. As the bell clanged out 2-5-3, this walking city directory had no need to

193

consult the chart. "That's Quail and Western," he would tell the nearest reporter. Then he would give the name of a tavern or neighborhood grocery near that corner, and identify by name the bartender or store owner. That was the signal for the reporter to call the resident informant to determine whether the fire was worth sending a reporter and photographer to the scene.

And rare was the obituary that Ray couldn't expand from personal knowledge of the departed. In his head he carried the biographies of hundreds of citizens in all strata of Albany's social structure from the soup kitchen lineup on lower Hudson Avenue to aristocratic Mayor Erastus Corning II and other families tracing genealogies to the Albany Regency and the patroon era. He knew how each fitted into local history.

When the notorious New York racketeer and Prohibition beer baron, Legs Diamond, was shot to death in 1931 in Albany's most celebrated murder mystery, Ray O'Connor had the rare distinction of viewing the corpse before the police arrived. Diamond, one of the most publicized gangland bosses of the post-Capone era, had been acquitted of felony charges in Troy the preceding afternoon, and after celebrating with friends at an Albany night club, had disdained his room at the Kenmore Hotel on North Pearl Street in favor of retiring to his "safe house" hideaway in a quiet rooming establishment on Dove Street. There at 5:30 a.m. he was assassinated by two men with guns.

The murder was never solved, but Lowenberg and other city room contemporaries insist to this day that Ray O'Connor knew all about it and kept the secret to the end. Bill Kennedy, the former Times-Union police reporter who wrote a novel based on the Diamond killing and won a Pulitzer prize for *Ironweed*, also an Albany-based novel, confirms the story that O'Connor was in the room on Dove Street before the cops and had "had a very privileged, close-up look at Jack Diamond dead."

Kennedy, who came on the Times-Union some years after I left the AP, says in his book, *O Albany*, that O'Connor, still on the night desk, taught him how to cover the police beat by telephone. Quoting Kennedy's book: "He cared about little else. He was a sad and lonely man, a generous and likeable grump

194

with almost no teeth and a bad foot, or maybe two, and he believed in the full moon: that it drew the crazies out of their lairs and drove them to phone up the Times-Union city desk and ask irrational questions."

The identities of the men who fired the bullets into Diamond's head will never be known, but researchers, including Kennedy, concede that someone tipped off O'Connor and his reportorial pal on the Times-Union, Joe O'Heaney.

Whatever can be drawn from fact and legend, there is no disputing that Ray O'Connor represented a breed of newspaperman no longer found in newsrooms today.

*　　*　　*　　*　　*

On the AP, the editor on "the desk" commanded the state wire for that eight-hour leg, directing traffic to and from each point throughout the upstate network. In such circumstances I had moved a number of breaking stories in the bulletin-take format, employed when an important spot-news story was worth breaking into the state wire and flashing the bulletin, accompanied by the customary alarm bells jingling on teletype machines across the state. In crises of this nature, the procedure was to type each sentence on a separate sheet of paper, called a "take," hand the paper to the puncher, and bang out the next sentence, always staying one "take" ahead of the puncher's flying fingers on the teletype keyboard.

The bulletin ritual was necessary because the UP was in the same race to be first on the telegraph editor's desk in metropolises like Buffalo and Rochester (and Watertown) that subscribed to both wire services. Near deadline an editor might use the first lead reaching his desk and ignore the other. Losing a race as vital as this was unacceptable and unpardonable.

As part of my function on day rewrite I had taken bulletins on the phone from the Capitol, whipped the takes out on the typewriter and fed them to Toni Adams on the day desk. I had also phoned in stories while covering important news breaks outside the office—natural disasters, jury verdicts, prominent court cases, death of a public figure and the like. On one dramatic

195

occasion I had phoned bulletins from the scene of an airliner that had come in short of the runway, clipped a radio tower with a wing tip and pancaked into a trailer park off Central Avenue; and as editor on the bureau desk had sped copy from the phone to a puncher on the hungry teletype.

Even when we moved hot copy with incredible speed we rarely got a kudo from clients or our own boss. We were expected to consistently deliver efficient, professional performances under competitive pressures, and if that was big league, then we were big leaguers, even in a place like Albany. Presumably it was no different in Washington, London, Cairo, Moscow or Des Moines, or with the correspondents on the Korean front.

*　　*　　*　　*　　*

After several months I was entrusted with "the relay," the single wire that condensed the cream of the state wire, A-wire, sports wire and other special wires, and relayed selected copy to several dozen small afternoon papers via a special circuit. This compact version of AP's service was necessary because the smaller upstate cities had dailies like the Geneva Times that lacked the resources and capacity to handle even a small proportion of the reams of copy gushing from a bank of machines. For me this was a fun job. It was also a day-shift job, a plum envied by most of the people on the nightside.

The hours were ideal, 7 to 3:30, and I enjoyed scanning the full output of the various wires with the authority to select anything and everything I felt telegraph editors on the smaller dailies would need or like. Having put in five years in that capacity in Geneva, I felt I knew just how much of a mix was appropriate, and where to cut and trim. The challenge was in being ruthless with the black pencil, cutting stories relentlessly. It was imperative to wrap up the sports before 8, move prime stories before 10 and the top state stuff before 11, then the shorter stuff and a few "brites" (AP jargon for short items of humorous or human interest). It was also vital to keep the wire available for bulletins on late-breaking stories.

One of the most interesting angles on this job was scanning the front pages of the papers on the circuit to see how they

196

(150)

SCHENECTADY, N.Y., OCT.25-(AP)-A STUDENT AT UNION COLLEGE CONTENDS
THAT EMBRACING A SKIDMORE COLLEGE GIRL IS LIKE "MAKING LOVE TO A
COAXIAL CABLE."

WRITING IN THE COLLEGE PAPER, COLUMNIST DAVID MARKSON OF ALBANY
SAID SOME SKIDMORE GIRLS WORE "DEADLY BEAR-TRAP ARRANGEMENTS" AS PART
OF THEIR UNDERGARMENTS.

A SPOKESMAN AT SKIDMORE IN SARATOGA SPRINGS SAID THE GIRLS WERE "SO
BUSY WITH OTHER THINGS" THAT THEY HAD NO TIME FOR COMMENT.

IN HIS COLUMN, IN THE CONCORDIENSIS, MARKSON DESCRIBED THE LAST
TIME HE DATED A SKIDMORE GIRL:

"EVERY TIME SHE MOVED I EXPECTED A COUPLE OF THOSE CONCENTRIC HIGH
TENSION WIRES TO POP OUT, ZOOM ACROSS X X X AND BURY THEMSELVES
BETWEEN MY FAVORITE RIBS X X X."

MARKSON WARNED SKIDMORE:

"IF OUR LOVE MEANS ANYTHING, YOU HAD BETTER STOP OUTFITTING YOURSELF
LIKE THE INSIDE OF AN ALARM CLOCK THAT IS APT TO BUST APART AT THE
SEAMS IN ANY GIVEN MOMENT.

"BEFORE SKIDMORE CAN HOPE TO SEE MORE OF UNION, UNION WILL HAVE TO
SEE MORE OF SKIDMORE."

*An example of the kind of "brites" that can be adapted from reading
a sheaf of upstate newspapers. I wrote this story from an item in the
Schenectady Gazette.*

handled the copy I was relaying to them. I was also appreciative
of the fact that if Kay Jones hadn't been doing that, I might not
be on the AP in Albany.

*   *   *   *   *

I had been on the relay desk only a few weeks when the
feared ogre of the bureau, Henry Leader, as state editor made one
of his periodic examinations of the content and selection of copy
going out on the relay wire. Henry was the most passionate
guardian of grammatical and rhetorical perfection to be found
anywhere in New York State journalism, or perhaps in any other

Henry Leader

state. He considered it his executive duty to mark up the copy filed by bureau staffers like an English teacher red-lining essays of high school sophomores. The ardor and vigor of this vigilance forced dayside people to review the files of the previous day and nightside people to see, upon arrival, what the peerless Leader had done that day to the copy they had filed the previous night.

In my prior stint on the receiving end of the relay in Geneva I was beholden to a whim of my boss at the time. Al Learned had insisted that I pencil in the word "was" whenever the wire copy reported that someone drowned. Al believed that people did not drown of their own accord, hence he disapproved of Albany's style. For five years I dutifully applied the pencil on each such "fatal" that came over the teletype.

I was joyfully filing my wire one morning when, among editors toiling and teletypes clacking in chorus, there was a roar from Henry's desk. "Who's editing the relay?" he shouted to all four walls, pretending to look around the room as if he didn't know exactly where the relay desk was located or who was stationed there. His outcry jolted me into an answer. "I am," I admitted, bracing for a possible attack.

Henry was wearing his gray fedora, as he often did in the office. He got up, strode over to my station, his face livid under a frightening scowl. "Would you step out in the hall for a moment, please?"

I complied meekly, wondering what felony had aroused this day's tirade. In the dusty hallway he closed the door to shut off the cacophony of the machines, held out the stapled relay file of the day before, and pointed to a small piece of editing.

"Is this your handwriting?" he demanded, obviously trying to keep his voice calm.

I followed his trembling index finger to the word "was" in pencil above the carat I had inserted before the word "drowned" in a one-sentence fatal I had relayed from the state wire. "Yes, Henry," I confessed.

He stared into my face from close range, his emotion taking him to the brink of apoplexy, the veins in his neck nearly bursting. "Permit me to ask you a question," he said. "You've just fallen out of a boat in the middle of the lake, you're about to go down for the third time, and you're calling for help. Do you shout, 'Help, help, I am drowning,' or do you say, 'Help, help, I am being drowned?' And if it's the latter, who in hell is drowning you?" He didn't wait for an answer. He yanked the door open and, slamming it behind him, returned to the clatter within.

In the five years we worked together on the AP, Henry and I became fast friends with a high degree of mutual respect. I recall that I later bested Henry in grammatical combat on two occasions, which gave me special stature among bureau staffers, and it is sobering to realize I cannot remember details of either encounter, other than they were friendly, with Henry conceding in gentlemanly decorum. In this context the dialogue in the hallway remains permanently etched in my mind.

Henry was the epitome of the newspaperman's newspaper-man. For my part, I can safely say that I have never again used the passive voice in marine fatals.

23

Deadline Every Minute

Most of the bureau staffers disdained the relay desk as somewhat juvenile, but to me it was the most delightful, though perhaps the least challenging, on the whole roster. It was, however, one of those assignments that was too good to last. I had been enjoying the relay desk only four or five months when a new hire arrived, and I was "promoted" to the dreaded midnight shift, the one the rest of civilization sometimes terms "the lobster shift." On the AP, the 12-to-8 was called simply "the Early."

The Early man started his stint each night at the Times-Union and ended it at the Knick. That involved the black suitcase ritual in reverse at 2:30 a.m., which meant he had roughly two and a half hours in the night office before returning to Beaver Street to await dawn and relief in the person of the day editor, in that order.

The Early was by its very nature a roster assignment dreaded by all AP staffers, especially those who were married. For me, still unclaimed as a husband, it was a welcome opportunity for a new experience, being in command of AP's New York State wire for eight hours each night.

I had hardly had time to settle into this authoritative position before I was initiated into the responsibility of being on the desk for one of those fast-breaking bulletin procedures. In previous encounters I had been the rewrite man taking dictation, shoveling the "takes," one sentence to a sheet of copypaper, to the desk editor, who in turn slapped each take on the teletype console so the puncher could send non-stop.

Not so automatic this time. I was not only in the double role of rewrite man and desk man, but I had to write the story as our correspondent was describing the situation. That particular split-second race to be first with a bulletin remains in my mind not so much for its content as for the astonishment of the stringer in Utica who was unabashedly awed by the AP's speed and efficiency when he phoned in his story.

When I arrived on Sheridan Avenue as usual that evening, Kay Parker, finishing up her regular tour on the night desk, alerted me to a developing story that might produce a new "top" at any moment. There had been a breakout at the Herkimer County Jail several hours earlier. Several inmates had jumped a deputy, taken the keys to his car and sped off. State troopers had set up roadblocks in central New York, and our nightside correspondent in Utica, who was the wire editor of the morning paper there, was on top of the story.

Thumbing through the flimsies (carbon copies) in the ever-present file on the wire desk, I briefed myself on everything that had gone out during the sixteen hours since ending my previous stint, including the bulletins Kay had filed at the time of the jailbreak. At midnight Kay and the night puncher went home, leaving Bart Bardossi, the rewrite man doing the "overnights" for the PM wire, the oncoming puncher and me to man the fort.

A few minutes after 1 a.m. our Utica man phoned. "They got 'em," he said, trying not to sound breathless or excited. I clamped on the headset and rolled paper into the typewriter as he was talking. With a dozen upstate morning papers only minutes away from closing the final edition, there was no time to take notes, so I banged out a bulletin lead and handed it to the puncher. Bart, sensing the situation, left his post to roll in new sheets for me while I wrote the takes. Our stringer wasn't dictating, but as he described the scene in a patch of woods on U.S. Route 20 near West Winfield, I whipped out short takes as he was speaking. State troopers had flushed the three fugitives

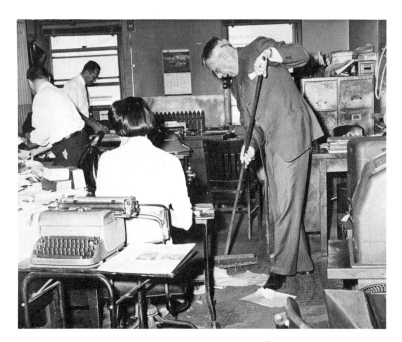

Few photos were taken in the din of the crowded, noisy AP office that served as bureau headquarters in Albany. In this rare shot, Paxton is attempting a housekeeping chore, unheeded by Toni Adams at the day desk. Typewriter in foreground is assigned to the relay desk, off-camera to the left.

from the woods, and during a scuffle on the road a trooper had inadvertently shot himself in the foot. Suddenly the man on the other end of the phone stopped. "Wait a minute," he said.

"Can't," I said, thinking how close to final deadline every upstate AM paper must be. "No time. Keep going!"

"Holy Christ!" he exclaimed. " You got the lead on the wire already! And I'm not finished yet! Wow!"

*   *   *   *   *

I enjoyed the Early, perhaps because I was single, perhaps because I was full of enthusiasm in my first year on a wire service, perhaps for the challenge and responsibility that came with directing traffic on the state wire. If there was a fringe benefit, it was the apparent freedom of working week after week without ever seeing any bosses— meaning the bureau chief and the state editor.

Despite the topsy-turvy lifestyle it created, there were some positive factors on the Early. The hours were regular, Monday through Friday with weekends off. There were fewer S-wire deadlines on the Early than on either the day desk or the night desk, and fewer bulletin-type stories like Herkimer, but there was plenty of copy to move and enough steady action to satisfy anyone.

Normally the first hour—midnight to 1 a.m.—was relatively intense, making sure the morning papers in major cities across the state had everything they would need in the countdown before the final edition, usually around 1:15. After that the emphasis shifted to setting up the overnight roster of stories for PM papers.

During my occupancy of the early desk in 1951-52, the highly controversial U.S. Senator Joseph McCarthy, a zealous Red-baiter notorious for questionable anti-Communist tactics, was conducting a series of hearings on behalf of a Congressional panel called the Un-American Activities Committee. It was continuous page one fare. When his quest in the Alger Hiss affair led him to Albany to extract closed-door testimony from a "Mister X," the fallout spilled into the Albany bureau.*

Virtually all the McCarthy excitement in Albany was handled by the day desk and night desk during conventional hours, but one morning as I was preparing to close the night operation at the T-U, the New York bureau sent Albany a query from a client. It was 2:25 a.m., and Bardossi, for once, had finished his chores early and had gone home. The message relayed a question the New York Daily News wanted Senator McCarthy to answer, adding that the client, which at that time

---

*Mister X later was identified as Whitaker Chambers, who was revealed as author of an incriminatory secret document known as the Pumpkin Papers. The revelation and the content of the documents caused a sensation at the time. He was thought to have been living in the small village of Cambridge, Washington County, just north of Albany.

had the largest circulation of any newspaper in the United States, was holding its final edition for the answer.

Thus alerted to an emergency, I abandoned my packing chore and called the Hotel Ten Eyck, where I knew the senator was staying. I was reasonably sure the famous man would decline to answer the question, and assumed that the Daily News assumed the same, but that assumption was no excuse for not contacting him. It was imperative that I get through to the senator regardless of the hour.

The switchboard operator predictably refused to ring the senator's room. The celebrity guest had left instructions not to be disturbed. I identified myself and my client, and insisted. When she again refused, I demanded to talk to the night manager. This time the dialogue was brief; the hotel agreed to put me through.

The senator answered the ring, obviously roused from sleep. To my apology for waking him he was gracious; he understood my position. To my question and its source he said he could not offer an answer at this time. I thanked him for accepting the call and wished him a speedy return to restful slumber. The dialogue had been polite and businesslike, devoid of what might have been rancor, and consumed barely a minute and a half. I filed my response to the Daily News on the wire and resumed packing the files prior to addressing the next crisis, the nightly decision as to which of downtown Albany's two acceptable all-night eateries to favor for "lunch" on the half-hour break en route back to the Knick building.

Meanwhile, somewhere out there, in another time zone, some edition of some newspaper was going to press. On a global wire service like the AP there was literally a deadline every minute, even if it was comparatively peaceful in the middle of the night in Albany, New York.

24

The Early Birds

It can be said that we Early Birds saw an entirely different side of the planet than Ordinary People, but it is not true that after long exposure we developed extraordinary night vision like owls, tigers, cats and other species that thrive on the nocturnal. We lived in a different world, but we adjusted to it, at least to a tolerable degree. There were, however, some aspects that defied adjustment, such as getting off work in the dazzling glare of the morning sun and, weary from eight hours of intense labor, having to choose one of two options— relax over a leisurely breakfast and the morning papers before bed, or unwind with a few beers and a dart game at the Eagle Tavern.

In those first weeks on the Early I faced a monumental decision as to how to pattern a lifestyle. What kind of a meal to eat after the day's (night's) work? The Day Desk relieved me at 8 a.m., at which point I was reasonably tired and certainly hungry. Albany's citizenry was having breakfast, but does a fellow who has just finished a full eight hours of steady travail turn to such culinary rewards as cereal, eggs and toast? Does a working man crave a glass of grapefruit juice after work, or a couple of beers?

For a while I played it each way. At the Eagle Tavern there were Albany cops getting off duty and dropping in for a few beers and a dart game before heading for home and bed. They were good fellows, and I could relax for an hour or so, then walk three blocks to Lodge Street and put a few lamb chops or some ground round on the stove, boil some spuds, take a vegetable out of the freezer, and read the New York Times before hitting the sack.

In that routine I slept from noonish into early evening, then had a shower and a legitimate breakfast. Thus fortified and feeling fresh, I was ready to confront a new day, if that's what it was, on the AP down the hill a few blocks at the Times-Union on Sheridan Avenue.

The other system also worked pretty well. Off work at 8 a.m., a light snack or a semi-breakfast, and bed. Up at 5 p.m., take a shower, cook a modest dinner, read, call a friend or two or catch a movie or a catnap until time to go to work at 11:30.

Working the Early, as I did for fifty consecutive weeks, required several basic adjustments in personal bionics. I had been sharing a small top-floor apartment on Lodge Street with a family of roaches a block and a half from Albany's downtown hub intersection at State and Pearl Streets, but in November I hooked up with a fellow AP man, Fred Davis, to lease a small but attractive basement apartment at Madison and Lake in an old residential section. During our joint tenancy Fred was filing the relay wire, a steady dayside assignment. Accordingly, he slept nights and I slept days, an arrangement that allowed us to live in reasonable harmony in close quarters that otherwise might have bred a degree of incompatibility.

Living with Fred on Madison Avenue, however, had a limiting effect on the Early's lifestyle options. Fred was a creature of habit and orderly convention, which translated to dinner at 6. Dinner meant meat, potatoes, vegetable, salad and dessert. We agreed that each of us would do all shopping and dinners for two weeks. The other would do the dishwashing, housecleaning and other domestic chores. For me that meant a mandatory performance in the kitchen on a regular schedule for two straight weeks. In the alternate weeks I could sleep late, i.e. after 5 p.m., but only at the risk of missing dinner altogether or, at best, settling for a warmed-over repast.

This schedule had its good and bad features. It was indeed a delight to roll out of bed, take a shower, pour a drink if in the mood, and pick up the evening paper while Fred, invariably wearing an apron, was toiling diligently in the small galley off the living room. It was not so luxurious when I had to set an alarm in order to have a full menu ready for Fred when he came home from the office. It was also difficult to keep the schedule in the summer months, especially after finding some fellow tribesmen, two Ski Club friends who worked approximately the same hours I did. Coming off the job early in the morning on those lazy July days I often teamed up with the third-shift superintendent at the big Schaeffer Brewery in Albany and a nurse who was a night supervisor at the Albany Medical Center Hospital. This unlikely triumvirate fell into the routine of meeting after work and going for a swim and a picnic, perhaps twice a week, at places like Crooked Lake and West Sand Lake. At 8:30 a.m. we had the beach and picnic area all to ourselves until mothers and children arrived in late morning. On such occasions a six-pack or two of Schaeffer's was highly appropriate with sandwiches and other goodies following a cooling swim.

Even after a year on the Early it was painfully obvious that there was no easy way to accept a lifestyle that called for rolling out of bed at 5 p.m. after a blissful eight-hour slumber to find Fred Davis in our little galley on Madison Avenue waiting to serve a full-scale dinner. Who would want a pre-prandial martini in that format? And with Fred such a stickler for a synchronized schedule, I found it uncomfortable to keep him waiting for an extra ten minutes while I showered and shaved before sitting down to a full-course dinner complete with gravy.

*　　*　　*　　*　　*

There was only one job in the bureau considered more distasteful than the Early. That dubious nomination went to the Early-Early, bureau label for the nightside rewrite function. The hours were inhuman—8 p.m. to 4 a.m., thus providing the worst of both worlds, but what was even more cruel was the fact that the Early-Early had split days off—Thursday night and Saturday night. Continued exposure was known to break the mental and physical endurance of our hardiest.

The nearest approach to a redeeming feature was that it was strictly a writing job. The incumbent was responsible for determining which stories from the nightside cycle should be given second-day leads and redone for the next day's afternoon papers. Upon arriving for duty at 8 p.m. and reading the complete file of everything the Night Desk had put on the wire for AM papers, the poor serf on the Early-Early had to rewrite each story for PM's. In the process he had to conjure up a fresh lead and, with no new input, rearrange and abridge the original piece to make it look like an update, which, of course, it wasn't. We became quite skilled at giving an old story—old because it had been in the morning papers—a new coat of paint, sometimes merely by lifting the sixth graf into the lead and reshuffling the identical facts.

*   *   *   *   *

Life on the Early was tolerable when there were such good guys as Bart Bardossi and Harvey Travis to work with. They were the closest of my friends in the bureau, certainly two of the most genial characters I encountered in all the time I toiled in the newspaper business.

For most of my year on the Early desk, Bart was the rewrite man on the hated Early-Early. Harvey was on the "swing"—working everyone's day off. A swing man was necessary when staffers worked five days a week in a seven-day operation. Actually it was six and a half—the New York bureau covered from midnight to 4 p.m. Sundays, hence the swing man worked the day desk Monday, night desk Tuesday and Wednesday, the Early-Early Thursday and the Early Saturday. (I put in several months on it and found it tolerable, certainly a big cut above the detested Early-Early.) During my year-long stint on the Early, Harvey was my partner as Bardossi's replacement one night a week— the Thursday night-Friday morning stint.

Bart was a pleasant fellow and a Phi Beta Kappa from Columbia University. He had come to the AP from the Ogdensburg Journal, the only daily in St. Lawrence County and a neighbor and semi-competitor of mine in Massena days. Our careers in the North Country hadn't overlapped; Bart was a few years younger and had been in Ogdensburg after I had left Watertown, but he had preceded me on the AP.

Harvey had several years on us both in age and seniority. He was easy-going, warm and friendly, with a cherubic countenance that featured a constant smile and a perpetual twinkle. He was quick to laugh and loved a joke. He was also a thoroughly professional newsman, and had been managing editor of the Endicott Bulletin, a small Southern Tier daily that was overshadowed and later absorbed by the combined Binghamton Sun and Binghamton Press. Harvey had the most even personality in the bureau, ever unruffled. He spoke softly at all times; I cannot recall ever hearing him raise his voice in anger or protest. Under fire on the day desk he treated a pressure-packed bulletin crisis on a breaking story with the same clear-headed command that he would apply if he were taking a one-sentence fatal phoned in by a stringer in Hoosick Falls.

*   *   *   *   *

If breakfast and dinner on the inverted clock of the Early presented bionic or gastronomic options, there were no such problems with lunch on the Early. Lunch from 2:30 to 3 a.m. in the relatively deserted streets of New York's capital city was an easy choice. At that hour in that era there were only two acceptable eating places in downtown Albany, the Famous Restaurant and the Plaza Grill, and we quickly got tired of both. The Famous was spectacularly misnamed, for it was neither famous nor a restaurant; it was an all-night cafeteria with shiny counters and tables under glaring lights. Its alleged fame might have extended across the river to Rensselaer on a clear night but hardly much further.

The Famous sported a brightly lit facade on dimly lit Broadway almost directly across the street from the stately Union Station. It featured shiny white porcelain tables and counters, and drew its patronage from the standard wee-hour assortment of cab drivers, cops, truck drivers, trainmen, winos and insomniacs. The fare was predictably ordinary, except for its specialty, a Western on a bun, which would get a kudo from Julia Childs if she ever found herself in such a commonplace beanery. It was a relatively clean place, inexpensive and totally dependable, and at that hour presented no parking problem.

210

In downtown Albany, it is four blocks straight uphill from The Plaza (foreground) to the Capitol, looking due west. The tower behind the Capitol is the 31-story Alfred E. Smith state office building. The skyline has changed drastically since this photo was taken in the mid-fifties, especially on the south side (left), where several office towers and the Empire State Plaza, featuring a 48-story building that is the tallest in the state outside of Manhattan, now dominate the scene. The Plaza Grill can be seen on Broadway in the lower left. The Famous was two blocks to the right.

Of the two eateries, the Famous had the better menu. The Plaza, only a few steps from the Knick, had better hamburgers. It also had a bar; in fact, it was a bar supplemented by a tiny kitchen in the rear, just large enough to satisfy a state law that mandated food service as a requirement for a liquor license.

The Plaza, at Broadway and Beaver, was on the first floor of a small building that had once been the Plaza Hotel. In the later hours the bartender had time to leave his station long enough to put a hamburger or cheese sandwich on the grill in the back galley while we two AP editors relaxed with a Carling's Black Label on draft or a green bottle of Carling's Ale. On the nights we chose the Plaza over the Famous we were often the only customers on the premises.

25

The Great Public Yawn

Liberation from the Early, by design or coincidence, came two weeks prior to my marriage in 1952. There was no indication from Paxton whether it was a wedding present or it was time to give a successor the experience of the midnight desk. It was, however, coincidence that the new man was Dick Hunt, the same fellow who had taken over my old job as telegraph editor in Geneva when I departed for Albany. Dick was a good friend and an outstanding newspaperman.

My new assignment was a plum. Paxton dispatched me to the Capitol bureau, where I became the freshman on the AP's three-man staff of legislative correspondents. Amidst the euphoria of the wedding and honeymoon I realized that I had achieved a pinnacle, of sorts, in New York State journalism by becoming a member of the elite press corps covering the Capitol. Up to then I had been too busy and too happy in my job and among new friends to spend time on career goals; besides, I was never one to be aggressively ambitious.

Not that I hadn't thought about being a legislative correspondent with a daily by-line flashed across the state on the AP wire. As telegraph editor of the Geneva Times, cutting and sorting a steady stream of stories rolling out of the AP machine

New York's unique Capitol has 77 steps and manicured tulip beds at the head of Albany's State Street hill.

at my elbow, I saw those by-lines from Albany, Washington and the UN become familiar household names. In my first year and a half in Albany some of those names and stories were still coming across my desk. Perhaps I could be forgiven for thinking I might become one of them.

Now, after a year on the midnight shift, I found myself on the brink of a new adventure. I also liked to think that in assigning me to "The Hill" Paxton was not showing compassion for a bridegroom, but instead had detected in me some promise, however small, as a writer.

Writing for the AP was truly a challenge. With wire space at a premium, AP writers were trained in the Rudolph Flesch school of terse, bare-bones prose—direct sentences uncluttered by adjectives, and sparing use of participial or descriptive phrases except for identification. The AP style was stereotyped but effective, and we fell into it by constant exposure eight to ten hours a day.

As the rookie in the Capitol bureau I was assigned to the Assembly while the older hands, Bill Davidson and Bob Jensen, covered the Senate, the governor and other bigwigs. The AP had a room of its own just off the entrance to the third-floor fortress occupied by the Capitol press corps. The press complex consisted of a large central room crammed with desks and file cabinets of reporters from a dozen or more newspapers. The room was dominated by the high ceiling common to the mishmash architecture that made New York's Capitol unique. The ceiling was high enough to permit a mezzanine, which housed additional cubicles for more newspapers, plus an alcove on the mezzanine that accommodated a round felt-covered poker table and a refrigerator for light refreshment, notably malt beverages.

Outside in a tiled inside corridor, tucked between large stone pillars that overlooked an interior courtyard, were five or six more cubicles occupied by resident correspondents. Besides AP, the largest contingents were in the New York Times bureau, Gannett News Service and our special rival, United Press.

Of the individual rooms the largest was the AP office, spacious enough to accommodate desks for three writers, a puncher and voluminous files. In short order I was initiated into the footrace from the Assembly floor to the intercom phone in the AP cubicle in order to dictate a bulletin or a breaking story to the rewrite man downtown. This launched another sequence in the familiar sentence-by-sentence "take" routine feeding the key puncher. Even in mid-morning this was necessary, for we had to deal with early deadlines in Syracuse, Rochester, Buffalo and New York City, where the noon editions had to be on newsstands for lunch-hour crowds.

On the AP at the Capitol the reporter, having moved his bulletin for the early editions, took a moment to catch his breath, then sat down to write—against the ticking clock—the same story with more color and a deeper perspective for the home editions of afternoon papers along the line, the regular edition that went to most subscribers by way of carrier boys on bikes after school. Later in the day the reporter would have still another rewrite of the story, an update for morning papers, which had to be ready when the night wire opened at 4. For major stories this meant writing the same story three times, not counting new leads, called "new tops," that might have developed hour by hour during debates in the legislative chambers.

Occasionally Paxton, in a burst of administrative vigilance, would glance through the wire copy after lunch and call an editor in Utica or Syracuse to make certain the AP bulletin had signed off, as usual, ahead of the UP. Sure enough, the UP bulletin cleared at 10:57, two minutes behind ours. The AP had "won" again. Routine.

Henry and Pax getting out an Election Night lead at a makeshift work station in the Capitol bureau.

One of the ingredients that provided an extra dimension or excitement in covering Albany's Capitol scene was the national visibility of its chief occupant. Throughout most of the nation's history the governor of the Union's most populous state was, in varying degrees, a national political figure. During their terms in the monstrous pile of masonry at the head of Albany's State Street hill, many New York governors had been either presidential candidates or potential candidates or, if neither, a powerful influence in the smoke-filled rooms at party conventions. Just in this century the list was impressive— Hughes, Al Smith, two Roosevelts, Lehman, Dewey and later Harriman, Rockefeller, Cuomo.

By the time my career landed me on the third floor of the Capitol, Thomas E. Dewey was in the middle of his fourth term as governor amid speculation that he might not seek a fifth. Harry O'Donnell, the AP's top legislative correspondent, had taken the job of Dewey's press secretary, thus creating the vacancy on The Hill I was now filling. O'Donnell was replacing Jim Hagerty, a former Albany legislative correspondent, who had left Dewey's staff to be press secretary to President Eisenhower in the 1952 presidential campaign opposite Adlai Stevenson.

Governor Dewey, an intensely vain man of small stature physically but a giant politically, was a master at strategic timing of major announcements to news deadlines of important newspapers. He enjoyed sending a courier to the Capitol press room to call out, in Paul Revere style, a summons to an immediate news conference in the governor's office. Even on short notice, sometimes as much as ten minutes, the occasion never failed to draw a large contingent of reporters to the executive sanctum on the floor below.

The first time I had to cover this sort of charade I made a costly mistake. As the crowd of reporters filed into the room and lined up three deep around the governor's desk, I was congratulating myself for getting a front-row position. Moments before the governor started to speak I realized my gaffe. There was a strict rule that no one could leave the room until the conference was over, and here I was, twenty feet from the only door, trapped by a wall of humanity between me and the narrow exit. On every subsequent occasion I made sure of a position against the rear wall, no more than six inches from the doorknob, one eye on the UP man, the other on the governor and my note pad.

I also took time to practice the escape route to the AP interphone one flight above, studying the course like a ski racer scouting a World Cup slalom course. The strategy was to take the shallow stone steps of the twelve-foot-wide staircase three at a time, and sprint diagonally on each flight to achieve as straight a line as possible between the broad landings. In the process of full flight I was writing the bulletin lead in my head, mind racing as fast as legs, mentally aligning the order of facts and quotes for a story that not only had to win the bulletin race with the UP, but also had to have a better lead and superior content.

For a while that sort of challenge was fun and exciting, but soon it wore thin. I began to envy friends on the morning papers who didn't have to file their stories until late afternoon. They could enjoy the luxury of a social wait for the elevator, an archaic oversize cage with folding latticework gates that an elderly operator coaxed slowly from floor to floor.

It was fortunate that only a small percentage of our stories required bulletin treatment. Most were straight analytical, interpretive or reportorial pieces that had to be filed for either PM or AM papers— or both. Dayside stories had to be rewritten for the night wire serving the next morning's papers, and stories that missed the afternoon editions had to be redone for "the overnight" so that wire editors on afternoon papers would have an update waiting for them when they came to work in the morning.

All these things constituted the glamor side of journalism in the fast lane. More typical were the weeks of uninterrupted drudgery covering routine stuff. There were long hours of trying to stay awake during endless dull debates on the Assembly floor, and dreary afternoons scanning hundreds of newly introduced legislative measures so clogged with unreadable legalese that the basic intent was difficult to find. For me, the freshman on the crew, it meant the drudgery of writing the daily "bills roundup,"

The "Million Dollar Stairway" is a tourist attraction in the Capitol, fancier but just as broad and steep as the one in the east wing I had to climb (and traverse) on the dead run.

a summary of what could be found of interest, if any, in the mountain of legislative measures introduced that day in the Senate and Assembly. There were literally hundreds, many strictly germane tò a locality such as Tompkins County or the City of Batavia, or so lacking in general interest they could be quickly skipped. All were written in ponderous language. It was a thankless chore, finding in the endless pile half a dozen that were either significant, of timely general interest or had potential as a humorous item or a squib with human interest appeal.

Overall it was a great experience, a new and fascinating environment, a chance to work alongside experienced newsmen and make new friends in our proud profession, plus a ringside view of government at work. No matter if most of it was dull debating, political bubble-blowing and wheels spinning in a cumbersome and lethargic democratic system. There were some good stories if you kept your eyes open or dug for them, and in the swarm of bloated egos and self-serving politicians, there were enough good guys and competent legislators to keep things mildly interesting.

From our privileged vantage point, observing the State Assembly in action often was discouraging. It was frequently dismaying to see the ineffectiveness and incompetence of a surprising number of legislators who had been elected, apparently in good faith but more probably in ignorance, by voters in their home districts. Some were indifferent, resenting having to spend time—but not public money—in legislative office. Others were blatantly political, playing dramatically to an audience, their insincerity apparent.

I still get a chuckle remembering one occasion when I was sitting with Eddie Kelly of the Buffalo Evening News in the press row under the dais facing the Assembly. Eddie called my attention to the desk of a legislator in the front row of the tiered chamber on our immediate left. "Are you familiar with that stalwart lawmaker?" he inquired, pointing to the gray-haired occupant, natty in a business suit.

I said I didn't know who he was. Eddie took pleasure in filling me in.

The Assembly chamber in New York's Capitol. The row of seats facing the chamber at the base of the podium is for the press.

"That," he said eloquently, "is The Honorable William J. Butler, Assemblyman of the Third District, Erie County, Republican. Watch him for a few moments. You will notice there are no papers on his desk, nor any books or manuals beside his chair."

As he spoke, Butler left his seat, walked up the carpeted aisle toward the rear of the chamber, and paused at a colleague's desk to chat. Neither conversant paid any attention to the legislator near the center aisle who was addressing the chamber.

"Notice his diligence and dedication to the issue on the floor," Kelly continued. "In a moment you will see him stroll toward the entrance door at the rear of the chamber, first lingering to pass some time with several buddies. Then you will see him disappear into the ante-room, thence to the corridor and to the Assembly Lounge. Eventually he will return, perhaps even before lunch, but then again, perhaps not until tomorrow."

"Does he ever introduce a bill?" I asked.

"Ah, now you have touched a sensitive nerve," intoned my informant. "It was last year, no, I believe two years ago, he did introduce a legislative measure. As I recall, it involved the placement of a historical marker on the site of an old courthouse. I feel safe in telling you that his bill passed without debate. It is also safe to say that in this astute chamber of lawmaking, Assemblyman Butler represents the total disenfranchisement of several hundred thousand constituents in the Third District of Erie County, New York."

Eddie was a fine tenor in the LCA show, the gridiron-type production written and staged annually by members of the Legislative Correspondents Association. Every newsman on The Hill was expected to take part, most of them on-stage, in the three-act musical extravaganza in full costume. Those who couldn't carry a tune could carry a spear. The staging took place at the annual LCA Dinner, in those days an all-male black-tie event at the unconscionable price of fifty dollars a plate—ten times the cost of a blue-plate dinner at Keeler's or Jack's, Albany's two nationally-renowned restaurants. In the audience was every high-ranking political and judiciary personage in New York State, plus big names in the corporate and financial world, and a dozen or more national figures. They all came to see what outrageous spoofs the Capitol press corps was putting on, and many among the top office-holders and party leaders in the audience were treated to satirical characterizations, highly humorous but rarely complimentary, of themselves. More significantly, they came to be seen at such a prestigious event.

The Legislature convened the first week of January, rehearsals for the LCA show got under way in early February, and the gala show was staged in mid-March shortly before the

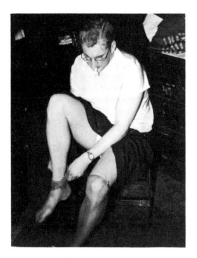

In one LCA show I was cast as Senator "Christine Jorgensen" Morse, a takeoff linking the Oregon senator who switched parties to the world's first publicized sex-change. On stage I wore nylons, skirt, padded bra, blouse and wig. At the dress rehearsal a photographer caught me without nylons, right, with ex-AP writer Charlie Palmer, in Scout uniform as VP candidate Nixon.

legislative session normally ended. Our writer-producers, Tom Stowell and Warren Weaver, enjoyed composing clever new lyrics to popular tunes, and we enjoyed singing and dancing to them. The rehearsals rarely got started before 9:30 or 10 in the evening, which made for long, weary days, sometimes fourteen hours or more, especially in the final weeks before the show. But it was good fun and close camaraderie.

There were long hours of overtime more nights than not, even without rehearsals that lasted past midnight. In his smooth administrative style Paxton annually convinced us that the AP couldn't possibly afford to pay all that overtime, particularly in a non-union shop like Albany. He assumed that the Capitol assignment was personally important and prestigious to us, hence worth all that extra effort. He eased his conscience by a concession he felt would compensate— overtime pay the final

223

hectic fortnight of the legislative session and, after adjournment, a week off with pay that didn't count against our regular two-week vacation allotment. There was, of course, no alternative but to accept.

It was during those bonus weeks that some of us began to see a different picture. We had taken for granted that the lofty prestige of the LCA with its by-lined experts, combined with daily contact with big-time political leaders on a first-name basis, stamped us as first-line journalists at the top of our trade. Not only were editors of major newspapers depending on us to furnish authoritative "inside" reports of the vital functioning of state government, but so were thousands of people who looked to newspapers for information that affected their daily lives, their jobs, their taxes, their lifestyles under state laws and regulations.

Thus it was sobering, if not downright disheartening, to discover that an overwhelming majority of New York State's fifteen million inhabitants weren't reading our stuff. Furthermore, they didn't care about the things we were writing about.

My dear friend and colleague Bill Davidson came to this conclusion each year when he and wife Elaine took their post-adjournment week off by returning to their native habitat down in Sullivan County. Relaxing on R&R with the boys on his old news beat in Calicoon, where he had grown up, Bill got a disturbing glimpse of the real world. Hardly any of the local politicos, including county judges, town supervisors and business leaders, had bothered to read the stories from Albany during the recent session, and few had more than minimal interest in what the governor and the Legislature were doing.

"And we knock ourselves out getting all this stuff out, and nobody reads it but the editors," he complained when he came back. "I don't know what we're doing this for."

I got a similar jolt after my second year on The Hill. I was having a blissful week at home on my R&R week—in return for a hundred uncounted hours of unpaid overtime—when my wife summoned me from working in the yard. "It's long-distance," she said. "Mr. Farley."

Along Capitol Corridors - By Nat Boynton

ALBANY (P) — The Democrats' new minority leaders are pepping up an otherwise dull Legislature session with a nice display of showmanship.

A pair of polished speakers and quick-witted debaters, the freshman floor leaders are giving legislators and sideliners more color for their money—although the minority cause is as futile as ever—and it's not an election year.

All hands agree that Sen. Francis J. Mahoney and Assemblyman Eugene F. Bannigan have livened up the infant 1953 session, and there are indications they're not even warmed up yet.

Both are New York City practicing attorneys with long courtroom experience and savvy.

Both are working under warps, using the caution that comes with new responsibility, but old-time capitol observers think there's a good show on stage.

———

The new leaders took their posts simultaneously, filling vacancies caused by the deaths last Sepember of Sen. Elmer F. Quinn and Assemblyman Irwin Steingut.

Bannigan has the most color, showmanship and tattersall vests. In contrast to Steingut's coolness under fire and long experience, Bannigan is a fiery speaker and an explosive debater with a sharp flare for humor.

In his college days at Manhattan he won prizes for Latin and public speaking. For a while recently he had his own TV show.

But the aggressive, ruddy-faced Brooklyn leader is careful of his oratory on the Assembly floor. He is speaking for his party now.

He is guided by the party's veteran strategists, but privately he will tell you, "What can you do with 52 votes?"

Assembly Republicans have 98.

———

On the sedate Senate side, Mahoney's calm, polished oratory is less spectacular than that of his Assembly counterpart. Oldline senators, however, look for a good—and perhaps refreshing — show when the new minority leader puts his scholarly vocabulary to work.

Mahoney, like Bannigan a Manhattan College man, has been a practicing lawyer in lower Broadway for 30 years. The son of a longshoreman, Mahoney did a little stevedoring himself while working his way through college.

In his new post, however, he inherits a familiar situation: Plenty of words and applause and not enough votes. The Senate lineup this year is 37-19, Republican.

Washington Scene - - - - - By George Dixon

Virtually every AP paper in the state used our weekly political column on the Op-Ed page. Some, like the Hornell Tribune, lumped it with its counterpart from Washington.

I had written my senior thesis at college on James A. Farley as the political kingmaker behind Franklin D. Roosevelt's campaign for the presidency in 1932, and he had taken the time to visit me backstage before one of the LCA dinner shows. He was living in New York City as a corporation executive, retaining a close connection with politics and continuing his longtime custom of keeping in touch with many friends and contacts. He had apparently liked me well enough to include me on his list, and after several such phone calls I realized I was one of the sources he liked to tap to keep posted on developments at the state capital.

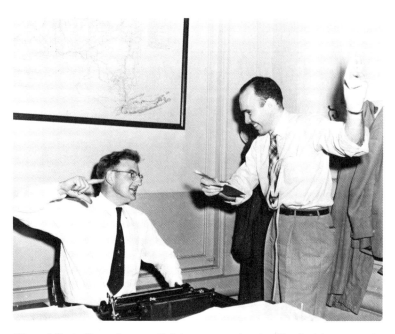

Two AP staffers share a light moment in the Capitol bureau. At right is Fred Davis, my former roommate.

This particular call was vintage Jim Farley. Warm greetings, brief family chit-chat and then political gossip. "How's Dewey doing with that auto-inspection bill he was having so much trouble with? Is he going to get it through?"

I had to explain that the Legislature had adjourned more than two weeks ago, and in a particularly stormy session had held the car-inspection bill over to the following year's session for further refinements. Inwardly I was shocked that the astute Farley didn't know this. I was even more horrified when he remarked: "Say, it looks to me like Tom Dewey is acting more and more like a candidate. Do you think he'll run again this year?" It was hard to believe that my distinguished caller was unaware that the governor had recently ended speculation— in that gubernatorial election year of 1954—by announcing he would not seek another term. Bill Davidson was right—from Calicoon to the Waldorf Astoria Towers our stories were widely unread.

I liked Jim Farley immensely and admired him as much as any of the big-name political figures I was accustomed to seeing in action. He sent me occasional notes and clippings, and an autographed copy of his book, *Behind the Ballots*. One of my proudest moments came while I was chatting with a friend on State Street in Albany one spring morning. Farley had just arrived at Union Station and was walking the few blocks to the Ten Eyck Hotel in May sunshine with several other men en route to the annual meeting of the New York Central board of directors.

As the group approached, my friend remarked: "Say, that tall fellow looks like Jim Farley."

"It is," I said. "Would you like to meet him?"

He looked at me incredulously. When I greeted Farley as he passed, he stopped and shook hands. "Hello, Nat! How are you, and how's that young son of yours?"

When I introduced him to Jack Toohey, I assume my local stock rose several points. "I may not wash this hand the rest of the day," Toohey said.

Within a few months all three of us who had covered The Hill for the AP for the previous two years left for new opportunities. Davidson became the first public information director for the new Thruway Authority (to be joined a year later by my old friend, Harvey Travis), Jensen went to the Washington Post, and I embarked on a new career as a writer and editor in the big General Electric plant in nearby Schenectady. Were those departures spurred by energy-draining hours of unpaid overtime, or by hours of trying to stay awake during dreary proceedings in the legislative chambers? Or could it have been the Great Public Yawn?

Well . . . maybe a little of all three.

V

*Corporate
Diversion*

26

Wearing the Monogram on Pajamas

Journalists who defect to the field of public relations are often frowned upon or envied—sometimes both—by colleagues who remain true to the core. Purists tend to regard deserters as selling out for the dollar bill, cashing in on their skills and contacts.

Today the field of PR is so large and diversified that it is almost inevitable that after a few years in newspaper work a reporter or editor turns to an easier and more lucrative life as a "flack"—the term once used by loyalists to describe a defector, but now relatively archaic. Flackery is only part of the expanded field known as communications, where it is now not only possible but popular to graduate from college and go directly into some form of PR without ever having worked on a newspaper— or any other boulevard of journalism.

I became one of these renegades after three sessions on The Hill as an AP legislative correspondent in Albany. My reasons for jumping ship were somewhat different from those of brethren lured by the lush political enticements found in a wide spectrum of state agencies as well as the infrastructure of the Legislature itself. Not that I didn't need to improve on the peonage wage AP staffers toiled for, especially with a first-born infant at home. I was disillusioned with the political scene as displayed inside that magnificent and monstrous conglomeration of masonry, the New York State Capitol, and I was dismayed by the low morale and poor working conditions in the AP bureau. I was looking for asylum, especially when my two associates in the AP's three-man staff in the Capitol, Bill Davidson and Bob Jensen, were leaving.

Jack Dumas, who had covered the Legislature for the Schenectady Gazette before taking a job in the General Electric News Bureau, tipped me off to an opening in the big Schenectady GE plant. I liked the looks of it, especially since Schenectady was about the same commuting distance. The sadness of deserting a profession I thought I would never consider leaving was quickly supplanted by a feeling of liberation.

*　　*　　*　　*　　*

Writing news releases for Schenectady GE's Community Relations unit was a far cry from previous literary efforts. After having been on the receiving end of many thousands of releases floated by PR people, I now found myself one of them, and it was a simple matter to emulate the familiar style and format of the news release. In fact, it was easy, because I knew well what editors would like and what they would look for. After all, that's why I was hired.

Foremost among my new chores was a commission to seize every opportunity to publicize happiness and good fortune as the lot of GE employees at every level. The objective was, of course, to create and preserve a favorable atmosphere for the next round of union negotiations. In the eyes of management, a union member who is convinced that the company treats him so well—presumably voluntarily—would be reluctant to go on strike.

In Schenectady the illusion worked beautifully. It didn't take long for me to adjust to the new habitat; the salary was only a modest improvement, but I was impressed with the quality and spirit of the people I was working with. Of key importance also was the fact that in this, only my third change of employer, I didn't have to move residence, and my wife and I really liked where we were living in suburban Albany.

There were all kinds of writing jobs within this corporate giant. In my first year with GE I switched to the News Bureau, the publicity arm of a large in-house full-service advertising and public relations agency. I spent the next eighteen years in various functions for GE's Advertising and Sales Promotion Department (A&SP), most of it stimulating and enjoyable.

In the News Bureau I spent a year in the labyrinth of the General Engineering Laboratory, where highly talented scientists, several of them internationally recognized, worked on long-range technological developments. This laboratory had given the world scores of technical breakthroughs that subsequent generations take for granted. One of the most fascinating of many challenges was extracting detailed explanations from scientists, many of whom were virtually incapable of describing their creations in understandable terms.

In frustration, unable to translate into comprehensible English the workings of a technical innovation, I would say to an inventor-engineer: "Let's try it this way. You are asked to describe this invention to your son's sixth grade class or his scout troop. Try to put it in sequence and terms these kids could understand." That didn't always work, but it helped. Once I asked a physicist: "Have you ever tried to tell your wife how you came to develop this phenomenon?"

After the laboratory stint was a year publicizing large jet engines, then three years in one of the best assignments I've ever had—creating and editing a sophisticated slick-paper marketing magazine called Trend. Its audience was the Apparatus Sales Division, which served GE's electric utility and industrial equipment markets worldwide. Along with exposure to a lot of good people, a lot of domestic travel, abundant professional challenge and interesting projects, I had almost total license to select and write in-depth articles and, best of all, I had a rare immunity from the tedious approval process that permits nervous executives to kill or stifle effective writing and withhold supplementary information.

But once again, like those journalistic Edens of Massena and Geneva, the magazine deal was too good to last. In one of the frequent reorganizations that corporations love to make, the Apparatus Sales Division was split into two new divisons, Industrial Sales and Electric Utility Sales. With new, ambitious vice presidents joining the executive circle, neither of the new divisions was willing to take on the budget for the magazine, and a publication I was intensely proud of was allowed to die without ceremony.

It was ironic, I thought, that I had survived W.W. II as a low-grade aircraft mechanic flying in planes for whose operational safety I was responsible, yet two magazines of high professional quality, *Harmoneer* and *Trend*, had gone down under me through external circumstances.

* * * * *

The next turn in my corporate meandering took me into the audiovisual field, even more fascinating, highly creative and far more challenging. It was one thing trying to translate the words and phrases of a research scientist or electronic engineer into sentences the public could comprehend; it was still another to develop a 25-minute presentation—slides and a cued script—for a GE vice president to give to a prestigious audience. The presentation might be for a stockholders' meeting, a worldwide sales meeting, an assemblage of Wall Street financial analysts or of electric utility presidents buying multi-million-dollar turbine generators and nuclear power plants. Given the high stakes, the power politics of corporate board rooms and the prima-donna personalities of the executives involved, this was the most demanding writing environment I had ever encountered.

Most of these projects were enjoyable despite the arduous hours, the incredible pressures of production deadlines before big meetings, and the whims of clients in an agency atmosphere. Almost every assignment was competitively sensitive in the light of executives constantly jockeying for pole position in the cut-throat push to the top spot. Here the insecurity and personality shortfalls of high-salaried corporate administrators often were exposed in spite of their polished efforts to project an image of capability and confidence.

234

In our pooled audiovisual operations we writers and slide producers were many levels below the people we were writing for. We possessed zero managerial clout, but we had a key role in their fishbowl appearances before audiences that included their peers and superiors. For them, each trip to the podium had the potential of being pivotal in their respective careers. If ever there was a place where pushing and shoving behind scenes was on display, it was during preparation for these excursions to the executive lectern. In this atmosphere my only ambition was to be allowed to operate as counselor and coach for my speaker; I wasn't pushing for a better job, just perhaps a word or gesture of appreciation when the talk went well.

In ten years of writing for scores of executives at various levels, it was inevitable that I would make firm friends as well as accumulate detractors. The relationship of a speaker to his speech writer was as intimate or cooperative as the "client" wanted it to be. Some were very appreciative of the writer's professional skill and perspective, others took his expertise for granted or were arrogant. At the very top level some were warm and friendly, others cold and indifferent. Those who appreciated our role were generous with their time and accessibility; others were aloof and treated us like hired hands. At our humble level we had glimpses into the personal makeup of these bigwigs that many of their daily associates might never see.

I soon found that a characteristic of mine set me apart from most of my half-dozen or so colleagues in the Schenectady writers' pool. Having been a newspaperman for so many years, I was not in the habit of kowtowing to any of the alleged superior beings in officialdom or society. No one—governor, Supreme Court justice, bank president, department head, even the boss in the office—was going to push a newspaperman around during pursuit of a story or an objective. GE, on the other hand, was structured more like the military, where a lower rank was expected to show a sense of humility and subservience, including an occasional "yes, sir" when appropriate.

I could accept this in the Army but not in private industry. The vice presidents I was dealing with had the political and financial clout that comes with high corporate station, but with few exceptions they were no more intelligent, no better educated nor possessed of more social grace than I. Most of them had more plaques and certificates of special distinction in their offices and impressive achievements on their resumes than a fellow who had spent his life in journalistic labor without distinction, but I would not want some of these characters in my living room, mixing with my family and friends.

I recall with warmth Dr. Charlie Reed, a renowned industrial chemist who headed an important GE division then headquartered in Bridgeport, inviting me to dinner in his favorite restaurant as we were concluding a slide session in his office that lasted until 8:30 p.m. I also had a high regard for Reuben Gutoff, a rising star in Reed's division, who played tennis with me—a little too well—during a break in a top-management conference in Florida. On another occasion Gutoff invited me to join him and some staff people for a drink in his motel room after a long rehearsal.

I was disappointed when Gutoff, a capable executive apparently impatient with his progress toward the GE presidency, took a job with another company, but I was glad to see later that he was heading it.

It was at that informal little session in Gutoff's room overlooking the pool, that a young department manager regaled the small group with tales of a recent business trip, his first to the Orient. His description of a visit to a mixed bath in Tokyo drew gales of laughter. The narrator was Jack Welch, a brash young fellow who not only became chairman of GE a decade later, but changed the whole course of one of the nation's largest investor-owned corporate entities. Later Jack Welch had power and a salary of a million and a half dollars, but reputedly few genuine friends. He must have lost many in his climb to the corporate penthouse.

I never wrote a talk for Welch, but I did write one for Reg Jones, his predecessor as chief executive officer, when Jones was a division general manager. There was no reason for Jones to remember a speechwriter he had worked with once in the past, but even in the company's highest position he called me by first name and paid me a compliment after looking in on a rehearsal I was conducting for an important presentation in Denver. Proof enough that it is possible to make it to the top and still be a good guy.

*   *   *   *   *

One of the toughest taskmasters I ever encountered was a vice president in Schenectady named Wells Corbin. He was a shirt-sleeve executive, all-business and intensely demanding. The writers in our small pool dreaded being assigned to him, but I had to admit that I grudgingly admired him. We had our clashes, especially when he wanted to throw out 75 percent of a script we had been working on for two weeks, and take a new tack two days before D-Day. On rare occasions I thought I detected a hint that he liked or appreciated me.

I had respect for Corbin because he ran his business the way he thought it ought to be run, was not afraid to go jaw-to-jaw with his superiors, and was more interested in running a tight ship than in playing the game of executive chairs. If he got promoted, fine; if not, there were plenty of good places for him to go. Most important, he had been through the mill himself and knew the problems his subordinates faced every day. Corbin was a refreshing oasis in a company that believed an executive with proven management capability could run a successful operation even if he had no previous background or knowledge of the product, the market or the nature of the business.

Perhaps that is why we ran into some real turkeys in the speechwriting game. In my eyes the most notable example of the fallacy of putting a successful manager of one business in charge of another, totally unrelated, business was a division head at Electronics Park in Syracuse I had once written for. Len Maier had been promoted to an executive office position in New York that put him in charge of most of the company's public and personnel relations, a far cry from engineering and manufacturing. He not only had little exposure to the PR field, but he had a personality that was ill-fitted for the role.

Early in his new capacity Maier was asked to keynote the kickoff meeting for a company-wide sales campaign, an assignment of high visibility in the executive structure. Ray Bonta, our audiovisual section manager in Schenectady, a

237

mousey little man who spent a career worrying about everything and everybody connected with his job, assigned me to Maier. Bonta made sure I realized that Maier's latest advancement lifted him to a position atop the pyramid of boxes in the organization chart that traced the administrative pecking order for our part of the vast corporation. That placed Maier in a direct succession three or four management tiers higher than Bonta's own boss. I promised to be a good boy.

That promise turned out to be hard to keep. In launching any speechwriting project, the first move always comes from the client, a comprehensive briefing by the speaker or one of his staff people. Maier and I got off on the wrong foot when I waited a full week for the summons to New York. When the call from a staff member finally came, it reached me at home late on a snowy Saturday barely five days before D-Day, which was the upcoming Friday. That was cutting it far too close in writing and producing a major slide presentation. Maier would like to see me in New York at 4 p.m. the next day, Sunday.

I told Maier's staff man, whom I knew quite well, that I couldn't make it that soon, but I would take the first train Monday. He was aghast. "But he wants you here today," he kept saying, implying that at Maier's lofty level he expected everyone to dance attendance.

I replied that I considered such a demand unreasonable, and that I had personal commitments on a Sunday I shouldn't be asked to break on a few hours' notice, especially after waiting several business days for the call. Sorry.

I reported to Maier's office at 11 Monday morning. He granted me audience at 3, wasting most of another critical working day. The briefing was brief, and we agreed on key points and basic structure.

"When can I see the draft?" he asked.

The normal interim would be two days minimum, but we had barely three working days to produce the final presentation—forty or fifty slides as well as the cued script. I would have to get a big bite into the first draft that night.

"This time tomorrow," I said, knowing that was cutting it close.

"I'd like to have it tonight," he said.

"That's pretty tight," I said. "I need more than a few hours to write a 25-minute talk."

"You can do it," he said.

"How about 8 a.m. tomorrow?" I heard myself saying, hanging my neck out.

"Do I have a choice?" he said grumpily, seemingly miffed at the apparent impudence of an underling.

"Not really," I said. "I need tonight to work on it."

Thus began a project that was memorable as the most distasteful in my working life. I finished his first draft at 2:15 a.m., delivered it at 8 in my own typing, complete with false starts and revisions XXX-ed out, and inserts pasted in. I made a photocopy so that Ted Batzell, my artist friend from Schenectady assigned with several others to New York for the duration of the overall program, could start designing the slide art—charts and graphs that would be given to an art studio to make flats (at an average cost of $70 each).

Back in Maier's office Tuesday after lunch, I received the extensive notes he had scrawled on every page of the clean copy his secretary had hurriedly typed. I wrote a new draft that afternoon, met with Maier, and wrote Draft Three late that night. On Wednesday morning he decided to change the sequence and introduce a new section of major proportions. Batzell and I put the visuals for Draft Four into production at the commercial studio on East 44th Street without taking time to get the speaker's approval—production time was far too tight, even with expensive overtime past midnight at studio rates.

Thursday morning Maier complained he had been unable to find me Wednesday night (I purposely didn't tell him the location of an office I had borrowed on the 27th floor where I could work in peace). Thursday afternoon he decided on a new approach, the format for which made $3100 worth of glass-mounted slides and charts unusable.

Batzell got help from a second artist designing slides, we alerted two art studios for an all-night session, and Maier assigned a typist to work that night. I wrote another draft—was it the sixth or eighth?—and in my mind I drafted my resignation from General Electric, along with a resolution to the board of directors that Maier be fired for incompetence. This time Maier, as might be expected, had some new suggestions, but I explained he had run out of time, and there would be no further changes in either script or slides. He didn't like that, but retreated when I explained that when he took to the lectern on the morrow in front of his audience, with a cleanly typed and cued script and a projectionist observing the cues, he would be free to make all the changes he desired.

After a pleasant weekend recuperating with my family on the ski slopes I was back in my Schenectady cubicle on Monday, confident that no future assignment could ever be that much of an ordeal. A day later Bonta informed me that Maier had told him that the speech had gone well, but that he complained that "I couldn't always find Boynton when I wanted him." The implication was that I might have succumbed to external distractions when I should have been working on the speech.

Bonta was shocked when I told him I would never write another sentence for Len Maier—ever. "But he's our boss's boss's boss," he said. "We're all responsible to him, you know that."

I was well aware of that, I said, but Maier, I explained, is an uncouth slob, an insecure, inept individual who should never have been allowed to hold such a position. I explained that I had worked four straight fifteen-hour days, that Maier's aimless executive gymnastics had put five or six other people through five days of needless jumping through hoops, and had wasted six or seven thousand dollars of GE stockholders' money making slides at $70 each, then throwing them away, meanwhile incurring huge expense working staffers and art studios far into the night at double overtime. I wasn't asking for any kudos, or even a thank-you, but I was in no mood to listen to any complaints on this one. Never again with me, I told Bonta.

There was nothing more to say. I never saw Maier again except at a distance at corporate meetings.

*   *   *   *   *

The staging crew, which handled projection, props and electronic controls in whatever auditorium we were using, had the office next door to ours in Schenectady. They also had their own problems with prima-donna executives.

Doug Crossman was the staging chief, and never one to be pushed around by anyone, let alone a top executive. The company's high standards demanded that each slide appear on the screen the very split-second the speaker uttered the cue word, whether it were a photo or the headline of a chart. Doug and his boys were trained in this regimen, and so were the writers.

Whenever a speaker tended to stray from the typed script, we had to straighten him out. Not everyone liked this, especially Milton F. Kent, vice president of the Power Generation Sales Division.

All of us at one time or another had written for "Mink" Kent, a down-easter from Maine. I had known him during my Trend magazine days, before his ascendancy to high rank. Mink, an accomplished salesman, was one of those speakers who believed that prepared scripts were inhibiting, and that a speaker who talked extemporaneously, maintaining steady eye contact without glancing at the text in front of him, was certain to hold the attention of his audience.

Mink paid little heed to admonitions of lowly writers and projectionists—until the day Crossman crossed him. I was sitting with Doug in the projection booth, each of us following the minutely cued script, when Mink departed from the text and began "winging it."

"God damn him," complained Doug. "How the hell does he expect me to punch his cues when I don't know where the hell he is in his script?"

A moment later he discovered Mink had skipped a cue altogether and now was somewhere on the next page. "Hell with it," said Crossman, swinging around in his chair, putting his feet on an empty chair, his back to the projector and the screen. He stared at the rear wall of the booth, waiting for the inevitable.

"Can I have the next slide, please?" came Mink's voice over the audio. Crossman swung around, his jaw tightly clamped in anger, and punched the hand-held "pickle" advancing the projector. Then he again swung his chair to the rear, his back to the screen.

241

Poor Mink, still winging it, had to interrupt his talk again. "Next slide, please," he called. Crossman again punched the pickle, still refusing to glance at the script, his jaw clamped in disgust.

Afterwards Kent was furious. He came to the booth and began to chew Doug out, but the angry professional interrupted.

"Mink," he began, speaking deliberately in a parental baritone. "I never interfere when you go out and sell big steam-turbine generator systems to power companies. At the same time, I don't want you messing me up in my job. You are supposed to follow the script so we can flash the slides on cue. You didn't do that. Don't make that mistake again. I'm sorry."

*   *   *   *   *

In direct contrast to the inflated ego that some GE executives developed as they rose to lofty levels was an internationally known scientist named Dr. Thomas O. Paine, a senior vice president. He had worked in Schenectady's vast engineering and research laboratories after serving as an officer in submarines during World War II, but subsequently had left GE to join the U. S. space program. His fascination with space technology and his expertise therein propelled him to become head of NASA and thus a key figure in the Apollo program that put man on the moon. Somehow GE lured him back to the fold, where he was put in charge of the Power Generation Group, a complex of divisions and departments that served the electric utility industry around the globe. This business was at the corporate core of General Electric, and the company had long been recognized as the world leader in the field.

In the wide spectrum of GE businesses, this was also the field in which I was the most comfortable. Our small band of writers and producers in Schenectady had to be versatile in order to take assignments wherever we were needed, but we did have our individual specialties. I had spent most of ten years in the field of power generation and transmission, including many trips to nuclear power plants and reactor manufacturing facilities. With this experience, it was natural that I would find myself frequently in Paine's orbit. The assignments ranged from internal company meetings to elaborate presentations to assemblages of top executives of the nation's utility companies, Wall Street financial analysts and GE management conferences.

Tom Paine was by far my favorite of all those executive "clients." He was the most brilliant and most admirable man I worked with in all the years at General Electric. He was also a superior person and a good friend.

It was strange, in a way, that we worked together so well, for our first encounter—when he personally rearranged the slide tray the night before his appearance without consulting his writer or projectionist—was nearly akin to the Len Maier syndrome. Like Maier, Paine had no qualms in making changes, some of them major, right up to the last few hours of the final-final deadline, often with small regard to the repercussions these changes might have on slide production and the timing of slide cues.

But there the resemblance stopped. Tom Paine was not only an excellent writer in his own right, but he had a keen appreciation of visual impact. He also had grace and humility, two qualities, along with good fellowship, that the Kents and Maiers could never be accused of possessing. Whereas Kent and Maier, even on our first-name basis, made it clear that they considered themselves a cut above me intellectually, professionally and socially, Paine accepted me not only as a social equal, but also as every bit as respected a professional in my field as he was in his. (Kent once asked me to carry his luggage.)

As an executive he was firm and authoritative. His associates tended to regard him as aloof, but they had deep respect, almost awe, for him, perhaps because they recognized his credentials and stature. When it came to basic intellect Paine was in a class by himself among GE's top management fraternity. A doctoral degree does not necessarily guarantee culture, but Tom Paine had both; he and his charming wife Barbara, an Australian, were patrons of music and art, were voracious readers, abreast of political, economic and social developments of our civilization. With most of the other vice presidents, once the

Tom Paine

dialogue strayed from the corporate specialty at hand, meaningful conversation soon deteriorated or evaporated altogether.

During this period I handled a number of Paine's presentations, including one that embraced the first computerized slide graphics to be put on film in GE history. The innovative technique, called Genographics, was developed by GE in Syracuse and introduced at Paine's Power Generation Group conference at Napa Valley. By today's standards it was crude, but at the time it was exciting.

Through these activities I inadvertently became custodian of Paine's extensive slide library besides being his personal script writer. It was fascinating to be exposed to a man who could grasp virtually the full spectrum of science and history, and relate technological developments to political, economic and social trends.

In view of Paine's stature and achievements, I felt the General Electric Company was wasting this substantial talent by positioning him as a group vice president in Power Generation. Although I never heard Tom utter a word of complaint, it was plain to see that he was uncomfortable in the high strata of marketing nuclear power plants and giant steam turbines to presidents of electric power companies. These were the prime customers in a multi-billion-dollar business where the accent was on salesmanship.

When a midwestern utility company was shopping for a new generating plant, it was customary for a top executive to parlay that into trips to New York, where he and his wife would be extensively and expensively entertained by GE officers of appropriate rank. Both corporations justified the lush outlays as routine business. However, the spectacle of Tom and Barbara Paine, opera buffs and patrons of art and classical music, spending a mandated social evening hosting the president of an inland power company and wife in a round of nightclub entertaining and banal conversation was almost ludicrous. Often the visiting executive's background was in corporate accounting and, typically, while a trainee in the auditing section, had married a grade-four clerk-typist with a background in high-school cheerleading or secretarial school.

The Paines lived in a tasteful apartment in Manhattan's East Fifties only a few blocks from GE's corporate headquarters, and I often worked there as well as in the corporate tower. I always enjoyed the sessions at the apartment, but the most memorable—shades of Len Maier—was a New Year's Eve I spent alone in the basement auditorium of 570 Lexington, putting the finishing touches on a five-projector extravaganza, the silence broken only by the hum of the projectors and the click of the slide trays as they moved. When I called Tom's apartment shortly after 1 a.m. to say I was ready, he came down promptly to the lonely booth for a run-through that lasted well past 2 o'clock. His pronouncement that the presentation was acceptable was reward enough, and we headed separate ways on New Year's Day to meet again in two days at the management conference in Florida.

Among dozens of clients in the speechwriting phase of my career the good guys far outnumbered the Maiers and Kents. A number of them exemplified the kind of capability and personal integrity an executive of an American corporation should have. But toward the end of this period I was becoming disenchanted with what seemed to be an increasing amount of travel and longer assignments away from home. By mere chance I had been thrown repeatedly into the company's large computer business, and from late 1967 to early 1970 made seventeen trips to that division's headquarters in Phoenix. One assignment lasted seven weeks, several others two and three weeks.

By 1972 I had one child in college and two in secondary school, plus a small cabin on Lake George that I felt I should see more of. I could think of no other kind of job in General Electric with any appeal, and not being interested in higher-paying jobs merely for the money, and being geographically selective, I had turned down several offers from other parts of the company. As that word got around I could see why few people would be interested in offering me advancement. At the same time, my own superiors, realizing I preferred to be a fixture and was no longer a target for head-hunters, tended to give the available pay raises to younger writers more apt to be lured elsewhere.

Despite the demands of the corporate octopus on my time and energy, I had been able to develop several free-lance accounts, known to the trade as moonlighting. Working out of my house in Slingerlands, I was putting out several newsletters on a regular basis and handling some public relations work for several Albany contacts I had developed over many years. It was a welcome change of pace, and I was beginning to consider further explorations into the world of freelancing as a means of escape from the incessant travel and pressure of the corporate carousel.

The straw that broke the camel's back came one summer during a long and tortuous assignment with my computer time-sharing friends in Bethesda, Maryland. Of all the places on this spinning ball, few have less appeal for me than Washington, D.C., damp and chilly in winter and unbearably hot and sticky in summer. It was dreary enough spending five evenings a week in a motel on Connecticut Avenue—five because my clients wanted me on the job at 8 a.m. each Monday—but battling the hordes and humidity at Washington National Airport on the Friday breakaways was intolerable. Twice Allegheny Airlines, known to us as "Agony Airlines," cancelled Friday night flights that August when I was desperately trying to get to Lake George, and I resented having to leave the lake at noon on Sunday to make a flight in Albany that would get me back to detested Bethesda Sunday night. The two themes that dominated my mind in these crises were: (1) there's got to be a better life than this, and (2) my modest salary does not compensate for this kind of torture.

By September I landed a new freelance account, helping the publicity operation at Russell Sage College in Troy. It wasn't a big account, but when added to the four or five others already on hand, I felt it was enough of a push to turn my moonlighting into full-time freelancing.

It would be risky, taking a sizeable cut in income in such a pivotal family circumstance, but I felt confident that the liberation would provide ample time to develop new accounts and expand the present ones. Meanwhile, my colleagues at GE couldn't believe a man in his fifties, only seven years short of minimum retirement age, would give up what they thought were generous pension benefits. Nor did they believe me when I told them that I had researched the pension picture and concluded that GE, for all its bluster in community relations, had one of the more meager retirement plans in American industry. I took the plunge.

*   *   *   *   *

It was especially satisfying to be able to mail my one-sentence letter of resignation from Bethesda in August, giving sixty days notice. By the same token, it was appropriate that the Napa Valley management conference of power generation people enabled me to end my GE career writing for my friend, T. O. Paine. In the euphoria of the impending career switch, I didn't mind that the Napa project delayed my termination date by several weeks in October.

For a while the new venture went well, showing more promise than actual growth. I found that many former GE friends who had defected to other companies were interested in my being available to help on special projects. Prospects for the coming year were good, but just before Thanksgiving I got the biggest and happiest surprise—a call from my close friend Dave Jones in Schenectady, asking if I would handle Tom Paine's talk at the annual GE Management Conference in Clearwater, Florida.

With the help of another good friend, John Duncan, who had supervised the writers' pool in the audiovisual section in Schenectady, arrangements were quickly made for me to have access to the art, photo and audiovisual production facilities I had so recently surrendered. Paine, it turned out, had asked for me, either unaware—or pretending to be unaware—that I had left the company. It was a simple matter to register me as a vendor under contract, a maneuver that gave me a lucrative freelance assignment and made Paine and GE people comfortable because I not only knew the company and the speaker well, but had worked three or four Clearwater summits in the past, one with Paine himself.

As the week-long Clearwater grind was ending, Paine asked me to come to his New York office the following week to discuss several upcoming speaking dates on his calendar. I was delighted. For the next several years Paine was in demand as a speaker, and often took me with him as his personal script doctor and projectionist, a role I relished.

One of his favorite themes was showing how technological innovations had influenced world history from the dawn of agriculture and primitive water transport through the ages of exploration and industrial development to the Age of Space. We produced several variations, tailored to the respective audiences, which ranged from the American Physical Society to a seminar of California high school science award-winners and a number of university campuses. The depth and scope of Tom Paine's knowledge made these presentations almost classic, and I felt grateful in having a role in them.

This happy partnership lasted until Paine extricated himself from GE and became president of the Northrop Corporation. There he found a vital outlet for his talents, for

Northrop was involved in the space program and, as a bonus for Tom, it was based in California, his favorite habitat.

Meanwhile I found myself busier than ever with no escape from deadlines. I wrote and produced slide presentations for Singer, ITT, Gulf and Western, Continental Can and International Paper, but this time I was in a position to accept or decline each as it came, turning some down because of travel or an undesirable geographic location.

The nucleus, however, remained the collection of small but enjoyable freelance accounts in the Albany area—banks, colleges, legislative lobbies, small businesses and others. These activities, especially in publicity projects, often brought me into contact with old friends on the Albany and Schenectady papers, where a sentimental oldtimer like me never failed to experience that comfortable feeling like coming home.

VI

Uniquely Weekly

27

Ink in the Blood

There was still lots of newspaper blood in my veins a decade or more after defecting from the AP. The Albany newspaper scene had changed substantially, notably as the result of the takeover of the afternoon Knickerbocker News by the morning Times-Union. That meant the Knick, clearly the highest-quality paper in the Gannett chain, had become a Hearst paper like the Times-Union. Now they were sharing quarters along with business and production staffs while vigorously proclaiming editorial independence from each other. This insistence, only mildly transparent and universally disbelieved, was designed to assure the community that competitive journalism was not dead in Albany.

I got to know both papers very well very quickly when I joined the AP staff in Albany back in 1951. I had kept in touch with city room staffers from the days we worked in that insufferable attic in the old Knick building and the airless night office at the T-U. The Knick of that era was a highly acclaimed paper with a staff of top writers, several of whom, like Emmet O'Brien, Dave Beetle and Arvis Chalmers, were among the best on The Hill.

During those years the T-U had one journeyman reporter assigned to the Capitol and, to handle the Civil Service constituency, a young eager-beaver was assigned to cover state offices. For the bigger legislative and political stories the T-U used the AP's daily production, four or five by-lined pieces on major developments. Papers across the state used AP by-lines and datelines; the Times-Union ran the identical stories under an open dateline, leaving the impression, intentional or not, that these stories were produced in its own shop. The first few times I saw stories we had written under pressurized conditions from the Capitol appearing without AP credit in the T-U, I was resentful; later I came to accept the practice as the T-U's indifference to competitive coverage.

In this context, however, I was still surprised when, introduced to Gene Robb, publisher of the Times-Union, at a dinner party in Loudonville in 1953, I got an inadvertent glimpse of the T-U's perspective. I was well into my second year covering the Legislature and the governor's office when Robb, sitting next to me at a gourmet buffet in the comfortable house of mutual friends, declared in all sincerity that the Times-Union had "the best legislative coverage of any paper in the state."

I was so flabbergasted I could only smile, thinking not only of the talent on the Knick staff, but of the Buffalo papers, other Gannett papers, Watertown Times, Syracuse, Binghamton and others whose Albany correspondents clearly surpassed the T-U's. Could it be that Gene was unaware that the Times-Union depended primarily on our AP dispatches for basic Capitol coverage? Although Gene at the time was fairly new in his job, his remark was all the more astonishing because Robb, a likeable and capable fellow, was one of the few, if not the only one, in a succession of Hearst publishers in Albany who had been a working newsman at some point in his earlier days. Poor Gene, seeing all those open datelines, assumed the stories were written by his own people.

Union printers on the Albany dailies, frustrated by a deadlock in contract negotiations, filled both papers with eye-catching typographical errors, much to the amusement of readers. I knew Gene Robb well enough to write this letter, all in fun.

NATHANIEL A. BOYNTON
1749 NEW SCOTLAND ROAD
SLINGERLANDS, NEW YORK 12159

April 10, 1967

Dear Gene:

I think the people of the Capital District owe you an expression of appreciation for continuing to provide a high level of news coverage and interpretive analysis in the face of the publisher's chronic bugaboo --- rising costs.

I'm not just sentimental when
I'm not just being sentimental when I say reference to fabrics my wife purchased at your store that the family newspaper never will be displaced by "electronic journalism." I am fully convinced there prize won by Connie for selling Girl Scout cookies never will be a substitute for being able to read the news when you want it want it without a series of commmmmmercmermmcials spliced between every news item.

As a longtimef ormern ewsman and editor I am grateful for the talent and integrity of people like Bob Fichtenburg, Dave Beetle, Arvis, Bob Illing-SHRDLUSHRDLU½..$$% etaoin etaoin 888   Kay Harrin others on your staff and I think we are fortunate in having people of this caliber serving our area.

Gene, you would have been pleased to hear the comments of a group of us in my home Friday night at the Washington press corps calling LBJ "Big Clyde" during a discussion of the changing responsibilities of the newspaper in the light of shifting influences, economic emphasis, changing social forces over the PICK UP SECOND LEAD
last 20 or 30 years. Here is what the group said:

I'm glad to hear that you are well on the road to recovery and that your trip did a lot for your health. I send this note to you with warm personal wishes, and in good faith to a good friend.

Sincerely yours,

Nat

255

It was hard to admire the Hearst product in the Empire State's capital city. The bigwigs in the corporate tower in New York City demanded only a healthy bottom line on the balance sheet, not necessarily quality journalism. The accent was on sales promotion, cost efficiency, visible community citizenship and careful collective bargaining. The result was a showcase of mediocrity. In the case of the afternoon paper it was more than that; the once-prestigious Knickerbocker News had become an example of journalistic neglect brought about by the milking process—stripping a newspaper to the bare minimum in order to preserve lucrative national advertising contracts.

By the time the merged Capital Newspapers moved to a new, modern plant near Albany County Airport, Robb had upgraded the Times-Union, and had made his morning paper dominant in Albany's newspaper scene. Unlike Ray O'Connor's day, there were editors and reporters working regular evening and night hours. For its part, the Knick had swallowed and digested the Schenectady Union-Star, in the process depriving the people of that fair city of what had been a hard-hitting, aggressive afternoon paper. By the late sixties the Knick and the fading Star had moved the deadlines of their home editions from early afternoon to mid-morning, a policy that inhibited coverage of that day's breaking stories. The move resulted in the virtual disappearance of the Knick-Union-Star from Schenectady and began a circulation decline in Albany that continued for a number of years.

In the new building there were still a few holdovers in the city rooms, and it was natural for me to drop in for an occasional visit, especially during my post-GE stint as a freelancer with a string of small public relations clients. By chance the Times-Union itself indirectly—technically, anyway—became one of my client accounts.

That strange twist came about when Robert Danzig, who had been appointed publisher after Gene Robb's untimely death, became aware of a phenomenon of the times, the Great Northeast Tennis Boom. The advent of indoor courts was sending former tennis players flocking to buy new racquets. Novices swarmed to sign up for tennis lessons. In Albany an energetic young financier, Sanford Bookstein, opened the first indoor tennis club in eastern New York, and several other investors were breaking ground with the same intent.

From Danzig's sanctum the word went down to Tom Cunningham, T-U sports editor, to install a tennis column. Cunningham, whose insatiable passion for thoroughbred racing tempered his interest in other popular sports disciplines, admitted to only a surface familiarity with tennis. He called Bookstein and lamented the distressing edict from the top boss. Where would he ever find anyone to write a tennis column?

Sandy, one of the most affable and enterprising of local entrepreneurs, explained that among the charter tennis players who frequented his new emporium in Latham was a former sportswriter now moonlighting from GE as a freelancer. Sandy dispatched me to the Times-Union sports department the next day. It was near noontime and it was August, and Cunningham was hurrying to the parking lot to make post time at Saratoga. In three minutes we agreed on fifteen dollars for a once-a-week essay, to start the following Wednesday.

Over the next four years I never ceased to marvel at the popularity of that column, which Cunningham christened The Net Set. While the abrasive Bud Collins in the Boston Globe covered world-class tennis, the Albany Times-Union and the Schenectady Gazette had the only local tennis columns in the Northeast. I thoroughly enjoyed writing mine, and was delighted with the sizeable audience it attracted among a burgeoning population of tennis addicts. I was especially pleased when Cunningham would call me in, as he often did, to help with the Saturday-night avalanche of football and soccer stories phoned in from local schools and colleges. It was like old times, working in a newspaper office against deadlines. The pay was microscopic, but the nostalgia was intoxicating.

That happy relationship ended abruptly after four years. With the tennis boom at its height, Albany's best-known (and only) tennis writer perpetrated an unwitting and unforgivable no-no: he bought the weekly newspaper in suburban Delmar.

When word of that dastardly deed reached Danzig, Cunningham called me. Was it true I had acquired the Spotlight?

Net Profit
Is Love of
The Racquet

By NAT BOYNTON

"Everybody in my family likes tennis." said Stacie Battaglia. "so I want to learn to play too."

Stacie is a 10-year-old lefthanded tennis player who spends Friday afternoon swinging at — but not always hitting — bouncing balls at the Tri City Racquet Club's preteen clinics. Her pronouncement reflects the spreading appeal of tennis among families in the land and its growing popularity among the small fry.

"EVERYBODY" IN Stacie's family adds up to nine. which is almost enough to start a tourament without leaving the premises 11 De Lucia Terrace, Loudonville. She has six brothers and sisters and sports oriented parents. Sister Mary Jo, for one, is Albany Academy for Girls' No. 1 field hockey player.

The Times-Union used several logos for the tennis column and occasional feature articles before settling on The Net Set.

If so, he said, Danzig was ordering him to drop the tennis column. My first reaction was shock—several thousand happy tennis players and fans would be deprived of one of their innocent pleasures, the column in the Times-Union.

I had never had occasion to talk to Danzig personally, but in this crisis I called him to plead for a stay of execution. No, I was told, there was no way that the Capital Newspapers could publicize Nat Boynton with a by-line, now that I had a competing publication. No, Danzig would not consider any compromise, the decision stands. Sorry and good-bye.

Suddenly two things penetrated my cranium. One, was it possible that the mighty Capital Newspapers empire, covering a hundred municipalities in seven counties, was concerned about supposed competition from a miniscule weekly, nearly bankrupt at the time, covering two towns in a corner of one county? Two, it began to dawn on me that I had been in the trade longer than he, and through the column and other contacts was probably more widely known; I realized he had shown me it would be the height of folly to permit a competing leviathan to exploit *my* name and talent. With gusto I dashed off a piece in my first Spotlight issue, proudly informing my readers of the incident of an elephant swatting a flea.

28

Return to Roots

The changes that had taken place in the Albany newspaper scene in the years since my departure from pure—as distinguished from adulterated—journalism were in the front of my mind when, at a time of life when mature people should know better, I found myself sole owner of a hometown-type weekly newspaper.

The route that led back to basic newspapering was a circuitous one. The final steps were motivated by an unlikely combination of sentiment and economics. There was no dramatic event or circumstance that propelled me into such folly, no overwhelming emotion, no consuming desire to attain a personal goal or pursue political office.

Yet there was a hint, however small, of all these things in the decision to rescue, from the brink of extinction, a small weekly newspaper that purportedly covered the Albany suburb where our family had lived for some twenty years. To say the Delmar Spotlight was in trouble would be too mild; it had died without knowing it.

Meanwhile I was having serious financial problems of my own. I had been making a basic living as a freelance writer, speechwriter and public relations consultant in the Albany-

Schenectady–Troy area since leaving the parental security of General Electric. In nearly twenty-five years in the community I had many good friends and contacts among local businessmen, state and government officials, corporate executives, and staff people in nearby colleges and newspapers, but freelancing is a risky pursuit, acutely vulnerable to the slightest economic, social or political tremor.

A widespread business recession in 1974 had deepened substantially in 1975, to the extent that many in my base clientele were forced by budgetary restraints to cut back or eliminate the kind of projects I was doing for them. Between Memorial Day and Labor Day, 1975, I was able to earn less than nine hundred dollars, far short of the minimum to feed a family, let alone subsidize my three children in college.

There were, however, several good things that came from enforced idleness. One was having time to do more bass fishing in Lake George, the most beautiful lake in America, than in any other summer of my crowded life. Another was having time to join a sizeable group of neighbors in an intense campaign to block an aggressive land developer from dealing a king-sized setback to Slingerlands, the close-knit residential community where we lived.

The zoning imbroglio in suburban Slingerlands that summer not only cut into bass fishing but lured me directly into taking over the weekly paper that was supposed to be serving the community. The combination of a political battle and the chance for another shot at grass-roots newspapering swept me up like a flood tide from a bursting dam. Whetting the temptation was the prospect of compensating for the indifference of the Albany papers. Here was a zoning fight of unusual intensity given only token attention by the Times-Union and the Knickerbocker News. There was no coverage at all in the Spotlight.

But then it might have been unfair to expect coverage from the Spotlight. The little publication was primarily a free-circulation advertising paper, concentrating on meeting notices, church items, weddings, engagements, graduations, honor rolls, Scouts activities, Little League and personal items.

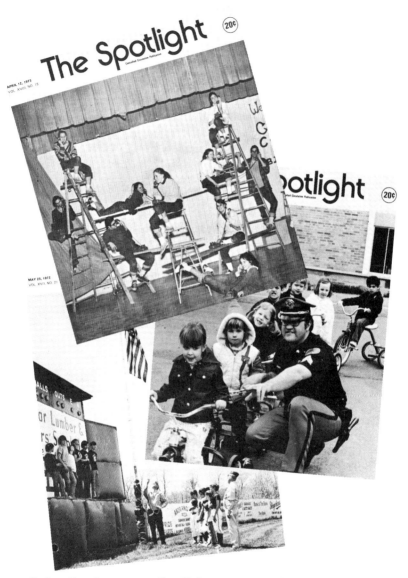

Before the changeover, Spotlight covers were devoted to civic events such as a bicycle safety program, Little League opening day and the high school play.

The Spotlight didn't even look like a newspaper. It appeared in mailboxes each week in magazine format on 8-by-11 bond paper. That gave it an attractive appearance, but inside the content was lightweight. It had no editorial staff and no reporter on any beat. Its news content was supplied entirely by items mailed in to a scrubby office in Delmar, largest of several communities in the Town of Bethlehem, or dropped off by publicity chairpeople of local organizations and by proud parents. In the sixties and early seventies it had flourished with forty-eight and occasionally sixty-four pages, and in 1973 achieved the admirable average of forty-four pages per week for the year. But by mid-1975 the advertising volume and news content of the once-popular publication had evaporated almost to the vanishing point.

The neighborhood campaign to enlist support from the Bethlehem Planning Board in blocking the intrusion of insensitive developers needed favorable publicity. That was my job on the vigilante committee. I was well aware of the deteriorating quality of the two Albany papers, but had paid little heed to the Spotlight.

In this scenario I found myself haunted by a persistent thought: if this sophisticated upper-income suburb had no editorial vehicle of substance and no communication channel of its own, why not create one? Could the comatose Spotlight be revived? If it had no editor, would it be interested in acquiring one? If not, would there be a chance, even remote, of buying the paper, or buying into the ownership? If that and all else failed, was the time ripe for starting a new paper, a hard-hitting newspaper to give Bethlehem and its rural neighbor, the Town of New Scotland, the quality news coverage they deserved?

In scouting the situation I quickly discovered the circumstances of the Spotlight's adversity. A competitive publication launched by the Albany dailies to bulldoze surburban weeklies into oblivion had delivered a death blow to the Spotlight. The struggle to survive had seriously undermined the health and vigor of its publisher, Robert King, and the business recession, forcing cutbacks in advertising budgets, had severely eroded the paper's revenue base. The combination of these three elements had left King and three part-time employees hard put to get the paper out each week. The product was a shell of its former self.

King had been on the advertising sales staff of the Times-Union before taking over the little suburban pennysaver. His professionalism soon elevated it to a major force in the suburban towns of Bethlehem and New Scotland. He kept a small office staffed by a part-time receptionist and had two other part-timers helping to sell ads. He sent all news and ad copy to a local typesetting shop and contracted the printing to a small non-union print shop in Albany. Over a span of eighteen years he had built the publication into a profitable operation until the collapse of 1974-75.

My cautious approach to Mr. King, whom I had never met, brought mixed reactions. He was vague and elusive, but two statements registered. No, he couldn't possibly afford an editor, even at the pittance I suggested. Yes, he would entertain an offer for the paper if the price was right. Working through his daughter, a highly intelligent woman who ran a successful brokerage business of her own in downtown Albany, I arranged to examine financial statements, and the negotiation process began.

The numbers on the accountant's balance sheets confirmed what was obvious from the printed pages of the publication—that the business was deeply in the red. The gap between advertising revenues and operating costs—printing, postage and payroll—was averaging more than six hundred dollars per week on the debit side.

King's astute daughter welcomed my approach as an opportunity to extricate her father from being engulfed in fiscal quicksand, and enthusiastically bent to the task of expediting the sale. The purchase price was relatively miniscule for the incoming owner, a scarred old newsman returning to the wars after a lengthy diversion in the corporate world, but a financial escape hatch for the outgoing proprietor. The new corporation could start, however shakily, free of debt accumulated by the former entity.

The challenge was clear—and ominous. Could the patient—a small local news medium not quite twenty years old—be nursed back to health from what had been life-threatening illness before available capital needed for the tranfusion ran out?

It certainly was worth a try. Fresh sources of funding were limited, but there were several encouraging factors. The paper now had an experienced professional editor for the first time, and there was an abundance of new energy on the premises. Besides, even an established base of only a few dozen advertising accounts and a microscopic paid circulation of 343 subscribers* among a bulk mailing of 6,000 copies was a better deal than financing the startup of an entirely new publication.

At least, it seemed that way in the beginning.

---

*To qualify for a second-class (controlled circulation) mailing permit, a publisher was required to have some paid subscribers. Apparently King's occasional appeals and promotions brought in enough subscriptions to satisfy the requirement, but the files in 1975 showed the total had declined drastically.

29

Vivat Rex

Rescuing a newspaper from the brink of oblivion, even such a small one as the Spotlight in Delmar, N.Y., called for a strategic game plan that had one major objective: creation of a full-fledged community newspaper dedicated to providing full, unbiased coverage of local news. That theorem meant providing a medium to boost businesses, organizations and personalities in the local constituency in keeping with the credo that the (name of hometown weekly) "is the only paper in the world that cares about (name of locality)." By the same token such an enterprise would have to have the economic support of its readers and merchandisers to fulfill its mission.

In this context it took less than thirty-six hours for the new publisher, who also was the paper's first-ever professional newsman, to be confronted with one of those time-honored tests of journalistic integrity that are dear to chroniclers of the industry—accepting a major advertising package without becoming beholden to the grantor.

I had known for some time that the scheduled transfer of title and creation of a new corporation in that third week of October would permit just one issue of the paper prior to the biennial municipal elections. My maiden publishing venture would thus appear in print just five days before the balloting on the first Tuesday of November. I also knew, as an established local resident, that the Town of Bethlehem, which encompassed the shady suburban streets of Delmar and Slingerlands and several other residential settlements, had an entrenched Republican administration that was next to impenetrable—so formidable that no Democrat had ever been elected to a local office since the town's incorporation in 1793.

Files in the Spotlight office, even in their bequeathed disarray, showed that the incumbent GOP strategists were accustomed to contracting for several hundred column inches of political advertising in the issue just before the election. That bonanza, padded by several sizeable ads from Democrats and a few from both parties in adjacent New Scotland, would more than double the anticipated revenue from all other sources that week. Facing a built-in overhead that had averaged some seven hundred dollars in excess of the average weekly intake, I was itchy for that plum, especially since this was the final week— and for me the only week—of the political season.

I had a nodding acquaintance with Bert Kohinke, the dominant power in the ruling party in Bethlehem who was town supervisor as well as Republican chairman. Suddenly, in the home stretch of the 1975 town campaign, Kohinke and I had a new relationship, political boss and local editor.

I had already drafted the lead story for the first issue of the first newspaper I had ever owned, enjoying every minute of the nostalgia it brought of those long-ago intrigues—almost a generation earlier—of St. Lawrence County and Massena village politics and those sometimes turbulent conflicts in the legislative chambers of the Capitol a stone's throw away in Albany. This was to be the first political analysis piece in a paper that had never done one. I had researched it carefully and had written it objectively; besides, I lived here and knew most of the key personalities on both sides in both towns.

When Kohinke called to say that the double-truck centerfold ad and several full-page display ads were ready to be picked up, I took off eagerly for GOP headquarters two doors from town hall. Sure enough, it was all there, copy and layouts, plus the four-figure check that would go a long way toward covering the checks I would have to write the following Monday for printing and postage, let alone the modest payroll that did not have enough room for me.

Kohinke was beaming with congratulations and good wishes for the new venture. He was also careful to explain that as a neophyte I might not be aware that the Spotlight had always made certain that the news content reflected the best interests of the establishment. He was, he added, confident that I would carry on that noble tradition.

I assured him that I had had extensive experience not only as an editor but as a reporter covering state and local government dating back some thirty-five years. Furthermore, I promised him that he and his associates could expect fair coverage in the news columns of the Spotlight henceforth and at all times. He seemed momentarily puzzled by this statement, but when I said I was sure we would get along just fine in the days ahead, we shook hands and there were smiles all around.

If Kohinke was shocked or disturbed by the unprecedented spectacle of a Spotlight election preview that several days later gave equal space to Bethlehem's energetic but vastly outnumbered Democrats, he did not mention it to me. He never asked for preferential editorial treatment in any way, and long after retiring from both political posts he never failed to give me a warm, friendly greeting whenever our paths crossed in the postoffice, drug store or a social function.

Since that episode, leaders of both parties have aired grievances against Spotlight news stories on several sensitive occasions, which was to be expected: it goes with the franchise. The only comfort was in knowing that if both parties were peeved at us, we were certainly doing a good job at being politically independent.

*   *   *   *   *

From the start the priority was to pull the paper out of the red. The two immediate objectives were to increase advertising volume and to convince local citizenry that they now

The Spotlight

Controlled Circulation Publication

VOL. XX, NO. 44
OCTOBER 30, 1975

Graphic newsweekly serving the towns of Bethlehem, New Scotland and nearby communities

TOWN ELECTIONS 1975

Political shouting, not much tumult

In off-year elections the spotlight is on local races, those municipal arenas the big-time politicians lovingly call "the grass roots." But on the town and county level, the local campaigns mean everything to the candidates, because this is where government is intimate and for a few weeks neighbors are running against each other.

In the unique framework of U.S. politics the "outs" do most of the shouting because they have to. The "ins" are automatically on the defensive because whatever they've done in office is fair game for atack from the challengers.

Games as usual

This week the combatants move into the home stretch for Tuesday's showdown at the polls. Democrats in both Bethlehem and New Scotland, challenging incumbent Republicans, have done most of the noisemaking, as befits the party wanting in, and only in the last two weeks have the defenders emerged. Both GOP slates, headed by Supervisors Harry L. Sheaffer in Bethlehem and Stephen P. Wallace in New Scotland, have followed the time-honored political precept of letting the challengers have their fun before moving up the answering guns.

In Bethlehem, supervisor candidate George Harder, a Delmar attorney practicing in Albany, has hammered at the Republican town board with charges of indifference and failure to communicate, including delaying release of budget information. In New Scotland, Guy Paquin (pronounced pay-quinn), has hit the administration's budgetary and assessment policies. Both Harder and Paquin have complained the incumbents are holding back sizeable sums of unspent revenues.

An unfriendly press

Bethlehem Republicans contend also they have taken a shellacking from Albany's daily newspapers, which also is fair game. The Knickerbocker News jumped in with a two-part editorial broadside, and Mrs. Ruth Bickel, seeking to retain her seat on the town board, declared she was misquoted in a Times Union news story. She said she was "shocked" at the report, but apparently felt somewhat better when the Knickerbocker News gave her the local lead headline that afternoon in carrying her response.

Tax rate down

Meanwhile the Sheaffer team last week unveiled a preliminary 1976 town budget of more than $3.4 million, up from $2.9 million for the current year but with a projected reduction in the tax rate of five cents per thousand valuation. At the same time they cautioned voters that Harder was unlikely to cut much time out of his Albany law practice to spend at town hall, a job Sheaffer says requires "more than full time."

On the county level the excitement is concentrated on three-cornered contests for county executive and comptroller. The hopes of the Republican challenger Gen. A. C.

On the county level the excitement is concentrated on three-cornered contests for county executive and comptroller. The hopes of the Republican challenger Gen. A. C. O'Hara, an able and experienced administrator, have been damaged more severely by one of the most easily forgotten campaigns in recent years and by a lack of support from the GOP organization than by the aggressive drive of Theresa Cooke, Albany's efficient but maverick reformer. Neither stand much chance of ousting the well-entrenched Democratic organization man, Jim Coyne.

Bethlehem: old targets for new guns

By adhering to a proven axiom in practical politics — incumbents should stand on their record and avoid direct confrontation with the foe — Bethlehem Republicans drew fusillades from Democrats in the daily press.

George Harder, running for supervisor, stated that "for some unknown reason either the Bethlehem town board or the appointed supervisor has pulled the shades down to obstruct the view of local citizens." He suggested the 1976 board "adopt the Vermont town meeting concept of government" involving citizen participation in key decisions.

Issues are scarce

"They are having a hard time finding issues," the Republicans shot back. "Harry Shaeffer is a full-time supervisor, putting in a full day at the town hall." The GOP claims Harder "has indicated that if elected, he will devote only one-third of his time" to running the town.

In the battle of press releases, Democrat Hank Dullea pointed to a rubber stamp board and Democrat Sue Coyle pumped for a town master plan. Republican William Johnston Jr. claimed the opposition was "telling only half-truths," pointing out the $515.000 that has set aside in a capital reserve fund to build a town hall appears on the public record every month in the supervisor's report.

Meanwhile Edward H. Sargent Jr. is assured of another term in the county legislature with endorsements by both major parties.

New Scotland: a pique at the books

Guy Paquin, a flamboyant 30-year-old Clarksville resident in his first try at politics, has spearheaded a "Wake Up New Scotland" theme centered on town assessments and budget policies of the present board.

He has charged that the board's policy includes "under-assess our friends, overassess everyone else . . . ignore the drop in equalization rate each year caused by too many low assessments . . . (and) prepare annual budget secretly" until after election.

At the picturesque town hall

The lead news page (Page Seven) of the first issue under new ownership carried a pre-election roundup plus a bi-partisan analysis of the campaign in each of the two towns. The cover, retaining the full-page photo format, featured a Hallowe'en theme.

269

had a genuine newspaper rather than a diluted pennysaver. The image problem was pivotal: advertisers demanded visibility for their ad dollars; visibility meant that the paper had to be accepted and read. At the time of the changeover it was safe to say that few publications in Bethlehem households were as widely unread as the Spotlight. We had to achieve respectability before pursuing paid subscriptions from King's six thousand postal boxholders.

The game plan was simple: put out a good newspaper with good coverage brightly written, and launch some promotions that would get people to notice the new style and character. To achieve these goals we needed a couple of lucky breaks as well as carefully structured therapeutic strategy. In the first year of the rescue operation we had both.

The timing of the changeover one week prior to the odd-year town elections was fortunate indeed, but there were other breaks in our favor. One was that we were getting in at the start of the Christmas shopping season, which meant a sharp escalation of advertising revenues after the doldrums of summer and early fall. Another was an opportunity to move from the dreary, cramped and rundown Spotlight office to a more comfortable and more convenient location in the center of Delmar. Still another was the appearance of several competent writers and photographers who offered part-time contributions for affordable remuneration.

The first few issues had plenty of lively news stories and photos, but readers had to look inside to find them. To ease the public shock, if any, we retained Bob King's magazine format and cover style—a full-page local photo under the title logo. The only change on the cover was plastering a call-out overlay that shouted "The NEW Spotlight." (Looking back, I realized this was a mistake; we should have amplified the shock by coming out with a whole new cover format and bold headlines.)

As it was, the beginning was modest. Flipping inside, a page-turner would find the familiar church directory tucked among the up-front ads. The classifieds remained in the back of the book. The big departure from the old regime was creating a bright full-page news layout on page seven beneath another

270

A sad story of subdivision septics

Political preview: police, primaries and party problems

Town tidies technicality on Tipple title

Only a routine ratification of a "new" local law remained for the Bethlehem town board to

expected fireworks this week, some 50 Bethlehem citizens crowded into the town hall for

weeks ago Judge Con G. Cholakis upheld that allegation, and ruled the board

Fire fighters fake fire for film

Drainage dispute dogs development, detours detergents

For most of the past decade, homeowners in the Lauralana Heights residential develop-

"That's because they're in the sewer district, even though they are not on the sewer line itself."

lived at 11 Bedford Ct. for nine years. Her husband, Bernard Berkowitz, is a medical doctor

field installed in the back yard 3-4 years ago "at great expense," extended the drain

Boys buying booze balked by bogus ID

Annexation: taxation without information

Slingerlands gets a shot in the charm

A New Scotland property owner seeking to have his land annexed by the village of Voor-

said he would file a revised petition that would show a —

port in the Spotlight quoting tis as saying he planned the land fo-

Burger King on grill as citizens sizzle

A group of Elsmere residents were cooking up a ... ruptions

What's a wedding without Rice? A near miss....

When it took place, only a few people knew about that most unusual wedding. Judge Robert H. Rice of Delmar, retiring from the bench this

Scotland," realized he had overshot the mark, and turned back. When he still couldn't find the address, he went to the Toll Gate and telephoned. The groom answered. "It's a formal

Delmar in Rice's car. Half mile down New Scotland Rc the bride asked the judge: "I we're in Bethlehem now, wh can't we just pull over and b married right here, and ge

Alliteration always attracts attention. So do puns in heads.

271

Spotlight logo. This was the showcase for the best stories of the week. Not an ad violated the sanctity of this page.

Our better stories continued for several pages before getting into the routine stuff and other features. We blocked out a section just inside the back cover for letters to the editor under the heading "Vox Pop."

For the first time the Spotlight was compartmentalized. The net result was, in effect, a strictly local Newsweek, printed on bond paper rather than newsprint, and in black-and-white because we couldn't afford color. We also hoped it wouldn't take too long for the electorate to realize it was a genuine newspaper supported by advertising rather than a shopping guide accepting news items to fill out odd spaces between ads.

If this format worked nationally for Time, Newsweek, New Yorker and many others, the reasoning went, it ought to work locally for us.

*　　*　　*　　*　　*

To spread the word, we turned to "reciprocals" on selected radio stations, trading our advertising space for radio spots. This oft-used gimmick permitted the respective media to trumpet commercial pitches in the others' vehicles. For our part, this and other devices were designed to speed the day we could break away from free-circulation distribution and be on our own with paid subscriptions.

It came as a shock as well as a revelation to discover the ineptitude of radio advertising. I had envisioned radio as a potential competitor for mercantile ad dollars, and we did find several of our landmark retail stores diverting a modest percentage of their promotional budgets to spot commercials on the air, but it soon became obvious that competition from the electronic media was next to nil. Of two highly rated stations with the most expensive reciprocals, we discovered that a "beautiful music" station did fairly well, and a talk-show station we thought was popular turned out to be a high-cost dud, incredibly over-rated. One low-rated station did better than several middling stations, but we concluded that none was worth the space commitments we had to give them in trade.

272

By January, a little over three months from the acquisition, we took the big plunge, informing Delmar and Slingerlands people by a bulk mailing to our two largest zip codes that henceforth they would have to pay to read the Spotlight. That took nearly four thousand addresses off the list in one stroke.

It was a bold gamble with a lot at stake. How many loyalists did we have among the citizenry? How many of the advertisers we had won back from a competitive free-distribution paper would now desert us if we showed a significant drop in total circulation? How many clear-thinking advertisers would appreciate our sales pitch emphasizing that people who paid for the Spotlight would read the ads, and thus would respond more than people who threw out the Helderberg Sun, our "freebie" competitor, with unopened junk mail.

Amid the growling and grumbling that followed our ultimatum, envelopes with checks began arriving. The list of subscribers grew steadily if not rapidly. So did the roster of advertisers and the size of the paper. By the time of our move to the more appropriate and more visible quarters only a few hundred feet from Delmar Four Corners, we had more than two thousand paid subscriptions and were selling another 350 on the newsstands. We weren't out of the red, but we were getting closer. Life insurance policy surrenders, periodic borrowings and dependance on bank overdrafts were becoming less frequent. Life was indeed full of promise.

*   *   *   *   *

Our new tenancy was in an old frame house on Kenwood Avenue in the heart of Delmar that had been the homestead and office of the late beloved Dr. Van Woert. With the move came several other changes, notably a new cover format that offered headlines and key photos instead of the single photo tradition of the King regime, and the hiring of a local college student as our first journalism intern. The latter was a phenomenon welcomed by the beleaguered editor-publisher, who found it difficult enough to write all the stories, long, short and otherwise, in a 24-page publication, let alone 32- and 40-pagers.

Through all of these weekly editions we retained the 8-by-10 magazine-style makeup. In format, in appearance and in style we were one of a kind among our journalistic brethren in our section of the state, a phenomenon that gave birth to our new promotional catchphrase—Uniquely Weekly.

30

Enter Goliath

Of the three elements primarily responsible for the Spotlight's near-demise, the most devastating was the emergence of a competing weekly newspaper launched by the Capital Newspapers, the Hearst subsidiary that published Albany's two daily papers. The newcomer's mission was strictly predatory—to eliminate weekly newspapers in several suburban areas that stood in the way of an advertising monopoly.

In suburban Delmar, just south of the Albany city line where Bob King, an enterprising ad salesman, was publishing the Spotlight, the small, independent weekly's advertising revenue was already on a down trajectory because of a general business recession and because of King's declining health. Even in its heyday the Spotlight—and several other small weeklies in the Albany metropolitan area—posed no threat to the city papers. In the executive tower, however, there was a different view.

The two Albany dailies had enjoyed an unchallenged print advertising monopoly in their home territory since the morning Times-Union took over the afternoon Knickerbocker News in the early sixties, limited only in some outlying precincts by adjacent dailies in Troy and Schenectady. Even the regression of the Knick from a first-class newspaper under Gannett to a third-rate stepchild of Hearst's morning money machine had not weakened the stranglehold enjoyed by Capital Newspapers.

The lord of this publishing barony at that time was Robert Danzig, one of a succession of businessmen entrusted with preserving the flow of profits from the parent corporation's most productive satellite. In the Hearst corporate format the publisher is the business manager. As such, Danzig had minimal experience in the news and editorial end, but he didn't need any. Top editors handled all that. The publisher got involved only when there was trouble or when some new dictum from the Hearst hierarchy required a visit to the news operation.

Danzig got the idea for the blitz against the pesky little weeklies at a national publishers' convention. He was impressed by the success of several big-city papers using variations of a device publishers called the Zoned Edition. The technique called for a tabloid insert in the regular editions of the dailies and bundled for selected suburban areas. The insert was itself a weekly newspaper, distributed free and designed to compete with the small independent weeklies, none of which, the theory went, would be able to match the vast resources of the metropolitan giant. Extermination of the little fellows was just a matter of time.

Danzig returned from his conclave full of plans to establish a circle of zoned editions that would eliminate the weeklies in Delmar, Altamont and Ravena to the south and west, Rotterdam due west, Rensselaer and Columbia counties across the Hudson River to the east, and Cohoes, Latham and the burgeoning areas along Interstate 87, the Northway, in southern Saratoga County. The Spotlight, serving the upper-income bedroom suburb immediately south of the city with shopping centers of its own, was selected as the first target, a tribute Bob King could hardly be expected to appreciate.

The Helderberg Sun, first of the Danzig Sunpapers, made its debut in the spring of 1974. The geographic thrust was primarily Bethlehem and New Scotland along with the Town of

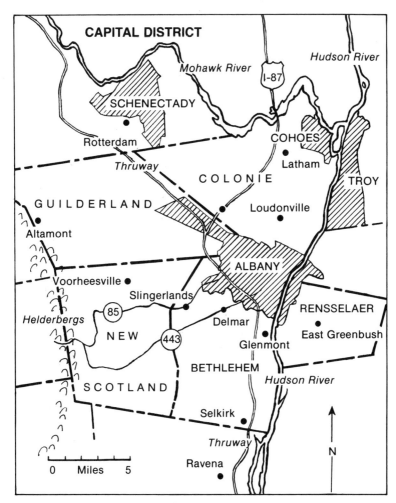

Hendrik Hudson's ship, the Half Moon, was alleged to have run aground on a mud bar in what is now the Town of Bethlehem, just south of Albany, in 1609. Bordering Bethlehem to the west is the Town of New Scotland, with hills rising to the Helderberg escarpment. The Sunpapers attempted to monopolize the suburban areas adjacent to the three major cities, plus outlying areas.

Guilderland, Albany's western neighbor. Those three townships occupied a prosperous and historic area spreading across a fifteen-mile-wide stretch between the Hudson River and the Helderberg escarpment.

The target area blanketed the entire scope of the Spotlight's circulation territory plus a substantial portion of villages and hamlets covered by the Altamont Enterprise, Albany County's most venerable (founded in 1884) weekly newspaper. The Enterprise, last of the oldtime broadsheet* "hot press" papers, covered Guilderland and the rural "Hilltowns"—crossroad hamlets that dotted the landscape of western Albany County rising into the Helderbergs and foothills of the Catskills to the south and west.

To accomplish this coup Danzig assigned one of his best writers, Grace O'Connor, as editor of the Sun. Grace was a first-rate professional, an outstanding reporter and feature writer who once had had no fewer than nineteen by-lines in one particularly fat edition of the Sunday Times-Union. On a later occasion she had jumped from an airplane to do a story on sky diving.

The new paper was to contain only "happy news" and personality feature articles generated by community correspondents, invariably homemakers eager for part-time writing that could be done in the house before the arrival of the afternoon school bus. The high-speed presses in the Capital Newspapers plant rolled out the Sun tabloids during unprofitable downtime between the last run of the Sunday Times-Union and the early mail edition Monday morning. The new paper, bright in a color format, was chock full of scout news, church notices, club items and all the tidbits the city dailies had no room for and the little weeklies thrived on. Not only did the Sun appear as an insert in Monday afternoon's Knick and Tuesday's Times-Union, but copies were stacked high in super-

---

*The term "broadsheet" is applied to conventional newspapers like most metropolitan daililes, as opposed to a tabloid format. Most are now standardized in a six-column width. The old Enterprise, like most papers until standardizing ten or twelve years ago, was eight columns wide, casting type and pages in hot lead instead of today's "cold-type" photo composition.

278

The fifth Sun in Hearst's Albany galaxy was the Riverside Sun. Sorensco covered southern Rensselaer County.

market checkouts, drug stores and newsstands, free for the taking.

The real blitz was directed at the advertising accounts that were the life blood of the hometown weeklies. Danzig turned loose a legion of high-powered sales reps in Delmar with instructions to sweep the place clean. The pitch was devastating—three times the circulation at half the Spotlight rate.

In that summer of 1974 Bob King was having enough problems coping with a slump in the national economy that had forced cuts in many advertising budgets. With the dawn of the Sun he watched in dismay as the clients who had sustained the Spotlight through its glory years succumbed to the tempting carrot dangled by Danzig's pros. The Sun's press run was 11,000, and with no one to challenge the sales reps proclaiming a

20,000 circulation to prospective advertisers, the base rate of $1.50 a column inch was a killer compared to King's $3 for 6,000 copies.

A year after its debut Danzig's pilot Sun had spawned two more Suns to the east and north, which in turn led to a family of five zoned editions. By this time the Spotlight was mortally wounded. Several times that spring, during rehabilitative absences of the beleaguered publisher, King's two part-time assistants scurried to put out sixteen-page issues, a technical violation of the second-class controlled-circulation postal permit that required a minimum of twenty-four.

Such was the scenario in Delmar when the change of ownership at the Spotlight shifted Bob King's publishing problems onto my shoulders. Now I was the little guy cowering in front of the onrushing bulldozer. How to stop it? Or, at best, how to live with it? I could think of only one answer: keep plugging by trying to put out a better newspaper. After all, we had the same outlay of "happy news" the Sun had, but we also provided "hard" news from town hall, police, politicians and the sports beat, which the Suns didn't have. In that arena we were up against the two dailies, formidable even in their casual coverage of the suburbs.

In this travail my thoughts often went back to my earlier heroes, Gordon Bryant and Henry Leader. They were top newsmen and fighters. So was I, dammit. My mind also drifted to the two newspaper publishers I had known so well—Harold B. Johnson, devoting ninety percent of his energy and talent to being an exemplary editor while delegating the business end to trusted lieutenants, and G.B. Williams, who ran the business effectively from the first floor while giving his editor upstairs carte blanche on the news pages. There was plenty of inspiration.

31

Ad Ventures

Newspaper editors and publishers live together because they have to, observing a form of uneasy truce. Editors are a proud lot, doggedly defending the purity of their mission and the sanctity of their independence from the slightest hint of commercialism. They tolerate publishers not only because publishers sign their paychecks but because someone has to run the business end of the operation, something an editor has neither time nor desire to do. On the other side publishers regularly regard editors as prima donnas, arrogant and demanding, so set in their idealism that getting them to see things in a rational way is like talking to an environmentalist or a Volkswagen owner.

In the editor's view, a good publisher is one who never dares to interfere with the news and editorial content of the paper. That's all right with the publisher, providing the editor stays clean and doesn't get the paper in trouble with advertisers and subscribers. In modern-day application, stemming from the baseball industry, this is directly related to the Steinbrenner Syndrome as popularized by the owner of the New York Yankees.

When I took over the Spotlight I suddenly found myself wearing both hats. As a fugitive journalist returning to the field I resurrected all my old lofty goals and principles, confident that on my own paper nothing would untrack me. It didn't take long to discover I was also the publisher, responsible for earning not only my own bread and butter, but that of the three or four brave people with me on what at that time bore only a slight resemblance to a payroll. That's when I came face to face with the advertising game.

Competitive journalism is a way of life in the jungle of mass media, but few reporters and editors are aware of, and certainly do not care about, the intense competition for the advertising accounts that pay their salaries. I was 58 years old and in my first few weeks of owning a weekly newspaper when I was initiated into the lodge where everything was measured in column inches and the battling was endless.

On the news side the rules were few and simple. You scored a beat on a story or you got beaten; you got your share of "exclusives" and you knew your competitors would get theirs. In the Watertown Times bureaus, where I and others received our competitive baptism, there were the sources that intentionally held up release of information so the local weekly could have it first, or at least come out the same day. It took skill and cunning to crack these barriers. On afternoon papers there was always the risk of the morning paper getting into print first with a breaking story; on morning papers it was vice versa.

On the Spotlight the competitive climate was far different. I was now the weekly competing with a daily. I could handle, or at least accept, the reverse of my old Watertown Times routine on the news front, but I found myself woefully unprepared for the street-fighting on the advertising beat. Here we had to justify our space rates by increasing circulation and readership. As if that weren't enough of a struggle, there was the predatory Helderberg Sun with slick professionals from the Hearst sales force hawking three times the press run at half our rates.

There was bound to be some kind of a tug between the pure and the practical, particularly in the small-town atmosphere of the two suburban Albany townships we served. The Town of Bethlehem, which embraced the core settlement of Delmar, was more densely populated, generally more sophisticated and more affluent than the neighboring Town of New Scotland, which was more rural and far more scenic. Between them, they formed perhaps the most tightly knit community in the greater Albany area, and certainly one of the most attractive marketing targets.

We automatically wrote off major chain stores and other big operations, pretended or otherwise. They made themselves consistently inaccessible to our sales reps. They didn't return phone calls or answer letters. Instead, we concentrated on the businesses in our own bailiwick. Bob King's regulars who had gone over to the Sun partially or in toto had to be lured back to the fold. New accounts had to be cultivated. The sales staff of three—one holdover and two newcomers—took on that challenge while I concentrated on developing a news format to attract the legion of lost readers. At the same time, I found myself using every contact I could think of to make advertising calls on my own.

It was slow going, but the ad volume gained steadily. As readership picked up, the progress showed in each week's issues of not only the Spotlight but the rival Sun. We were slowly getting thicker and they were getting thinner.

*　　*　　*　　*　　*

With a typewriter on a plywood plank and using the drawers and cabinets converted from the kitchen of the late Mrs. Van Woert in newly renovated quarters on Kenwood Avenue I found myself in the same competitive adversity in Delmar as the independent storeowners on Delaware Avenue and the Plaza. Hilchie's Hardware and the Garden Shoppe had to compete against the local K-Mart as well as big-name chains in Albany shopping malls. The small, family-owned drug stores had to resist the inroads of out-of-town discount chain outlets, notably CVS and Brooks Drug a block or two away. Local clothing stores, gift shops and appliance stores were going head-to-head with a Denby's department store in the Plaza in Delmar, and Sears was barely twenty minutes away. I could relate to all this: here was a small newspaper trying to survive the onslaught of two metropolitan dailies and the pirates aboard their zoned insert.

What chance did the little fellows, carefully rationing their advertising dollars, have against the bullies who had big-name agencies placing full-page blockbusters in the big dailies and expensive commercials on regional television? The ad agencies— except two or three friendly locals—had eyes only for circulation numbers in the overall metro market. They couldn't see, or didn't want to see, the demographics of the towns or the quality of the respective media.

To overcome this David and Goliath scenario, our strategy was to build the Spotlight into a crisp, attractive and well-written family newspaper with blanket coverage of everything local, and to capitalize on our unusual format. From its birth as a four-page advertising flyer twenty years earlier, the Spotlight had been printed on bond paper in magazine format. As a result, it was natural for households to keep it, like Newsweek, on the coffee table or by the reading chair from Thursday through the weekend or longer until everyone in the family had read it. In contrast, the Albany papers, including the tabloid Sun printed on cheap newsprint, would be tossed in the trash pile the same day they arrived.

We seized every opportunity to convince advertisers of our durability and lengthy "exposure time in the living room." Local business people recognized this as an extra value, and as our readership grew, our advertising volume gained, arduously but surely. But non-resident merchants and store managers found this extended-exposure feature hard to believe.

Jerry Gordon, a star member of our sales staff who spent several years moonlighting from a full-time managerial job, especially enjoyed this kind of challenge. Among the accounts Jerry covered evenings and Saturdays to offset a high Delmar mortgage and three maturing daughters was an appliance store on Delaware Avenue that a Delmar owner had sold to an established Albany appliance firm. The new manager kept Jerry at bay week after week, insisting that the parent store's ads in the Albany papers provided sufficient coverage in suburbs such as ours.

Jerry's perseverance eventually gained a small foothold. Obviously more interested in getting rid of a persistent salesman

284

than promoting appliance sales, the manager agreed to put several items "on special" and put a discount coupon in the next Spotlight. The coupon, he said, would also go in the Sun.

Jerry accepted the device to measure the comparative effectiveness of the rival papers as a welcome breakthrough of sorts, but pointed out to the store manager that because the Sun came out Monday night and Tuesday morning, two full days before the Spotlight, the many households receiving both papers would naturally bring in the Sun coupon and would have no reason to use the Spotlight coupon when it showed up later in the week. The manager was unimpressed. "That's your problem," he told Jerry.

Sure enough, a Sun coupon surfaced in the store on Tuesday afternoon. There were none on Wednesday, but on Thursday two Spotlight coupons came in. On Friday there were three more from the Spotlight, several more on Saturday, and, to the manager's astonishment, two more on the following Monday. The final score was Spotlight 12, Sun 1.

Jerry refrained from the I-kept-telling-you routine, restated the pitch on five-days-in-the-living-room, and brought in a signed thirteen-week contract. "He's a believer now," he announced.

*   *   *   *   *

We knew that our circulation area had the highest per-capita income among Albany's suburban population blocs; and even when we could document a higher readership saturation than any other print medium in our market, the chains and the New York ad people were not interested. Our numbers didn't have as many digits as Hearst and the throwaway shopping sheets could show.

In standing up to the powerful resources of the discount chains, the local Mom-and-Pop stores had one trump card, not spectacular, but recognizable and modestly effective—personal customer service, one-on-one communication on the sales floor or by telephone. In Hilchie's, Mullen's, Town and Tweed, Crystal Chandelier and other local stores the proprietors, clerks and customers knew each other, many on the first-name basis

285

neighbors use. Go to K-Mart or CVS, the hometown merchant would say, and if you can find a clerk within fifteen minutes, chances are it's a minimum-wage teenager who knows little of the product and can't answer basic questions.

And, the hometown merchant is quick to point out, with few exceptions the price differential is either minimal or nonexistent. Bill Candido, an enterprising pharmacist who had toiled for the Fay's Drug chain before opening his own store in Voorheesville, ran a survey on two hundred common shelf items, comparing his prices with allegedly discounted prices at Fay's, CVS and Rite-Aid. He was equal or better on 133 of the items, and less than five percent off on the rest.

Less apparent but far more vital to the community is loyal support of local civic and volunteer organizations. Home-town independent businesses habitually respond to every community cause; the chain outlets, with rare exceptions, ignore or reject such solicitations. In 1975 Bethlehem and New Scotland had seven independent pharmacies and one drug-chain outlet. Ten years later the score was two-and-two—one survivor in Delmar and one in Voorheesville.

In Delmar the big loss was Mullen's Pharmacy, which was more than a drug store. It was a community resource. Luke Mullen regularly gave his front display window to Girl Scouts, Progress Club, musical and theatrical groups and every neighborhood organization that asked for promotional help for an upcoming event, and rare was the Saturday when there wasn't a bake sale or benefit ticket table on the sidewalk in front of the main entrance. On Sundays before and after church the parking lot was alive with family cars picking up the Sunday papers. No one blamed Luke for retiring from the business, and he felt as badly as everyone else when the happy conviviality vanished in the CVS takeover.

That left Vince Rehbit at Tri-Village Drug as the last of half a dozen local independent pharmacies. It wasn't in Vince's nature as a soft-speaking community loyalist to voice resentment of the tactics of chain competitors. Each season of each year finds Vince writing a check to sponsor a Little League baseball team or a Bethlehem Tomboys girls softball team, or for some program ad, or a contribution to Pop Warner football, an ambulance drive, youth soccer program, high school booster club for field lighting, Christmas toys for needy children—the list goes on. Then he goes home to find on his TV screen a CVS commercial stressing the warmth and intimacy of having a prescription filled by "your own personal pharmacist, one neighbor helping another," or proclaiming that Fay's is "not your average drug store." He knows that's pure poppycock; that CVS and Fay's personal interest in their "neighbors" is in their money more than their health, and that neither chain has contributed one dime to the community. But does the public know?

The next afternoon when two high school juniors come to the store, he takes out a courtesy ad in the yearbook. It's a pure donation; he knows no one who sees the ad is going to change a shopping habit. On the way home that night he sees a goodly number of cars on the blacktop apron at CVS, where that same afternoon an out-of-town manager turned away those high school kids.

Vince was doing what many other individually owned business people do for their community, often without recognition. One prominent Delmar merchant enjoyed telling a succession of high school yearbook ad solicitors that he would take an ad three times bigger than the nearby K-Mart. Go get their ad, he would say, and when you come back you can have the bigger one. The kids leave elated and return deflated. He then makes his annual contribution, just one more in a ceaseless succession, trying not to resent the well-heeled chains that take money out of the community while refusing to give as much as a nickel back.

Not all the big chains are heartless. On our sales rounds that first year, it was encouraging to find in this pattern several notable exceptions. At the top of the list was McDonald's, always ready to provide free coffee and Big Macs for volunteer firemen fighting a wintry blaze, soda for perspiring athletes at a grade-school track meet and gift certificates for winners of local contests. The local manager recognized the promotional power of the hometown weekly, and was able to persuade his regional manager to authorize full-page ads in the Spotlight for giveaways he had dreamed up for St. Patrick's Day, Mother's Day, Valentine's Day and other inspirational Hallmark occasions.

The response to these ads was an eye-opener. On one area-wide promotion involving giveaway cartoon glasses the Delmar McDonald's, fortified by a Spotlight ad in addition to those in the Albany papers, not only ran out of glasses before noon, but was the only store in three counties that had to go to other McDonald's restaurants to keep up with the demand. That episode led to a profitable relationship between chain and local paper. When a new manager arrived, the sales story didn't save the account, but when the franchise was sold to a local couple, McDonald's became a regular Spotlight advertiser.

Another large chain that recognized the pulling power of the weeklies was Stewart's, a Saratoga-based dairy and ice cream maker with a network of bread-and-butter "convenient" stores across eastern New York. When its Delmar store won a company-wide contest for sales of ice cream by the half gallon three years in a row, the company gave most of the credit to the Spotlight ads. That was borne out the fourth year when a mail foul-up caused the ad copy to miss the Spotlight deadline, and the Delmar store finished far down the list of some eighty stores in half a dozen counties. In the years since, Stewart's, with several additional stores in the circulation area, has been a consistent advertiser in local weeklies along with regular TV spots.

*   *   *   *   *

Apart from the Impossibles, the hardest sells were Albany businesses that found it difficult to believe the magnetism of a Spotlight ad would outdraw the Albany papers in our area. By the same token, the most rewarding satisfaction came from these sophisticated metropolitan accounts who admitted that their response from an ad in our little paper had been surprisingly profitable. A Troy-based sporting goods retailer with a branch in a shopping plaza on U.S. Route 20 in

288

We ran this ad in the Capital District Business Review, but it got us more publicity than new accounts.

neighboring Guilderland who reluctantly let us run a full-page ad containing a long list of items on a one-day-only super-sale designed for the dailies conceded that fully a third of the early birds lined up waiting for the doors to open that Saturday morning were clutching the tearsheet from the Spotlight.

Not so the big agencies. A Deco-World chain headquartered in Rochester beholden to a Pittsburgh ad agency disdained our help in promoting the opening of a franchise in Delmar. We were the only paper to take a photo of the ribbon-cutting ceremony, but the ads went to the dailies. Within a year the retail space was empty and available, the sign removed, victim of a disappointing volume. Who could say they would have done better with us? We'll never know.

When Citibank, one of the nation's financial leviathans, erected a mint-fresh example of modern architecture on a vacant acre adjacent to the shopping plaza on Delmar's main commercial artery, our calls to the bank's regional office and the national ad agency were ignored. On opening day there was no noticeable rush, and as the weeks passed there were rarely more than a few cars in the gleaming new parking area. Today steady traffic on Delaware Avenue flows past a sparsely occupied parking lot holding primarily the cars of employees. Barely a hundred feet to the east a store-front branch office of a local savings bank, a regular Spotlight advertiser, handles a normal day's worth of transactions.

*   *   *   *   *

Truly amazing are the moods and whims of advertisers. Some are grateful for layout help and professional counsel, others insist on abusing the rules of good graphics. Some appreciate a good response to an ad, others grumble that the good response was short of expectations. One asked for a free re-run because of a small typo, refused to accept a twenty-percent rebate and cancelled an upcoming four-week schedule. Another, delighted by the response to a freebie reference in a shopping column that appeared periodically, signed a substantial six-months contract far higher than expected, but when a later feature boosting shopping in Delmar's Four Corners complex inadvertently omitted mention of one longtime business, the proprietor spitefully terminated a Spotlight account that had been on a regular schedule for twenty years.

Lee Holder, our receptionist and front office manager who generated a productive telephone sales operation for our Business Directory, was such a staunch Spotlight booster she suffered serious deflation when a painting contractor or blacktopper would call in to cancel a listing that had been running TF—continuously "'til further notice." She was only mildly pacified by the customer's explanation: "Lady, get that ad out of there, I'm so backed up with the response it'll be November before I can get caught up."

*   *   *   *   *

As varied as the moods of advertisers can be, the most puzzling of several hundred Spotlight accounts, large, small and intermittent, was that of a department store chain that began in Troy, became headquartered in Albany, was absorbed by a chain in Providence, R. I., and then disappeared.

Conditioned as we were to the fact that rich and uncaring corporate giants like CVS, K-Mart, Brooks Drug, Sears and even regional chains would stonewall any approach from a weekly newspaper sales rep, we never stopped trying. On rare occasions we made a breakthrough, albeit with mixed results. In the late sixties, Denby's, a successful Troy department store, flexed its muscle by expanding to several other locations in what retailers and chambers of commerce like to call the Capital District. Much to the delight of Bob King, then publisher of the Spotlight, one of the new stores was to be in Delmar. In the promotional extravagance leading up to the grand opening, complete with ribbon-cutting by county and town political bigwigs to an accolade of flashbulbs, King got a small piece of the growing chain's advertising budget for his little weekly.

That didn't last long, however. In due time the number game ad agencies love so dearly rubbed off on Denby executives,

291

and they concentrated their advertising on the dailies and the electronic media. King and the Spotlight were cut off.

If that was the attitude, however myopic, in the heyday of King's Spotlight, which several times exploded to sixty-four pages and once to seventy-two crammed with ads in 1969-72, what chance did the little crew that had pulled the paper out of the ashes have of landing a Denby's ad in 1976-77? The answer was clearly zero, but after repeatedly but politely turning down our pitches, including a carefully crafted flip-chart presentation using proven GE audiovisual techniques, the marketing vice president of Denby's tossed us a crumb.

This particular pitch was motivated by the occasion of Denby's adding a new section to the Delmar store—housewares and small appliances—and we offered promotional help. To our delight, the store took a full-page ad, announcing the opening of the new department and offering free coffee mugs to customers attending the gala inaugural demonstrations. To make it a true measure, the store gave the ad to no other paper, and there were no radio spots.

On the great day the store, which normally might have drawn fifteen or twenty pedestrians in the first hour of a typical Friday, ran out of coffee mugs forty minutes after opening the doors to a waiting crowd. An emergency call to the warehouse produced a new supply, but the throng gobbled that up before noon. The visiting representatives of the houseware distributors told the store manager they had never seen such a response, and by lunchtime the inventory of several of the heralded products had been exhausted. No one could have asked for a more classic example of the pulling power of a single ad.

And no one ever explained why it was the only ad Denby's ever gave the little weekly in Delmar. Our follow-up calls were graciously received at headquarters, there were hints there would be something next week, if not, certainly the following week. After several months we quit calling.

On the Friday morning of Thanksgiving weekend I was passing the local store and dropped in to pick up a couple of my favorite button-down blue Oxford shirts. Browsing the counters I suddenly realized there was only one other customer in the spacious store on what traditionally is one of the busiest retailing days of the year. Two people in a Denby's store at eleven on Thanksgiving Friday? Impossible!

I made what became my final call to the administrative sanctum on Broadway in Albany. No dice.

Within a few months the Albany papers reported the sale of Denby's financially troubled retail stores in New York's Capital District to a merchandising holding company based in Providence. No one on the Spotlight was brash enough to think we might have stalled Denby's demise, but we do respect the adage that the worst thing—well, almost—that can happen to people that don't advertise is nothing.

32

Uniquely Weekly

The struggle to establish the Spotlight as a credible paid-circulation weekly newspaper rather than a giveaway shopper was helped by two breaking stories that had enough substance and excitement to delight any editor. The first was the revelation that the U.S. Department of Labor was secretly negotiating to set up a Job Corps rehabilitation center for inner-city youth from New York and Buffalo in a rural section of the town, causing a degree of panic among peace-loving residents and motivating them to mount emotional resistance. The second was the decision of the Bethlehem Town Board to suspend and investigate their chief of police, an entrenched though controversial political figure, and bring a multitude of charges against him.

I threw myself into both stories with adrenalin flowing, reveling in each turn and development as in the old days on the news beat. In each case the Bethlehem town hall became a battleground for the Albany media, two daily papers and three TV news teams. For me it was a showcase example of my old Massena situation in reverse, when I was working for a daily paper that rolled all over the hometown paper. Now I was the local brat on the block, brushed over and ignored by the big-city bullies with their generic advantage—instant electronics and daily press runs.

To survive and be competitive in this kind of battleground it was almost instinctive to adopt the stance of the big national magazines like Time, Newsweek, Sports Illustrated and the like. They accept the theorem that there is no way a weekly can beat a daily to a spot-news story. What does Newsweek do when a blockbuster news development breaks a day after deadline? What does Time do when it goes into the mail 36 hours before a presidential election? What does Sports Illustrated do when it goes to press the day before the seventh game of the World Series? The answer is to offer a clearer insight, a more comprehensive analysis, a more intimate portrayal of key personalities, fresher angles, more in-depth reporting and more authoritative writing.

I was fortunate that the Albany dailies used the Bethlehem beat as a training ground for rookie reporters. By the same token, TV newspeople were content to take a few quotes from the central cast and report only the most obvious—or the most visual—spot developments. None of my competitors had the old Gordon Bryant imprint on their training. That's largely why our paper seemed to have more lively and more interpretive content, much of it "new stuff."

* * * * *

Both the Job Corps drama that first summer and the police chief hassle a year later provided lush opportunities for all these things. In each situation emotions ran high, rumors abounded and there were twists and turns that developed over several months.

In the Spotlight's private struggle against the Albany dailies there was one aspect that might have worked to our advantage or disadvantage, depending on the viewpoint: we had no editorial page as such, while the dailies each took strong editorial stands. We presented analytical aspects along with reports of the week's developments without offering editorial comment other than Letters-to-the-Editor from impassioned readers, and these viewpoints often clashed. The Job Corps and police chief intrigues were natural fodder for editorial writers, and both the Knick and the Times-Union jumped in with forceful opinions. Ironically it turned out that in each case they backed the wrong horse.

The Job Corps story would have been routine if the federal government in the form of the U.S. Labor Department hadn't been so incredibly inept. They also were consistent in their bumbling. As a result, the scarcity of reliable information spawned rumors and further misinformation. These factors in turn caused the town government to get angry at the federals, the townspeople to become disillusioned with both, and the resident Congressman to abandon his mediation attempts in frustration.

This kaleidoscopic scenario put the Spotlight on center stage through the first summer of its resurrection. Perhaps more significantly, the editor, who was producing virtually the entire news content of each week's issue because the publisher (the same fellow) couldn't afford to hire a helping hand, acquired an assistant in the person of a college journalism summer intern. The balance sheet was much improved, which was to say that instead of cashing in the last life insurance policies and adding more bank overdrafts, the cash flow was approaching the break-even point.

In the Job Corps drama there was some cloak-and-dagger sleuthing that stemmed from a stubborn reluctance of government officials to talk to the media. This produced so many unanswered questions in an emotion-charged situation that I embarked on what, for a fledgling newspaper, was a daring move: I sent my 19-year-old assistant on an out-of-state assignment as an investigative reporter. An investigative reporter taking to the road for a paper as dinky as the Delmar Spotlight was not only incongruous, it was wild.

Pulling this stunt required parental permission for my wide-eyed, enthusiastic star-of-the-future. Helen Burggraf was a Syracuse University sophomore whose family lived in Delmar. She had come to me hoping for a summer job, pay not important. She had talent as a sketcher and cartoonist as well as a writer. Two weeks after she had eagerly pitched in to help with the

Wagons roll, frontier style

*Story and sketches
by Helen Burggraf*

"Wagons, ho!!!"

With that cry, two outriders pivot their mounts and canter towards the highway. Stanley Rickard, driver of the first wagon, smacks his team's rumps with the reins, clucking them them. "Get up there, King!"

The four Belgians, their golden coats gleaming under mounds of silver-studded black leather harness, lunge forward. With a squeak of leather, a groan of wood and the grinding of gravel, the wagon lurches. We are moving!

The other five wagons fall into line behind us as we move out onto the road. Outriders direct traffic around the wagon train and relay messages between wagons.

I am riding the official New York State bicentennial wa-

ing the pilgrimage of one wagon from every state, provided this wagon. Wagon master Richard Menkins said that except for the ball-bearings in its wheels and hard rubber instead of metal wheel rims, this wagon is an authentic replica. It seems smaller and narrower than I would have expected, and higher off the ground.

The other wagons vary in authenticity. They were built by various members of the train, using a variety of materials and styles. Two have green canvas covers, one has rubber tires and one is painted red, white and blue with "Valley Forge or Bust!" lettered on one side. Menkins said the wagons are holding up "pretty good," while another driver added, "They're holding up better than the men!"

The horses have settled into a pace, clopping along with harness chains jingling like

These sketches of the wagon train and others by Helen Burggraf brightened our pages that first summer.

community calendar and the endless flow of "shorts," I took her out to Esperance, a village twenty-five miles to the west, and deposited her, by arrangement, for a one-day ride with New York State's Bicentennial Wagon Train. An entourage of a dozen covered wagons was slowly plodding eastward along U.S. Route 20 en route to a multi-state assemblage at Valley Forge. It was still two days from its scheduled overnight camp-out in the town park in Delmar when Helen climbed up beside one of the drivers with notebook and sketch pad in hand. She thus became the first reporter in the Capital District to contact the colorful caravan but, as luck would have it on a weekly paper, she was the last to get her story into print. Her sketches and heart-warming writing made the Spotlight coverage—three days after all other media had done their pieces—the best of the bunch.

Now it was July and Helen, a college student with six weeks of part-time newspaper experience, was on a train to Baltimore, where a remarkably parallel Job Corps situation had developed a year earlier. In a rural section of Albany County the Labor Department was taking over a former Vincentian Fathers seminary to convert its beautiful campus and facilities into a youth rehabilitation center, to the consternation of local residents. In suburban Baltimore the Labor Department had established a Job Corps Center in a former Jesuit seminary, causing concern among local citizens. The tie-in was a natural.

I called the editor of the Baltimore American, who graciously offered to guide Helen to the veteran reporter who had covered the story. That reporter would, in turn, take her to suburban Woodstock and Granite to talk to officials of the Maryland Job Corps Center, community leaders, local home-owners and police officials. I dispatched Helen with $100 in cash for hotel, meals and taxis, plus instructions to get all the infor-mation she could, talk to as many people as she could, and, please, try to come home before the hundred dollars ran out.

Three days later she was back on Kenwood Avenue with a sheaf of notes and her patented happy smile that seemed to reflect a new dimension of self-assurance and a noticeable hint of maturity. Her well-written reports were so professional and so informative that I could only wonder why the Knick or the Times-Union hadn't done the same thing long before. (Actually, the Knick sent a man to a Pennsylvania Job Corps center six weeks later to do a story backing up its strong editorial stand on the local controversy.)

By October, with Helen safely back in the shelter of her campus, our capable Congressman Sam Stratton and top Labor Department officials overcame the fumbling and bumbling of lower-level bureaucrats and succeeded in establishing the New York Job Corps Center in the Glenmont area of the Town of Bethlehem. In the process they also established communication lines with the host community that effectively put to rest the fears and insecurity of neighboring residents. It is warming to report that the facility, in a rural setting along the Hudson, subsequently established itself as a productive resource.

It is even more warming to report that over the same decade Helen Burggraf, putting aside talent that might have made her a highly successful cartoonist and caricaturist, went on to journalistic triumphs, first in Italy with the English-language Rome Daily News and later as one of the top by-line writers in New York City's fiercely competitive business press. Would that more journalists were blessed with the writing talent of this personable lady, so natural, so gifted. As this is written, she has become a wife and mother, but her keyboard will be productive, let us hope, for many years to come.

*   *   *   *   *

The police chief imbroglio erupted a year and a half after peace had been established on the Job Corps front. When the new leadership of the Town of Bethlehem's entrenched Republican party declined to renominate Bert Kohinke's hand-picked town supervisor for a new term, it touched off a series of political gymnastics that hadn't been seen in nearly two decades of Bert's unchallenged rule. From its seat on the fifty-yard line, the Spotlight hurled its non-partisan presence into the thick of the scrimmages, relishing every aspect of its first full local election campaign in its second summer as a paid-circulation newspaper.

The trouble that beset Chief Peter Fish was a by-product of an unusually heated town election campaign. The voting produced enough new faces to point the Bethlehem Town Board in a new direction and to reshuffle political priorities. Fish's explosive personality and harsh professional tactics made him either loved or hated by a sizeable segment of his contituency, and when the 1977 political gymnastics eroded much of his power base, he discovered how controversial and how vulnerable he was.

The board's action in suspending the chief and bringing in a special counsel from New York City with high credentials as a

299

racket-busting prosecutor touched off a succession of legal maneuverings that played like a soap opera. As the drama unfolded week after week, punctuated by occasional courtroom calisthenics, I could only offer a weekly analysis with little chance for timely spot reporting on-site. But I had town hall sources the competition didn't have. After one private Sunday morning session with the prosecutor, I took a chance on breaking a story for my next issue—still four days away—that turned out

The Job Corps in 1976 and police chief in 1978 made for lively reading and catchy headlines spread over several months.

to be virtually on-target, giving the little weekly a rare beat on the dominant dailies.

It was also ironic that as the town's legal jousting with the chief dragged along, the Albany papers took the editorial position that Bethlehem town officials were arrogantly harassing an experienced law enforcement officer of high integrity and proven accomplishment. In April, two months after the chief had been suspended, the Times-Union came out with an editorial and cartoon that chided town officials for what it saw as an inability to support the charges. The cartoon by Hy Rosen, the T-U's

This political cartoon supported a Times-Union editorial on the police chief suspension in Bethlehem.

affable and nationally acclaimed political cartoonist, depicted Bethlehem as a man in underwear and socks playing strip poker with Fish in full uniform. In its hand the town character was holding the deuce of clubs.

A month later the county grand jury indicted the chief on two counts of perjury. That case and other litigation, including a brush with federal authorities disturbed at learning he possessed copies of the income tax returns of two town officials, spelled the end of Peter Fish in Bethlehem, and he was not seen in town thereafter.

*   *   *   *   *

Stories like these gave us a chance to show our mettle, if any, but other material was plentiful. With two towns to cover, we had two town boards, two planning boards, two zoning boards and three school systems, plus the active and growing village of Voorheesville located in a corner of the Town of New Scotland. It was simply a question of doing what Gordon Bryant, my old city editor in Watertown, would insist on—cover the news beat, cover it thoroughly, and keep a constant eye out for anything that would make a story.

The news beat in Bethlehem and New Scotland was exciting and productive for any reporter willing to tap into it. Replacing Peter Fish in the headlines were such things as a citizen uprising in Voorheesville protesting a whopping increase in sewer rates, job action by the Bethlehem teachers union protesting stalled contract negotiations, a vigorous campaign to fluoridate the local water system that met widespread resistance, and a succession of torrid hearings on zoning issues in both towns. In the sewer flap in Voorheesville, we were the only paper to attend an angry protest meeting that filled a school auditorium, and the only paper to provide depth coverage of several other municipal controversies that stirred emotions of the citizenry to a high pitch. It was great fun.

In our magazine format we were one-of-a-kind among print media in our section of the state, and we exploited this as best we could by calling ourselves "Uniquely Weekly." Our promotional

Photo by Longabaugh

From left, councilmen Corrigan, Johnston and Bickel, counsel Harry Rezzimini, comptroller Martin Smith and Supervisor Sheaffer.

Plurality slim

Supervisor Harry H. Sheaffer, winning his first elective office after being appointed to fill Bertram H. Kohinke's unexpired term, had the narrowest margin in the major races last week. His plurality was 352 over Democrat George Harder, who lost to Kohinke by some 2,000 votes in 1971.

Councilman Ruth O. Bickel, also seeking the voters' mandate for an office she was appointed to last Jan. 1, won by 865 votes and Councilman William Johnston, Jr. was reelected by 755 in the unofficial tally of more than 11,800 ballots. Town Clerk Marion T. Camp ran far ahead of the ticket with a smashing plurality of 3,394.

Fewer voters

The vote total fell just short

393 DELAWARE AVE.

Battle of budget a routine fizzle

Bethlehem's annual public hearing on the town budget, a popular issue in election cam-

unexpended balances in several categories of the document, and on the b...

and career, ignored a suggestion from the ...

TOWN PLANNING

Subdivision site scene: blurry

Bethlehem's burgeoning residential development picture, showing all aspects of a boom in direct contrast to the nationwide slump in housing starts, continues to make headlines. The headlines are generated by developers trying to clear legal hurdles en route foundations, citiz protect their ne and the plannin the catalyst cor tecting the inter as a whole.

NEWS ANALYSIS

Public sympathy for teachers: small

Bethlehem Central teachers, frustrated by long delays in negotiations for a new contract, apparently have won little sympathy from the bulk of district residents in their work-to-rule and mass picketing job actions.

A random sampling of citizen attitudes toward the Bethlehem Central Teachers Association produced a box score that was overwhelmingly unsympathetic to association tactics along with a sprinkling of public apathy. Only a few citizens were adamant, and some indicated mixed emotions. The majority had such comments as "teachers worked harder 10 years ago," teachers are already well paid and have a retirement plan the average citizen could never hope for, and teachers "have lost all professionalism along with the love of children."

Other opinions indicated that "teachers did what they did because they had to," and "teachers are not radical." Most of the citizens polled agreed action such as work-to-rule will

not do much in accomplishing objectives.

Impasse continues

Negotiations for a new contract have been in various stages of stalemate and limbo since last March. A Public Employee Relations Board (PERB) factfinder's report this fall was accepted by the BCTA but rejected by the Board of Education.

While teachers in some communities went on strike, risking jail terms, heavy fines and a tide of resentment from taxpayers and pupils, teachers' job action has been relatively mild in Bethlehem. Local teachers have confined their protests to observing work-to-rule (performing only duties specified by contract and embargoing

after-school activities, extracurricular meetings and taking work home), and that only a few weeks ago. Last week about 70 teachers marched with hardly readable signs in the November darkness of Adams Pl. as the Board of Education gathered for its regular meeting, then filed silently into the meeting room after a divided show of hands called for by BCTA president William Cleveland. They stood quietly along the rear wall as the board completed its routine business without a word being exchanged between the factions.

Progress slow

Twelve hours later, on Thursday morning, Cleveland, board president Bernard E. Harvith and their negotiators

TOWN PLANNING

Residents roast Frye plan

A new clash between a property owners and a land developer has members of the B...

ed by Jay Barbas...
Detro...

303

The Spotlight

Controlled Circulation Publication

Graphic newsweekly serving the towns of Bethlehem, New Scotland, Albany County, N.Y.   439-4949

WORK-TO-RULE EDICT

Union to teachers: tell kids you're 'too busy' to help

At the bargaining table things were placid, just one negotiator for each side and the state-appointed conciliator, but in the community the cauldron was boiling. Bethlehem teachers, growing increasingly impatient over the deadlocked negotiations for a new two-year union contract, stepped up their pressure on the parents and the school board by implementing the work-to-rule procedure. The reaction of parents, disgusted at picket lines and other incidents reflecting the pressure on the pupils, gave indications the tactics might be backfiring into a public relations problem for the union.

For its part, leaders of the Bethlehem Central Teachers Assn. (BCTA) last week distributed a mimeographed instruction sheet to members spelling out guidelines for strict adherence to work-to-rule. The edict combined a bid for teacher unity with "pressure on the board of education to negotiate." Among the instructions to teachers were strict compliance with the 7-hour, 30-minute workday required by the contract, no extra duties, no extra help or tutoring during lunch or after school, and no preparation of special displays or bulletin boards. The guideline: "Simply indicate to students that you are too busy."

The district's seven-member school board was not scheduled for a regular business meeting until next Wednesday, Oct. 5. The contract impasse was almost certain to come up, either on the agenda or during the open discussion period, inasmuch as a negotiating session with the state conciliator is scheduled for Monday, Oct. 3, at 3:30 at the High School.

Board members and Supt. of Schools Lawrence A. Zinn have declined to make official statements during the stalemate, but one board member, commenting on the union's "contract now" campaign, observed that the board "has been ready since last June to negotiate, but how can you negotiate when the chief negotiator for the

---

Full text of work-to-rule instructions:

Purpose:

Focus attention on the fact that we want to settle the contract dispute.

Promote and demonstrate the unity of BCTA members.

Pressure the Board of Education to negotiate.

Meaning of "work to rule":

Teachers work up to but do no more than the contract calls for. The work day is 7 hours and 30 minutes.

Procedure:

The contract work day is 7 hours and 30 minutes. You should work only 7 hours and 30 minutes.

Teach only required classes and perform only required duties such as assigned supervisions and homeroom. The following are some activities that should NOT be held or performed:

• Extra help or tutoring during preparation or lunch or after school.

• Preparation of special displays or bulletin boards, etc. Simply indicate to students that you are too busy.

DO NOT volunteer for anything, for example, committee work, extra supervision (paid or unpaid).

• Do not plan any field trips.

• No voluntary participation at faculty meetings, future events - shows, meetings, parent teacher events, concerts, etc.

Teachers should be unavailable to school for anything except contract requirements. If you are ordered to perform a task, get the order in writing and obey the order - do not be insubordinate - see your building representative.

Utilize lunch time for lunch and nothing else.

Utilize planning and preparation for that purpose.

Teachers should not bring home any work.

Do things in a group whenever possible, ex. lunch.

Meet all deadlines - not ahead of time - at the last minute. Building reps will coordinate this activity.

Let management manage. Teachers should not do any administrator's job. For example, do not volunteer suggestions or solutions to problems that are administrative. Send discipline problems that occur outside classroom to principal, etc.

Building reps should keep a record of who is not participating in work to rule activities. Notify those individuals and remind them of the importance of unity. Each member should encourage all teachers to participate to the fullest, and when problems arise have members check with reps for advise (sic). Be sure all building faculty knows and understands the work to rule concepts and guidelines.

Additional activities and actions will be added as the need for further pressure becomes evident.

When the Bethlehem teachers' union instituted a job action during contract negotiations, we printed the leadership's instructions to the membership. This story caused shocked anger in the community, and earned the Spotlight the undying enmity of union activists.

efforts never ceased. We had some personnel changes, and with only three full-time employees (editor, sales manager and receptionist-bookkeeper) we depended heavily on part-timers for sales, circulation, news writing and photography. We continued to farm out typesetting and printing, as had Bob King.

The Big P's—Payroll, Production, Printing, Paper and Postage—were the high-ticket items. We were starting to break even and flirting with profitability when we took the boldest step yet. We signed a lease-purchase contract for a direct-entry phototypesetting machine, partitioned off a new facility in the basement of our rented quarters, installed a photo dark room, and inaugurated our own camera-ready page composition. After a few setbacks in the shakedown period, we acquired some new skilled people, and it was up-beat from then on.

Not that we stayed out of trouble. As editor-publisher, I still had to do all my own proofreading, distribute bundles of papers to twenty newsstands, take the trashbags to the dumpster, sign the checks and do other chores. The sales manager had to pick up the mail, do his own filing, supervise the sales reps and collect delinquent accounts. The bookkeeper, besides getting out the monthly billing to some 200 accounts, handled the front counter, answered phones, posted advertising ledgers, balanced the checkbook, clipped tearsheets, handled classifieds and subscriptions, did secretarial chores, dusted desks, changed the flowers, filed timesheets, and protected the petty cash.

Financially it was a marginal operation, but the gains were steady and prospects favorable. Everyone was having a good time, there was plenty of spirit and there was no question we were becoming a vital part of the community. People got mad at us for things we wrote and things we did, and we were accused of slanted reporting and biased viewpoints, but in any locality that kind of thing goes with the franchise. Overall we had far more boosters than detractors. The only critics I felt were off-base were those whose accusations of bias were based on quotes and statements we had directly attributed to identified persons; yet because such statements had appeared in the Spotlight, these people saw it as the Spotlight saying these things. I also was forced many times to bite my tongue when accused of doing a story "just to sell papers."

Editors have had to live with this sort of thing since the beginning of time. It's easy enough to dig yourself into editorial craters and tangle yourself in journalistic barbed wire without taking a broadside for someone else's opinions. And always remember, the longer a newspaper functions in a community, the more popular it becomes to run it down.

That's not what the editors keep striving to accomplish, but they take it as a Fact of Life. They also know that most of the dissidents will keep on reading the paper anyway, and even the most vocal critics will always find some good things to read in it, if only football scores or the daily horoscope, fraudulent as that may be. Even the people who love to hate their local newspaper would hate to lose it.

33

Eclipse of the Suns

For a while Danzig's Sunpapers, off to a strong start, flourished and the half dozen suburban weeklies struggled, but soon the pendulum swung the other way. It was purely a case of salesmanship, for most of the weeklies were presenting a better journalistic product than the renegade intruders. Grace O'Connor, editor of the Suns and a quality professional, was perhaps the only bright star in an otherwise dim galaxy.

We continued to push the concept among our local advertisers that the Sun was a throwaway insert, a "freebie" shopper reaching only a limited audience. We pointed to stacks of unclaimed Suns in supermarkets and newsstands five days old. We argued that people tend to throw away inserts and junk mail on sight but, we kept insisting, people who buy papers tend to read them.

When it became apparent that the Suns were causing little, if any, damage to the steady growth of their intended victims, I was moved to expose the perfidy of their sponsor, Albany's lofty and greedy journalistic octopus, as a service to readers and as a contribution to fellow publishers in the weekly field. At about the same time, across the Hudson in Rensselaer County, the most aggressive entrepreneur in our circle of publishers, Tony

DiBello of the Greenbush Area News, confided that he had abandoned preparation of a lawsuit charging the Capital Newspapers with predatory pricing, a violation of the Sherman Anti-Trust Act. His reason for calling off the pursuit, he said, was in line with our thinking: that the Suns simply weren't much as newspapers, and once the novelty wore off and the vapidity showed, they would no longer be a threat.

My contribution was in the form of a Spotlight column I had been writing sporadically, billed as an occasional commentary on the newspaper and radio-TV scene. I had christened it Media Rare, and to avoid having my by-line appear *ad nauseam* I frequently used a pen-name, Perry Galt, as an alter-ego. (Readers straying this far into my text will find the spurious Perry Galt as the central character in the following chapter.) The name of this imposter appeared as the author of the column in question, a Spotlight piece that traced the basic thrust of the Suns. The article also purported to describe a strategy session that predictably might have taken place in Danzig's private office relating to the impending failure of his community tabloids. It appeared in December, 1977 under the heading, "Blitz on the Fritz."

> A funny thing happened to the publishers of the Capital Newspapers on the way to exterminating the community weekly newspapers in their circulation area. The bulldozer ran out of gas and now needs a big push.
>
> It has been nearly three years since the Times-Union-Knickerbocker News publishing team made the decision to extend their Albany-area newspaper monopoly by eliminating the small independently owned suburban weeklies. The targets were the Ravena News-Herald, Altamont Enterprise, Delmar Spotlight, Greenbush Area News and Colonie Townsman. By comparison, these five papers were hardly more than flies on the giant's back, but were considered enough of a nuisance to warrant extinction.
>
> The flyswatter device to accomplish this noble objective was devastatingly simple: use the huge in-house resources of the Capital Newspapers to set up a string of low-budget tabloid weeklies of their own, feature strictly neighborhood news and cut-rate ads, print during off-peak hours, and distribute the papers free in target localities.

The Hearst bulldozer in Albany was designed to obliterate these local independent weeklies plus the Spotlight. Of the six, the Townsman and Reporter were the only casualties.

The business strategy was equally appealing: sell the ads at rates below the prevailing weekly's, promise far larger circulation, and fill the news columns with non-controversial items gathered by "country correspondent" homemakers for a by-line and a few dollars grocery money.

First to go into orbit was the Helderberg Sun, aimed at the weeklies in Bethlehem, Guilderland and Ravena. In quick succession the other satellites were launched: first, the Mohawk Sun in the west, the Sorensco Sun to eradicate the prize-winning Greenbush Area News in southern Rensselaer, and the Northway Sun and Riverside Sun to stop the foolishness in Latham, Colonie, Clifton Park, Cohoes and Waterford.

The father of the Suns and their oleo is Robert J. Danzig, a former Schenectady businessman whose function as assigned by the parent Hearst Corp. in New York is to concentrate on the lower right hand corner. That's accounting lingo for the bottom line of the balance sheet, not to be confused with the quality of the product.

To give the solar system a touch of class, the powers assigned one of the many fine professionals on their news staffs to edit the Helderberg Sun and all the little Suns that sprang therefrom. The choice was Grace O'Connor, the organization's most versatile and most productive resource. Grace still pumps out regular columns on sports cars and jazz, helps write and edit the Peppermint Page for kids, and once had 19 by-lines in one edition of the Sunday Times-Union. On another occasion this copper-haired young grandmother jumped out of a plane to do a story on sky-diving.

But now, in their third year, the Suns need more than heavenly Grace. The Helderberg Sun has been running eight fewer pages this fall than a year ago. Advertising lineage is way down. Many local advertisers have gone back to the hometown weeklies, preferring the proven readership and household welcome of the suburban weeklies to desperation giveaways. The Mohawk Sun and Northway Sun have never risen much above ground level, and the Sorensco Sun is up against a well-written, well-edited weekly.

The little weeklies have been hurt, but not fatally, and the Danzig timetable is behind schedule. Said one publisher: "Most of their news was in our paper the week before."

Last month a high-level meeting in Danzig's second-floor office came to grips with the sinking Suns. The business managers had two alternatives: beef up the zoned editions and make them into respectable newspapers, or put the blitz on advertisers by offering special discounts on top of existing discounts and push the combination rates to big advertisers even if it means giving the space away at less than a dollar a column inch.

The boys decided on No. 2 for obvious reasons. The Albany chapel of the Newspaper Guild, the newsmen's union, has just won the largest pay boost in years, which means publishers must cut down on editorial manpower rather than increase it. That alone was enough to rule out No. 1, but it also was foreign to the image of publisher Danzig, who can never be accused of putting the editorial quality of his papers ahead of the bottom line.

"When they give discounts during the peak season," observed one local publisher, "you know they're in trouble."

Last week the Suns rose in glory, full of heavily discounted holiday advertising, much of it non-local, that is not enough to cover production costs. But the publishers feel the loss is worth it if they can get rid of a couple of weeklies and become the only game in town. It was a courageous if arrogant decision, for the U. S. Department of Justice does not look kindly on people who make special efforts to build monopolies.

The decision to "flood" the Suns puts new pressure on the smaller local advertisers. Hometown businessmen who consistently give a boost to civic groups are not overly comfortable supporting an out-of-town slicker who cares for none of these things. They are also less than delighted at being put in the position of a family owned business contributing to the strengthening of the very kind of supermarket chain operations like Sears, Macy's and cut-rate drug chains that victimize the small businessman.

Meanwhile the pages of the Enterprise, News-Herald, Townsman, Greenbush News, Rotterdam Reporter and Spotlight will continue to carry the community news items the dailies don't bother with and the zoned editions will warm over next week or the week after. "We've got to give our people a good local paper," muses Tony DiBello, "because if we don't, no one else will."

In the executive suite on Albany-Shaker Rd. the forecast might read like this: partially Sun-ny today, cloudy after Christmas, reign diminishing, probability of precipitation 30 percent. The extended forecast: missed in the outlying areas.

A short time later I got wind of Danzig's reaction to the Galt column, courtesy of my good friend, Stan Levine, a onetime Times-Union sportswriter. Stan had as many friends and contacts in Albany as anyone I ever knew. He also had a close association with Danzig, for whom he worked as the Capital Newspapers' community relations director. "You really got to him," Stan confided at the tennis club one day. "He thinks someone in his office is leaking confidential information to you."

I told him I was just guessing. I said that anyone could figure that Danzig must have had a meeting —or several—to discuss the status of the Suns, and that at such a meeting the discussion would go in a predictable pattern.

"I know," Stan laughed. "But he doesn't." More laughter.

About a month after the article, I had to go to the Capital Newspapers to pick up an ad a customer wanted to run in the Spotlight as well as the Times-Union. As usual, I used the side door, which was the staff entrance, close to the employee parking lot and unfettered by receptionist rituals. This time I was astounded to find an elaborate electronic security system and a uniformed guard. I had to ask the guard to call the person I wanted to see.

Before leaving the building, I went around to Stan's office to chide him about the new high-security environment in, of all places, a newspaper plant. "Hell, that's your damned fault," he said, smiling broadly. "The boss now thinks you've bugged his office, and he can't sleep at night. He's all shook up." And he dissolved in laughter.

Meanwhile there were only a few death rattles among the intended victims. In the Latham-Cohoes area, the Townsman threw in the towel, a demise brought about more by the failing health of its venerable publisher than by the Hearst intruder. In Rotterdam, a Schenectady adjunct, a small paper just getting started decided the odds in bucking the Mohawk Sun were not worth the extra effort. These were the only casualties; the targets in Altamont, Delmar, East Greenbush and Ravena not only remained intact, but continued to thrive.

Toward the end the Suns set, one by one, but not before Danzig escaped to greener pastures. The aborted blitz to wipe out the annoyances in the hinterlands apparently hadn't impeded the flow of gold into the coffers in Albany. Danzig's reward for chaperoning those millions into the corporate bottom line was a promotion to the executive suite in New York City, where he was put in charge of all newspapers in the Hearst empire.

In Albany, it fell to one J. Roger Grier, imported by Hearst from the Trenton Times to succeed Danzig, to jettison two of the Suns. The original predator and last survivor, the Helderberg Sun, hung on until the spring of 1981. Despite the talent of the prolific and amazing Grace, its appeal to advertisers dwindled steadily; when it slimmed down to sixteen pages from its early zenith of forty-four and had difficulty selling peak-season ads at huge discounts at Thanksgiving and Christmas, it folded quietly, two weeks before its seventh birthday.

34

Fun With Fich

Journalists who stick necks out in print are fair game for brickbats, notably columnists who have a name and often a photo alongside the essay, editors whose prose appears as unsigned editorials, or reporters writing under by-lines.

I know. I've been all three.

In the late sixties and early seventies the Albany newspaper scene offered a favorite target in Bob Fichenberg, a highly capable newsman who rose to become editor of the Albany Knickerbocker News. Fich had a volatile personality, strong convictions and boundless ambition, all of which assured him center stage in a steady succession of controversies.

Fichenberg was managing editor of the Knickerbocker News when, to the dismay of newsroom professionals and thousands of readers, it was sold to the Hearst interests, which published Albany's morning paper, the Times-Union. That transaction not only ended the era of competitive journalism in New York's capital city, such as it was, but also launched the proud Knick on a toboggan slide to obscurity.

That took a few years. The Knick had long been widely recognized as one of upstate New York's premier papers. It was more than the Gannett chain's cornerstone in the state capital; it had a stable of talented writers, top-drawer political analysts and columnists, plus an experienced staff of local reporters and editors. By contrast, the Times-Union was inept, a product of absentee owners so uncaring that after 7 p.m., when the early "Metro" edition went to press, it presented the incredible spectacle of only two staffers, a night editor and one reporter, assigned to duty in the city room of a morning paper.

In the many changes that began the erosion of the Knick, Fichenberg was promoted to editor. He could see what the powers were doing to his paper, but he had enough ego to believe he could make a good run in a bad situation, and he basked in his new limelight. Nevertheless, it would be unfair to relate Fich's ascent to the Knick's descent. He was a respected newsman and writer, but in consensus his colleagues and associates took a somewhat dimmer view of his administrative credentials. Old hands, mindful of the ageless axiom that the most capable editor in creation is beholden to the dictums and budget restrictions of the publisher, insist that Fich brought on many of his own personnel problems.

In his sanctum off the city room, insulated by a secretary and administrative clout, Fich took to his executive role with relish. His temperament made him a controversial figure, and as he wielded his authority in the newsroom his circle of close friends and admirers narrowed. Personnel changes became routine. Bill Skirving, dean of police reporters in the competitive Albany-Schenectady-Troy battleground, was relegated to writing a streetside gossip column prior to being pushed into an early retirement. In another switch Fich gave the city editor job to Bob Illingworth, then fired him after a brief tenure. As a replacement he brought in John Schoolfield, a scarred veteran of newsrooms in Bridgeport and New Haven, to be city editor, but threw him out in the streets several years later for reasons poor John hasn't learned to this day. Fich's passion for purge extended to such unlikely outposts as the sports desk and the entertainment section.

During these turbulent times at the Knick, I had a seat on the sidelines with a good view. I was working for General Electric in neighboring Schenectady and living in Slingerlands, an Albany suburb where most subscribers still tolerated the deteriorated Knick, presumably either from habit, family tradition or the need to know what's playing at the movies. I was also enjoying, on the side, a devious gambit that enabled me to contribute a tongue-in-cheek column in the local weekly shopping paper that served Slingerlands, Delmar and other adjacent Albany suburbs. The column indulged in gentle needling of public figures, institutions and situations. For obvious reasons I had to write the column under a cloak of anonymity, delivering it to the local publisher through a neighborhood attorney pledged to protect the source.

I will never understand how or why Bob King accepted material from an unidentified source, but he apparently welcomed its content and spirit. Thus it came about that a feature called The Periscope written by someone named Perry Galt began appearing sporadically in the Spotlight in the sixties, poking fun at various well-known personalities and institutions. It was inevitable that one of the subjects of the spurious Mr. Galt, who was familiar with the Albany newspaper scene, would be the tempestuous editor of the Albany Knickerbocker News.

I had known Fich fairly well during years of hobnobbing with old cronies on both Albany papers and the Capitol press corps long after my AP days, and we enjoyed a pleasant relationship in the brotherhood. When Galt did a piece on the changing role of the afternoon paper under the new Hearst format, I had no inkling that it would stir up a storm in the lofty echelons of Albany's journalistic hierarchy. After all, the Spotlight was an inconspicuous free-circulation advertising mailer confined to a small community in the vast geographical complex served by the legitimate giant, and my fun-poking was regularly intended for the amusement of whatever constituency the local shopper had, plus, natch, myself.

In November, 1969 the Periscope twitted the Knick on several counts. It chided the proud established giant for changing the delivery of the home edition in residential Slingerlands from 5 p.m. by newsboy on a bicycle to 11 a.m. by contract carrier in a car. That departure, the ingrate columnist pointed out, climaxed a gradual evolution of the news deadline from the old 1:30 p.m. to the new 9:30 a.m. The net effect was to shut readers off from that day's breaking stories and to give them an evening paper printed only a few hours after that morning's Times-Union. "The potential of getting our afternoon paper in the morning is exciting indeed," wrote the masquerading Galt. "Think how wonderful it would be to have tonight's news at breakfast this morning..... Getting the paper read early frees up the cocktail hour for conversation, and in some houses, enables followers of Ann Landers, Mark Trail and the daily horoscope to get the dishes washed earlier and thus get to the TV (or even a committee meeting) without rush."

I had forgotten that Fichenberg also lived in Slingerlands. Most people paid little heed to the adolescent Spotlight's servings of church notices, Brownie troop activities, new brides and neighborhood children making the dean's list at college, but Fich apparently saw the errant column or was told about it. He fired off a heated letter to Mr. Perry Galt, denying all allegations.

The home edition, he insisted, starts rolling off the presses at about 1:45 p.m., only fifteen minutes earlier than it did ten years ago. Because of Galt's "sketchy knowledge" of the local newspaper situation, and because of the "inaccurate" information in the column, the irate Fich invited him to come to the Knick office for a tour "and a short course in accuracy in journalism."

In reply, the dastardly columnist wrote a personal letter above Perry Galt's signature, plus a follow-up column that gave full play to Fich's impassioned complaints. Galt also admitted that it was hard to explain how an edition that is printed at 1:45 p.m. can be delivered on New Scotland Road by 11:15 a.m. the same day.

During this period our paths crossed several times under amicable circumstances, convincing me that Fich had no inkling that I was his elusive protagonist. When, some six years later under surprising and unexpected circumstances, I became editor-publisher of that self-same little weekly paper, we found ourselves, in effect, not only neighbors in residential Slingerlands, but also legitimate fellow-journalists. Our relations as editors of our respective journals continued to be fraternal and friendly, however casual.

THE PERISCOPE By PERRY GALT

When the Capital Cities Newspapers move into their new multi-million-dollar plant near Exit 3 on the Northway, one of the things we can expect is to have our evening paper delivered earlier.

Just in the last few years the delivery time has been moved up from mid-afternoon to 11:15 A.M. and it wasn't so many years ago we didn't get the paper until 5 P.M. That was in the days when the local evening paper, whose name I can't recall at the moment (the one they delivered in Delmar before the Schenectady tion and keeping abreast of current events and commentary. This has become increasingly difficult since the Knick News has ceased to cover the Tri-Village area and has substituted pages and pages of Schenectady, Glenville and Schoharie news.

We talked to a former newspaperman the other night, and he

THE KNICKERBOCKER NEWS
UNION-STAR

ROBERT G. FICHENBERG
Executive Editor

ALBANY, N.Y. 12201

Nov. 21, 1969

Mr. Perry Galt
The Spotlight
154 Delaware Avenue
Delmar, N.Y. 12054

Dear Perry:

That was a very interesting column you wrote on the Capital Newspapers, particularly the section on The Knickerbocker News and Union-Star.

There was only one thing wrong with it. It was completely inaccurate.

You said, for instance, that "...The Knick News has ceased to cover the Tri-Village area and has substituted pages and pages of

This was the piece that touched off the flap, motivating Fich to write a personal letter to a columnist he felt was sniping at him.

317

Bob Fichenberg

Fraternal and friendly, that is, until, to my surprise and delight, the volcanic Fichenberg in the spring of 1978 erupted in another broadside at the Spotlight and its editor. This time, however, he was shooting at me as a known and identifiable target, not as an undercover agent.

No one but Fich himself will ever know what touched off this vitriolic, almost childish blast in his regular weekly column, a Friday fixture on the editorial page of the Knick. There were several targets of his ire that day, which happened to be Good Friday. One was local television news and the people on the Albany-Schenectady area's three network channels who, pretending to be journalists, dared to intrude on what had always been newspaper territory. Another was the Spotlight, a small suburban weekly newspaper that he accused of being nondescript, inept and several other things. Had he had a bad day on Thursday when he sat down to write it? Was he frustrated by Albany traffic jams caused by unrestricted triple-parking, or was his anguish caused by budget restrictions imposed by a publisher with no news perspective? Was his coffee cold that morning? Did he have corns that were acting up?

I liked my own suspicions best. I had no evidence, but I pictured Fich coming home to his fireside on North Helderberg Parkway and finding in his mailbox the Spotlight, and reading therein several stories his high-powered staff should have had earlier in the week. This must surely have been the case during the long summer of Bethlehem's war of nerves with the Job Corps and the subsequent storm that swirled around Bethlehem's volatile and beleaguered police chief. The Knick had been the first to break the Job Corps story, alertly spotting a routine Help Wanted ad placed by the U.S. Labor Department, but after capitalizing on this obscure tipoff, the paper failed to follow up its initial advantage until late in the summer. The Spotlight, meanwhile, made hay week after week. In the Peter Fish case the Knick—and the Times-Union—covered for the most part only town board meetings and press conferences without further digging. As a consequence it might have rankled Fich to get more information from the Spotlight than from his own reporters.

In his Viewpoint column on that Good Friday all these frustrations boiled over, and Fich unleashed fusillades in all directions. As one of several targets I caught this volley:

> The public developments so far in the intriguing story of the Bethlehem Town Board vs. Police Chief Peter Fish have been confined to legal sparring—charges, countercharges, court motions, etc. Still to be revealed are precisely what the town has, or believes it has, on the controversial and embattled chief.
>
> Meanwhile it's interesting to note how the Spotlight, a nondescript Bethlehem weekly, is tiptoeing around this story, as it tiptoed around the Job Corps Center issue and any other controversial story involving the town government. Instead, it is engaging in a vitriolic campaign against Bethlehem school teachers, who are an easy mark because, unlike town officials, they can't fight back.
>
> I had thought the reason for the sustained anti-teacher campaign was that the Spotlight editor once flunked high school English, which would be the logical assumption of anyone who reads the rag. . .

I couldn't have been more delighted. Getting this exposure in the Knick on Good Friday was the biggest boost I'd yet had in the quest for recognition of the Spotlight, despite the fact that the Knick's readership in the town had dwindled. It was also somewhat sobering to realize I could expect a fair-sized barrage of joshing from friends in the large crowd of worshippers at St. Peter's Church in downtown Albany gathering on Easter Sunday for well-wishing on State Street after the service two days hence.

But in the sunshine in front of the church that Sunday not one person mentioned the Fichenberg blast. No longtime Slingerlands neighbor, nor any of many Albany friends, had seen it. If they had, they would not have missed this opportunity for a good ribbing.

On Monday I put Fich's column logo, complete with his photo, in the upper right corner of the upcoming Spotlight cover, with the slugline: "The Knick gets touchy. Page 30." Inside I dashed off one of my periodic Media Rare columns, informing subscribers that I was unaware that the big-city Hearst daily considered our little weekly as competition. I explained that we had been so busy trying to get our paper out on time, leaving the Knick to its own problems, that we hadn't realized we were bugging its top boss. I mentioned that I had always thought our paper was pretty descript, and was certainly not a rag, inasmuch as it was printed on fifty-pound Premier Offset paper that I wished wasn't so expensive. I also assured our friends that we hadn't been angling for Fich, he "just jumped into the boat, and now we don't know what to do with him."

We did exploit it mildly. I reprinted the key excerpt with the Fich logo on our stationery and wrote a promotional letter to advertisers and potential advertisers. I wrote to Fich on the new letterhead, thanked him for the unexpected publicity, and asked, in the event we were still friends, how I should address him if I had occasion to meet him or call him. Bob? Fich? Mr. Fichenberg?

He didn't respond. As it turned out, he quit his job in a subsequent and unrelated flareup some six months later. The Hearst hierarchy, opting to create a new executive position for an editor with overall responsibility for both Albany

320

The Spotlight

April 6, 1978
Vol. XXIV, No. 12

20¢

Graphic newsweekly serving the towns of Bethlehem, New Scotland and nearby communities

Home-building surge buoys Bethlehem
Page 7

Eagle Scout in Elsmere Page 22

Knickerbocker News gets touchy
Page 30

Viewpoint
By Robert G. Fichenberg
Executive Editor

I had thought the reason for the sustained anti-teacher campaign was that the *Spotlight* editor once flunked high school English, which would be the logical assumption of anyone who reads the rag. But it turns out he's been miffed
The Knick, March 24

It was a squeeze to fit Fich's logo on the cover, along with the lead head and a photo of a new Eagle Scout. I explained that I felt I had to reprint the column because so few people in town read the Knick.

newspapers, by-passed Fich in favor of Harry Rosenfeld, an experienced Washington editor. That was too much for Fich. He resigned rather than report to a new level of management instead of the publisher, and even his detractors couldn't blame him for that.

Shortly after the announcement of Fich's acceptance of a job in Washington with the Newhouse chain appeared in the papers, I got a call from Francis (Doc) Rivett. Doc had put in a long stint on the Times-Union copydesk and sports desk in addition to being a prime mover in the local "chapel" of the Newspaper Guild. Like many other Albany newsmen, including myself, he had left what might be called the mother industry for greener and reputedly less hectic pastures, and had become a PR man with the state Public Service Commission. When I heard Doc's voice on the phone I knew something was afoot. He put on a businesslike tone: "Nat, some of the boys are planning a farewell

321

testimonial for Fich, to which he will not be invited. We thought you might like to be our toastmaster."

Months later at the annual luncheon of the Legislative Correspondents Association alumni, Emmet O'Brien, longtime chief of Gannett's Capitol bureau in Albany and one of the best newsmen around, recalled Fichenberg's Good Friday tirade with high glee. Emmet was a resident of Delmar and a loyal supporter of my struggles· to give the local weekly a semblance of respectability. He has since gone to his Eternal Victory, but I will long remember the wisdom in his observation at that luncheon, one of the last times I chatted with him. His ample waistband shaking with mirth, Emmet said: "If the editor of a newspaper is going to attack another newspaper, be sure it's a worthy foe. Pick on somebody big, the New York Times or the Washington Post, certainly not (and another peal of laughter) the Spotlight!"

35

Epilogue

By the spring of 1980 three elements at the Spotlight were evident. The paper had established itself as a solid and viable community resource, it had outgrown its cramped three-room office suite with the primitive typesetting facility in the basement of the house on Kenwood Avenue, and it was time for the editor-publisher, approaching age 65, to give up the seventy-hour work week.

There was a desperate need for editorial assistance in the form of a full-time news reporter-photographer, but although the corporation was now solvent, there was not yet a place in the budget for such extravagance. Advertising volume and the subscription list were rising at a pace that was steady enough to sustain several modest rate increases.

It was also becoming increasingly and painfully clear that we needed more space not only for operations but in the paper itself. That meant our attractive magazine format was threatened by the inevitable—a switch to tabloid format. Such a move would include a changeover from bond paper to newsprint, thus dooming forever the Uniquely Weekly product that for a quarter of a century had given the little paper in Bethlehem such a distinctive appearance. Would a tabloid newspaper remain on the coffee table in the family room for five or six days, as did the contemporary Spotlight? I dreaded the thought.

I kept that fateful decision on hold, but took two other actions. I signed a contract to buy a commercial building a block away, confident that I could entice one or two of my friends to join me in a modest real estate investment, and I put the paper on the market. My plan was to be free of administrative and fiscal burdens, then work for the new owner for one year before retiring. If the purchaser was an experienced journalist, such as a newsman eager to flee the jungles of New York or Washington for a life of skiing, fishing and fresh air, he would need my help writing and editing. If the purchaser's background was in advertising, circulation or in some other business, he would need an editor, and with me staying over, he would have up to a year to find his own man.

The fates were generous to both me and the community. When Dick Ahlstrom, a vice president of Gannett's Westchester Rockland Newspapers, turned up in Delmar, he explained that he had dedicated the two years prior to his company's minimum retirement date to finding a newspaper in a country setting. At the time he was based in White Plains, responsible for the building operations and production of ten daily newspapers and a weekly with a circulation of 70,000.

What would a man of this caliber want with a small operation like the Spotlight in Delmar, where the publisher's salary and corporate earnings were barely one-fifth that of a Gannett executive? I was curious, and also a bit wary of this genial, intelligent, energetic fellow. When I asked the question point blank, his response was straightforward.

"That's easy to answer," he said. "I have been responsible for a number of technical innovations in newspaper printing and production that have saved my employers many millions of dollars. Now I would like to put my expertise to work for myself instead of a large corporation. For nearly two years I have been searching for a newspaper I could have for my own. I love the mountains, especially skiing, but I have looked at properties in Pennsylvania as well as New York and New England. This seems to be the most ideal situation I've found so far."

The resulting transition could not have been orchestrated in a more ideal way. For buyer and seller it went according to script, a story with a happy ending for everyone.

Except it wasn't the ending; it was just another chapter in a continuing story. A fiction writer might add some embellishments, but I would have difficulty structuring a happier chronology. I became editor, free of accounting, bookkeeping, cash flow, production, newsstands, supplies and trash removal. I was back to my first love, the news pages, with a free hand, courtesy of a first-rate publisher-owner.

The purchase of the building to house the expanding operation also went through on schedule. So did the acquisition of a new editor. Dick Ahlstrom made the courageous move to tabloid form, and in subsequent years doubled the paid circulation, tripled advertising lineage, quadrupled personnel, computerized production and office operations, and expanded news and editorial coverage. Not only has he made the Spotlight a respected force in Albany County, but his warm personality and civic energy has earned him a leadership role in community activities.

In those years, so distant from the scrubby little room that housed a free-circulation "shopper" in a corner of the old bus garage in Delmar, Dick also has permitted me to reach the pinnacle of my career. I am now a sporadic contributor of news stories, story ideas and—the most fun of all—an occasional Media Rare at my own pace.

Meanwhile I live with my treasured and tolerant Barbara among the picturesque hills of New Scotland, six miles and one traffic light—but five hundred feet higher in altitude—from the Spotlight. In this cozy retreat I have a sweeping view of the Helderbergs, and all those reminiscences of Gordon Bryant, Harold Manning, Stubby Struble, Charlie Small, Henry Leader, Tom Paine, yes, and even Fich. Perry Galt, whose demise was due to exposure, should be this lucky.

VII

Media Rare

Hash stripe

hash stripe = **hash mark.**
hassel   hassle   *n.* A disagreement, dispute, quarrel, or argument; a struggle or fight. 1949: "A hassel between two actors touched off the ... riot...." Billy Rose, *synd. newsp. col.*, Dec. 2. 1953: "... The hassle over putting fluoride in drinking water." Nat Boynton, AP, Albany, N.Y., Mar. 5.
hassock   *n.* In baseball, a base. 1931: "The Crab bingled ... with the hassocks crowded." W. Pegler, *Lit. Digest. Not common.*

—Dictionary of American Slang

328

The Affluent Rich

I began collecting what I liked to call Unnecessary Redundancies (URs) in 1968 while writing for General Electric, and dashed off this essay for the pure fun of it. Appreciative friends gave it wide distribution via copy machines, but I never thought to submit it for publication. Several years later Edwin Newman, one of the journalists I admire most, published a book that treated this subject along with a serving of well-worn newspaper cliches. Newman went far beyond my effort, but I often wondered whether I should have—or could have—beaten him to this punch.

In the abundance of life in the U. S., Americans are a wasteful lot. They buy things they don't use, they use things they don't need, and they throw away more in a year than other nations do in a lifetime.

They are wasteful even in their language, inherited as it was from the first English colonists. Much of the waste comes in the prolific duplication of spoken and written words, especially the unwitting and unneeded adjective or modifier, the unnecessary redundancy, commonly used, blindly accepted and often undetected.

A colleague of mine renowned for his creativity in design was impressed by the "pair of twins" born to a neighbor family. This same fellow was so unimpressed by service in a New York restaurant that he "never went back again." Had he been back before he decided not to go back again?

Alan Truscott, bridge editor of the New York Times, has a chapter in his exciting book, *The Great Bridge Scandal,* entitled "Past History." I trust Truscott realizes that past history is the best kind of history we have, just as past experience is the most desirable kind of experience.

But then we must always remember that Columbus, according to legend and schoolbooks, first discovered America. We are not told who second discovered it. By the same token, I first learned about Columbus from my grandmother, that is, before I second learned it in first grade.

If Columbus talked and thought like one of my GE associates, he would have stated that he first conceived the idea that the world might be round while staring at the horizon. Whether he ever conceived that idea again is lost in, of all things, past history.

If Queen Isabella had been as astute as my boss, she would have immediately asked Columbus, "All right, but what about the follow-up afterwards?" Whereupon Columbus could have replied, "Your Majesty, I believe we would have good success with such a scheme." Ah, yes, signor, that's so much better than just plain, ordinary success.

As an itinerant traveler, Columbus got permission to proceed ahead, and thus found his new discovery. Old discoveries aren't worth looking for, let alone finding. In the latter case, some embarrassment could have been avoided by advance scouting, but then, as one of my neighbors once remarked, you can't always anticipate these things ahead of time. He said this in a moment of frank candor.

*   *   *   *   *

Newspapers are a goldmine of URs, not only in the prose of their own writers, but also in reporting the quotes of public figures or people involved in news stories. Here's a Page One wire story:

> WASHINGTON (AP)   Claiming lack of "mutual confidence" between them, President Nixon today fired Interior Secretary Walter J. Hickel.

Earlier, an explosion on the University of Wisconsin campus damaged the Army Mathematical Research Center and killed a graduate student. In a newspaper interview, Madison

Police Inspector Herman Thomas was quoted as saying: "We know of those who are potentially capable of doing this."

My friend Ed Swietnicki, highly respected business editor of the once-respected Albany Knickerbocker News, was pressed into service on election night last fall, and even the copydesk couldn't—or didn't—save him when he wrote: "The winner was the Democratic candidate and current incumbent, Thomas W. Brown of the 18th Ward." Poor Ed forgot some basic fundamentals.

It is a true fact (a kind most people prefer, actually) that the Occidental Petroleum Company, in an elaborate annual report to stockholders, described several "new innovations." I was told about this during an oral conversation with a neighbor who had attended the annual meeting. Conversations of this nature have positive advantages.

In my own newspaper days, back on the Watertown Times before World War II, we cubs were warned of dire consequences befalling anyone writing "widow of the late" So-and-So in an obit, which, it was said, was a more heinous crime than referring to the deceased as "a former native of this city." Yet the Albany Times-Union used the former twice, and I have a clipping of a Schenectady Gazette sports head that says: "Sears, former Vietnam Vet, Named Lineman of the Week." That's almost as credible as being a former graduate of Syracuse University.

With that old copydesk training I would have wielded a hard pencil on a headline like "Restoring Old Homes Keeps Past Tradition Alive" from the Lakes Region (N. H.) Trader. I also would have cracked down on my friend Scott Christiansen of the Knickerbocker News for writing about municipal budgeting for a boat marina. As a taxpayer I might've become angry if they let cars and planes use that marina. In fact, I might even go to my legal counsel, bearing in mind it was the Knick that reported that "the body of a Massachusetts man wanted in connection with an armed assault and holdup in Troy on Halloween was found dead in Pennsylvania Saturday, according to Troy police."

Perhaps that isn't so bad, now that gas stations are offering free gifts with every eight gallons, and banks advertise free gifts for opening new accounts. If there's anything that ruffles my good nature, it's receiving a gift I have to pay for. Besides, I probably wouldn't get one if I opened an old account.

*　　*　　*　　*　　*

The print media enjoy no monopoly on affluence in idioms, or, to paraphrase a condensed version, the wasteful effluent of language. Mike Wallace said on CBS the other day (and I heard him with my own ears, aurally as well as orally) that "people nowadays have a lot of nostalgia for the past." Even though nostalgia isn't like it used to be, I still like to think back on it in a sentimental way.

A business associate of mine at GE is a past master of the art of redundant phraseology without being aware of his talent. On a survey seeking a site for a business meeting, we were shown a Florida hotel terrace with a view of a palm-lined golf course stretching into the distance. "My, what a beautiful vista to look out upon," my friend remarked to our host. I was impressed, too, because less than an hour earlier, my companion, who outranked me, had said he considered us co-equal partners in the project. He also pointed out that this trip was a re-continuation of a job we had worked on together the year before.

I was forced to point out to him that I felt the Florida deal was a different variation of the earlier project. Anyway, that was better than an office compatriot who complained that management seemed to be "vacillating back and forth." But, then, everyone knows that the Mississippi River meanders back and forth and all around, a fact that is noticeably visible with your own eyes if ever you are in a plane flying aloft in the air above.

Irregardless, conservative economists are often just as profound. A nationally known expert remarked during a television panel discussion on the decline of the textile industry in Rhode Island and Massachusetts that "all of New England has suffered poorly."

At least, he wasn't too overconfident. It's best to be on the conservative side, like the General Electric vice president who said in a sales meeting presentation: "I may have overdone this a little too much, but you get the message."

If I have made any omissions in this little essay, dear readers, I'll count on you to fill in the missing gaps.

Surrounded on All Sides

In the sporadic Media Rare column in the Spotlight, I occasionally gave readers an update on my UR collection, which grew steadily. Here is an example.

Loyalists who have chuckled at some of the semantic misdemeanors recounted in this space on past occasions are asked to forgive if some are a bit familiar, but these UR's keep coming back, hence bear—if you will pardon the expression—repeating again.

Local radio and TV newspeople provide a steady source. I have to leave these perpetrators anonymous because they are, in some cases anyway, friends of mine, and I forgive them because they have not had the experience of working under fearsome, hammer-wielding city editors. Thus I pardon a Channel 10 Action News anchor for saying that a county effort to clean up a former GE dump site "was not sufficient enough" to pacify local residents, and a WROW newsman for reporting that the possibility of the governor calling the Legislature back to a special session "is definitely up in the air."

It's harder to resist naming the Channel 6 man who said the suspect of a police pursuit "was surrounded on all sides" just prior to his apprehension. Slightly to our south a weekly newspaper in the Catskill foothills had this headline on a Page One feature story: "Conservation Fire Towers: Obsolete Thing of the Past?" A more immediate neighbor, carrying a story on a scholastic basketball game last month, reported that "both teams were deadlocked at halftime."

That score turned out to be 29–29, and I was thankful that both, not just one, of the teams were involved in the tie.

To the west of us, a newspaper that should know better described a trailer mishap on the Thruway by stating that "the coupling in use was near the breaking point, and failure was imminent at any moment." When I mentioned this to a friend in Slingerlands, he produced a clipping he had been saving for me on a local zoning issue, in which an applicant was "looking forward to receiving favorable approval" of his development proposal.

These affronts to the language are not confined to the locals. The biggies commit their own violations, to wit: "Flyers Revert Back to Bully Tactics" (Watertown Times sports headline); "the river had receded back within its banks" (UPI caption on an Iowa flood photo); "Argentina's ruling junta" (also UPI); "Pirates Capture Final Showdown" (New York Times sports head) and, believe it or not, from a Wall Street Journal editorial, "the present Oval Office incumbent."

In some cases you can forgive the writer, but where was the copy editor when something like this flows across the desk? A by-lined story on rising taxes in the Albany Knickerbocker News a while ago pointed out that Mississippi residents "paid only $646 each per capita." I know the reporter personally, and could only hope that his English teacher is not a Knick subscriber.

One of my friends believes that Paul Harvey can do no wrong, but I find among my handwritten notes in the UR file two pleonasms attributed to this staunch defender of conservatism. On a landslide that engulfed a Japanese village, Harvey reported that 17 persons "were buried and suffocated to death." That shows how dangerous suffocation can be to good health, but in the same broadcast Harvey had this assurance on the Berkeley City Council's 6–4 vote to assist draft evaders: ". . . so draft evaders and pacifist extremists will have safe sanctuary in Berkeley."

Another rich vein is found in the observances of Dandy Don Meredith, one of my favorite sportscasters and ice-tea lovers. From him I learned on Monday Night Football that George Blanda "once kicked 89 consecutive extra points in a row." Later he reminisced that John Brockington and MacArthur Lane of the Green Bay Packers "made one of the best two-man tandems in the NFL."

Even the erudite Frank Gifford, in the same TV booth, didn't escape the malaise. In a recollection of his own, Giff told his public that Johnny Unitas was "a living legend in his own time." Does that make Frank an anachronism in his own time?

Under the proverbial glass-house precept, I can report that in my speechwriting days for GE corporate executives I was guilty of giving a senior vice president a script stating that "the marketing end (of process automation systems) is unique compared to other businesses." That's a different variation (ouch!) of a quote from a Cincinnati paper that "the Spring Wheat store she manages is more than unique—it's practically one of a kind."

The implication, of course, is the only one of its kind that exists today. Sort of like an experiment someone was just trying out.

Verbal Abuse

Delmar Spotlight, 1986

It would be hard to find a word in the American language, formerly English, that is more abused than the transitive verb *lay*.

Grammarians cringe every time they hear this simple, ordinary verb used in place of the word *lie* in constructions where the verb has no object. The rule here is clear and basic:

you can lay something down, or up, or whatever, but you can't simply lay down, that is, unless you are an athlete intentionally not giving your best to the game.

You hear colloquial crimes like these every day:

● Child to parent: "Mommy, I'm tired. Can I lay down for a little while?" (or vice versa from a mother who ought to know better: "You look a little tired, dear. Why don't you lay down for a while?")

● Nurse to patient, pointing to reclining table in examining room: "Lay here and the doctor will be right with you."

● Witness to police officer at accident scene: "There he was, laying right in the road."

When Bobby asks his mother for permission to "lay down," Mom should say, "What is it you want to lay down, dear?" When the nurse asks me to "lay" on the examining table for an electrocardiogram, I invariably ask her what she wants me to put there. In this situation I have so far successfully refrained from the obvious—the temptation to apply locker-room terminology by asking her not what, but whom? But I may not be able to hold out much longer, which means that in my next physical exam I'm going to come out with something like, "Okay, you get on there first," or "Okay, but shouldn't we go somewhere, like your place or mine?" If she is shocked, it's her fault; she asked for it.

And what, or whom, was the accident victim laying in the middle of the pavement? An egg, maybe?

Scarred old English teachers, bleeding from each new generation of linguistic felonies, and unable to stem the tide of rhetorical blasphemy, now await the day when *lay* is legitimized as an intransitive replacement for *lie* in cases like those in this text. My trusty old Webster sees this coming. Deep in a long list of definitive illustrations that outline a wide spectrum of proper usage for this unsuspecting little three-letter word, the Webster people concede what appears to be inevitable: *Now illiterate: to lie (be prostrate).*

I like to interpet that "now" as meaning it is currently illiterate, but soon won't be, rather than currently illiterate, but didn't used to be.

Lay is, however, accepted as the past tense of *lie,* thus the accident witness could properly tell the gendarme that the victim lay in the road (for a while, that is, but he's gone now), or a friend could inform you that the book lay on the table unopened. But be sure to say they were *lying* there, not laying.

Count the number of times in the next day or two you hear this defenseless little verb violated. In our daily commerce we can lay objects, bets, hands, plans, seige and many other things. Fish, fowl, insects and reptiles can lay eggs, and sailors can lay to. Tormentors can lay off, but employers have to lay off people, presumably employees. It's not even permissible for fugitives to lay low in the present tense. They can lie low, but if they lay low, we can assume it's all over—they either were caught or got away.

If you're going to lay in the sun or the sand this summer, you'd better have something in hand or someone in a like mood. Whatever you do, don't walk out on the beach and lay down. It's proper, and certainly preferable, to lie down, so be sure to make the right choice.

If you are guilty of this kind of verbal abuse, forgive me for laying it on you. I'm just trying to spare you some grief if anything like this comes up when you're talking with your grandfather or your English teacher.

The next time you're tempted to indulge in verb molestation, remember the old story of the couple sitting on the porch of the farmhouse on a warm summer evening, gazing at the distant hills. "Such a beautiful night," says Mom. "I hate to think of our daughter laying up there in the cemetery." "Yes," sighs Dad. "I'd sooner wish she were dead."

That Wandering Apostrophe

Delmar Spotlight, 1980

Now that it is possible to graduate from high school (and many colleges) without knowing how to spell, punctuate a sentence, or use proper tenses and participles, it may be asking too much to bring the apostrophe into line.

Actually, felonies perpetrated by semi-articulates against the apostrophe pre-date the abandonment of Latin in schools and the substitution of television for reading books. Whatever the cause, it is well documented that people abuse the apostrophe outrageously.

Some can be mildly forgiven, like "the Joneses' cat was in our yard last night" or the unpronounceable "Phyllises' hat rolled under the school bus today." Noboy wants to declare or write "the Jones' cat" or Phyllis' hat," mainly because they shouldn't. I go along with the New York Times writer who had an answer for the Kentucky woman wondering if she was "Charles' mother" or "Charles's mother." His advice: "Be Charlie's mother."

He could have replied that "Charles's mother" was proper. Grammatical rules not only permit but require an "'s" to be added to names or nouns ending in s. So it was Phyllis's hat that got away from her on the way to school, and it was Mrs. Jones's cat who was messing around in our yard. Of course, when you associate the cat with the whole Jones family, it's got to be "the Joneses' cat" because no one is going to take on the Jones's feline regardless (not irregardless) of whether it's good, bad or fixed.

Notice that last apostrophe sneaking in there. The apostrophe, versatile little devil, also substitutes for a missing letter when it's not getting involved in possessives. But here, of course, being it's English, we have an exception: the apostrophe is abandoned when the word "it" takes on a possessive. Medieval King James would look at his castle and notice *it's* stonework was getting a bit grungy, but modern-day Jimmy Carter would look at the White House and complain *its* front pillars needed a paint job. Sympathize with the Greeks, Romans, Spaniards,

French, Chinese, Arabians and users of other civilized tongues trying to explain to their children the difference between a contraction (it's) and a possessive without an apostrophe (its).

In my distant youth teachers frowned on contractions, presumably to keep us pure of mind in regard to the apostrophe in essays and compositions. Hence we did not use *didn't* even though we might've if we could've.

That was before the days of shake 'n' bake, to say nothing of brown 'n' serve. Modern usage has moved such idioms into new punctuational dimensions—the hyphen level—so we can have rock-'n-roll and that new business coming to Delmar called Stop-N-Shop. The capital signifies perhaps the investment needed to get it open.

Many of the assaults on the apostrophe stem from misguided attempts to make it serve in plurals. Drive around town and count the family name-signs that identify this house as "The Sturdley's" and the house down the street as "The Minestrone's." Which Sturdley is The Sturdley—Dad, or is Mrs. S. liberated? Once the principal occupant is identified, why can't (cannot) the house be labelled as the dwelling place of the whole Sturdley family, kids and all, instead of just "The" Sturdley? For myself, I prefer a nameplate stating simply "The Sturdleys" indicating who lives there, rather than "The Sturdleys' " proclaiming who owns the property.

At the risk of beating the horse, I will never forget the sign over a small but aggressive dress shop on Route 20 in Guilderland in the early '50s (apostrophe up front, not behind). As a lifetime collector of URs as well as a scarred defender of the apostrophe, I was intrigued with the foot-high lettering proclaiming the ladies' (not ladie's) apparel establishment as "The House of Gladwish's." For nearly thirty years I have been haunted by thoughts of Mr. Gladwish's intent: did he want the world to know that his wife was with him in the business, thus falling into the trap of trying to make the name plural by apostrophe, or did he want to imply that it was not only his (their) house, but his (their house's) house?

We'll never know. Meanwhile, here's a toast to the incoming '80s, the Joneses' cat, Charlie's mother, and assorted Sturdleys and Gladwishes. Rise 'n' shine!

Find Your Own Bookie

Delmar Spotlight, 1979

If Abner Doubleday turned another few degrees in his eternal resting place in Cooperstown the other day, the Times-Union and many other (but not all) newspapers should be credited with an assist.

When Abner invented the game of baseball, the most scientific form of organized exercise on this spinning planet, he couldn't have dreamed of the silly dimensions his creation would have in its second century. As if artificial turf, prima-donna players, greedy owners, million-dollar .237 hitters and free-agent pitchers unable to hold a two-run lead aren't enough to desecrate the memory of this genius, we now have the most ludicrous gambit yet—gambling odds on spring training games! Imagine that!

As a resident baseball expert, I have always felt I could supplement my income by betting the baseball odds on a regular basis. I say this in full knowledge of what a bookmaker told me 20 years ago when the New York Yankees were awesome in their domination of the game. When I asked how rich one could get by betting on the Yankees every home game for a season, he replied: "Oh, you wouldn't lose much."

Now the Times-Union and others beholden to the Las Vegas syndicates and The Reliable Jersey House are giving us baseball odds along with point spreads on football and basketball. Think of the benefits of this public service! It not only enhances our daily gambling habits, but it saves us time and tolls in calling our bookies to get the rundown on the morning line.

But these papers don't go far enough. How do they expect us to feed the habit when they don't tell us where we can lay our bets? To the dismay of many readers, especially parents anxious to get their Little League baseball players, Pop Warner football players and eighth grade basketball players started properly on a life of gambling, the Times-Union does not include in this service a list of recommended bookmakers, or even phone numbers where baseball or football bets are accepted on credit.

Naturally every parent wants to get the kids hooked on illegal addiction at an early age. But how can a father show his Little Leaguer how to read the odds and point spreads without teaching him how to keep secret the name and number of the family's personal bookie, especially when the phones change with every police raid?

What good does it do to show young Bobby that the Orioles with Jim Palmer pitching tonight are a good two-unit bet at 5½-6½ against the Red Sox at home if Bobby can't put down a piece of his lunch money with a bookie? Then there's the problem of explaining to Bobby that if Palmer doesn't pitch because of a blister on his thumb, the odds switch to pick-em, which favors the house, unless, of course, Jim Rice is out of the Boston lineup because of a hangnail, in which case, the odds shift back to the Orioles. The bookie isn't going to take the time and trouble to educate the kid, so Dad has to do it with the Times-Union, which gives us a daily rundown right off the Vegas wire.

When my son was of the impressionable age in Little League, I was never able to find a bookie, so I was deprived of the chance to show him the thrills of a lifetime of gambling. Today he is a young man who has to contend with the dull routine of making student loans and car payments rather than being in hock to his bookie.

I did make one serious effort to fulfill my parental responsibility. I went down to the OTB parlor in Delmar and, with the morning line from the Times-Union in hand, asked the lady to place three units on the Reds over the Phillies. She gave me a puzzled look. When I repeated the request, she said: "Oh, that sounds like it's baseball, and we don't take baseball bets here." When I asked her where I should go to bet on the Reds, she got huffy.

It's especially frustrating now that we have, for the first time, the opportunity to bet on Grapefruit League games. That should be great fun, especially when well-known pitchers go three innings without throwing hard breaking stuff and managers are trying to see if a rookie shortstop from Cedar Rapids can hit or throw.

So please, T-U and others, don't be stuffy just because this kind of betting is illegal. Expand your valuable service to include names and phone numbers of recommended local bookmakers. We can't teach our kids to gamble just on paper.

Never Argue with a Tennis Buff

Albany Times-Union, 1972

Tennis players are a clanny lot. They tend to consider themselves beneficiaries of mankind's purest form of athletic expression, endowed with classic origin and possessed of a degree of sophistication unattained by more commonplace activities.

This explains why you can never win an argument with a tennis buff. They are as unwavering in their rationale as conservationists and Volkswagen owners.

They will fraternize with golfers because they often have to share a country club locker room or someone's swimming pool with these boorish people, but they feel they do not have to be nice to commoners who pursue such vulgar pastimes as....well, bowling or pocket pool or pinochle. None of these, they agree, belong on the sports pages because they do not involve physical exercise or make any demands on the brain.

The bowler argues that directing a heavy ball along highly waxed teakwood toward a hypothetical "pocket" demands the ultimate in skill and technique.

Ah, yes, sniffs the tennist, but you perform this ritual only about 45 times in the space of two hours. Bowling, he snorts, is a beam-broadening excuse to get out of the house at night, a pastime in which the participants relax on their buttresses 94.7

percent of the time, quaffing malt brews and making the air heavy with fumes of tar, nicotine and Cuban hemps.

Besides, he yawns, it's just plain boring. Bowl three times and you've seen it all, leaving the rest of your lifetime to monotonous repetition.

Tennis buffs will, however, consort with skiers and sailors, mainly because most players do either or both of these things or at least endorse them as accepted forms of healthy exercise practiced in the fresh air and requiring skill and strategy.

Easy as it is to dismiss the lower forms of recreation, the tennis player finds himself outnumbered and often outmaneuvered by golfers. From April til October these garrulous hordes dominate conversation at the office, shop, lunch table, bar. Not only do they replay their Sunday matches all week, but they plot devious ways to get out of work early in order to get in 18 holes before dark.

But what ruffles the tennis purist most is the tendency of golfers to regard tennis players as second-class citizens who should use the back of the locker room. They concede it's all right to have a social drink with them once in a while, but you wouldn't want your sister to marry one.

Nowadays things are changing. The tennis player is beginning to get the recognition he has lacked in the past. His numbers are increasing, and with the expanding population has come respect and the beginnings of status. People with money have taken note, and have built indoor courts for him to expend his energy when it rains or even snows. Did anybody ever do that for a golfer? Where is the angel who will inflate a plastic bubble over a golf course, or put even a par-3 thing under a roof?

Let those guys go south to chase that little pill over those hills, scoffs the tennis player as he heads for Latham or Delmar with his racquet bag on the seat and the car-heater on full-fan.

With the new status has come confidence to stand up to the golf gang at the office and dish the gaff right back. For example:

"What bugs me about golf," he will say with newfound bravado, "is the way you have to be so quiet when your opponent is making a tee shot or a putt. Me, I like to attack my opponent, drive him back to the baseline, make him dive in the alleys or pass him at the net. Give him the business, make him sweat."

"Right-o," chimes in his doubles partner. "And don't forget, tennis is the only game where you can hit a hard volley into the pit of your boss's stomach (or a customer's) and he'll say, 'Ouch! Nice shot!' "

"I switched to tennis," said a reformed golfer, "because I didn't have time to give up most of the day to a golf game. It takes three hours to play 18 holes, and I can get a better workout playing three sets in an hour and a half."

"Tennis has a lot more action," the other fellow said. "And it's better on television. Watching golf on TV is like watching paint dry."

One unexpected twist of the new popularity is the widespread enthusiasm among the female of the specie. "I was a golf widow every summer," observed Mary Barvoets the other day at Tri-City. "Now I've discovered tennis, and Brooks is a tennis widower all winter."

Learning to Paddle

Albany Times-Union, 1973

Last week's Net Set essay on the history and socio-political evolution of platform tennis had such a deep impact on Bob and Julie O'Connor that they invited Barbara and me to actually play the game.

Now that your chronicler has tried it in the flesh, I can report that the world is a lot different.

In fact, I want one—a paddle tennis court, that is. Anyone interested in helping to defray the expenses of building this kind of a contraption in my yard in Slingerlands can call or write—or better yet, just send a check. Somewhere between $5,000 and $7,000 ought to take care of it nicely.

The invitation was for Sunday afternoon at Schuyler Meadows Country Club, and my first concern was what to wear. After all, this is an outdoor game, played with oversize ping-pong bats on a raised wooden platform enclosed in wire mesh, and it was the first Sunday in February.

Barbara was very helpful. "Wear anything that's comfortable," she suggested.

"Like sweater, parka, ski pants?"

"Sure, if you want to," she countered. "But the way you overheat you probably will be too warm."

"Okay, but what kind of a shirt? Open collar and sweater? They don't wear tennis shirts for this sort of thing, do they?"

"I doubt it," she said. "Anyway, hurry up or we'll be late."

She wore a turtle neck and a knitted sweater. I couldn't find a turtle neck on short notice, so settled for a sport shirt and light sweater, slacks and tennis shoes. Turned out anything goes— Julie showed up in a plaid skirt and knee socks; Bob had a jacket and wore mittens.

The day was gray and chilling, but not numbing. The dusting of snow from early morning had disappeared.

We started warming up on the court, and it took about six seconds to discover how different this was from tennis. The first time I swung to return a ball, it wasn't there, and fresh air whooshed through the perforations in my paddle. The ball bounced mockingly under my swing and dribbled undisturbed to the backstop.

A moment later, there it was again, an orange-colored sponge rubber ball coming at me, this time on a longer, higher bounce. Beautiful. This is more like it, I thought, and set myself to tie into a nice hard forehand and whistle it down the middle, low.

It was low all right. The ball thudded against the heavy paddle with a gutteral clunking sound and shot to the base of the net like a rocket.

But then things picked up and I got a couple back. One backhand volley felt so good and looked so beautiful I decided we were warmed up and could start the first set.

Julie took it easy and Bob got extravagant and we got some points, but it wasn't a close match. Barbara had her dependable cross-court forehand going, but both of us were having trouble on the baseline. Then we began to realize we shouldn't be back there in the first place. The game is at the net, close up, period.

"Not so much wrist," Barbara said as I flubbed one of Julie's crisp drives. "You're not playing badminton."

That helped some. We didn't cause any panic among the paddle tennis crowd, but we were having fun in abundance. Ralph Burdick came by and pretended not to be horrified at the way we were treating a graceful sport.

"You don't try to win the point on the first shot," he explained, patiently. "You use the first shot to set up a winner the next time."

My approach was to get the ball back, let alone try to strategize for a subsequent winner. The orange pellet dipped and banked around the boards, spinning and darting, sometimes skidding or dying.

Paddle tennis requires a careful touch. The court is exactly half the size of a tennis court, so it is easy to whack the ball out or wide. It was dismaying to belt a nice forehand down the alley, feeling like a hotshot making a winning drive, and watch the doggoned little sphere clear the baseline by two feet.

On the small court the action is fast and close, the speed of the ball dizzying. In my zeal to react quickly at the net I intercepted shots that the wise paddle tennis player lets sail.

"If it comes in shoulder high, let it go," someone advised Barbara.

"That means I have to think fast whether I'm playing tennis or paddle," she said.

"Think paddle," Bob said, laughing.

"There isn't time," said Barbara.

We served a lot of faults until we realized the game is designed for accuracy and agility rather than power. That's why the rules specify only one serve, like badminton. You won't get anywhere serving the ball hard, but you can spin it in or tease it into a corner or close to the lines.

So now we've played paddle tennis and it is great. There are only three courts in all the Capital District, and none of them are public. Maybe we should start a campaign for municipal subsidies to spot some paddle facilities alongside the tennis courts at neighborhood schools and parks. Then I won't have to solicit public subscriptions to build a court in my yard.

"You didn't play very well, but we had a good time," Barbara said to me as we left the court after losing four sets to Bob and Julie.

"That's because the ball didn't bounce properly and the paddle didn't always work right," I said.

"But you looked very nice in your blue shirt and that sweater," she said. "And now your cheeks are red."

"I'm comfortable," I said. "Maybe overheated a bit, and not very sartorial, but comfortable."

Kids Like Their Baseball

Geneva Daily Times, 1947

They were crowding around home plate, their bronzed dusty faces watching every move. Charlie Small was illustrating how to shift hands on the bat handle and feet in the batter's box to square for a bunt. Overhead the noonday sun beat down without mercy, and outside the park there were nearly 100 bicycles.

Ben Lady sauntered through the gate and trudged over to the closely packed group of youngsters crowding around the Redbirds' skipper. The rotund manager of the Kingston Ponies was wearing a clean white shirt, and his tan sun-hat was pushed far over the Lady brow.

"Hello, Charlie, what's goin' on?" Benjamin called, gruffly.

"Getting in a little bunting," said Charlie, straightening up from his stance at the plate. Turning to the youngsters around him, none of whom came to his shoulders, he said: "You boys know this fella?"

"Sure," they chorused. "It's Ben Lady," a 10-year-old said. "Hi-ya, Ben," timidly offered another.

"Nuts," said Ben. "There ain't nobody in this whole league can bunt right." Charlie laughed, picked up his glove and went out by the mound. The kids formed a line, and each took his turn as Charlie tossed baseballs. Ben borrowed a glove and squatted behind the plate in civilian clothes.

They paraded up to the plate, one after the other, while others watched intently in a circle a few feet away. Charlie called instructions from in front of the mound, and Ben continually interrupted the young batters to correct their hands or their stance.

And the kids could bunt, too. "Nice one," called Charlie when Boots Salone, aged 12, pushed one toward the box. "Now down that third base line," and he served up another. "Now down towards first." And so it went.

They were all ages, and they all played on some ball team in the Kiwanis leagues. There were tall boys and short boys, dark boys and blond boys. They all had one thing in common— they wanted to learn baseball.

All over the park were groups clustered around Redbirds players, practicing bunts. Jerry Murray had a group in the Geneva bullpen, Rupe Lewis and Chief St. Denis another in left field, Phene Willette another in center. Joe Schurba had one near the scoreboard, Norm Payne another in the visitors' bullpen, and Harry Lockwood another on the right field line. The sun was hot and the dust clung to the sweaty little figures, but no one cared.

One tow-headed youngster of 13 tore himself away from Professor Lockwood's class near first base and asked a bystander what time it was. Twelve-thirty, he was told. "Jeez," he said, wiping dust off his pants. "I gotta go. I'll be late for my music lesson." He trotted sadly toward the gate, swinging his glove, glancing back enviously over his shoulder.

After a while the faculty switched to pitching and fielding techniques. A group of would-be pitchers clustered around Chief St. Denis.

"Let's see your drop, Chief," pleaded a well-built youngster of 12. "Yeah, show us a drop," said his friend.

The Chief, stripped to the waist in the mid-day heat, grinned and asked for a baseball. "It's all in the snap of the wrist," he explained while the kids studied the way his fingers gripped the ball. "Drops, hooks, in-curves..." A moment later they were all spinning baseballs at each other while the perspiring Chief inspected their motions.

On the sidelines scattered groups of adults watched the classes with interest. "This is the greatest thing we've ever had for these kids," said an old-time fan. "We never had this in our day."

"You got some naturals out there, Charlie," said Lady, trying to light a two-inch cigar stub without igniting his beak.

"Sure, we have," said Charlie, smiling. "Good prospects, a lot of them."

"Great kids," said Ben. "You can't beat baseball, and they know it. It does your heart good to see them take it so serious. Now let's hit that Y pool and we can forget about all them doubleheaders comin' up!"

Ketchup with Pepper

Geneva Daily Times, 1948

Hardly anyone in baseball knows John L. Martin, but they all know Pepper Martin or they know of him. When he was playing with the Cardinals in the early thirties he stole everything but first base, and in the World Series of 1931 the Athletics had all kinds of trouble getting him out.

Pepper Martin is not a young man anymore, but his mind is alert and quick, and he is a man with a purpose. That purpose is to teach boys how to play baseball the way it should be played, how to size up a curve ball when it's coming at you, and how to get the jump on a pitcher to steal a base.

"The Wild Hoss of the Osage" the sportswriters called him when he was the most famous of the Gas House Gang. He is in Geneva for a few days this week directing the Brooklyn Dodgers baseball school at Shuron Park, and Saturay he's going to Plattsburgh to be a place-kick specialist for the football Dodgers of the All-America Conference. This is pretty good for a guy who is not so young anymore.

Pepper likes baseball, boys, Branch Rickey and hamburgers drowned in ketchup. He was sitting in the lobby of the Seneca late yesterday with Ron Burkman, the St. Lawrence coach, and Spike Garnish, coach at Hobart, after a six-hour workout with 42 youngsters at Shuron Park.

"What I can't understand," the Wild Hoss was saying, "is what has happened to all them good throwing arms. The youngsters you see around nowadays can't throw. Their legs are good, and some hit pretty well, but they don't have the arms."

"Funny how it goes," said Garnish. "I wish I knew the answer."

"It's got me," said Pepper. "Maybe they don't throw enough rocks or hickory nuts the way we used to when we were kids."

Dick Cameron, a Dodger scout, came in the lobby with Mrs. Cameron and Mrs. Garnish, and caught the end of the conversation.

"It's a shame, too," Cameron said. "When a ballplayer breaking in can't make it as an infielder or outfielder, it used to be he could always take a crack at pitching."

"Don't forget you got that broadcast," interrupted Spike. "We've got time for a bite before you go on the air, or do you want to wait until later and eat a steak?"

"Sounds good," grinned Pepper. "But let's get a hamburger first."

Spike threw up his hands. "What a man," he said, winking at Burkman.

The conversation got around to Rickey, who Pepper claims is the most misjudged man in baseball today.

"He's one in a million," said the Hoss. "He's loyal and understanding. He'll always hear your side of anything, even when you're talking contracts. The fellows that work for him think he's great. I'd do anything for him. He's a real square-shooter. The sportswriters don't understand him. He ought to run for president of the United States, that's how fine a man he is."

Somebody remarked that Paul Dean, a member of the old Gas House Gang, had signed as a scout for the Browns.

"That's good," commented Pepper. "Paul's a good fella, but how that guy can argue. He loves to have an argument, especially with Joe Medwick in the old days. But I see where Elmer's back now."

"Who's Elmer?" asked Mrs. Cameron."

"Elmer was one of the Dean boys," explained Pepper. "Seems one day before Diz and Paul broke into baseball they was riding in in an old car down by their farm and their brother Elmer was driving a Model T just ahead of them. They come to a railroad crossing, and Elmer got over before a long freight train went by, and Diz and Paul had to wait. After the train got by, Elmer was gone and they never saw him for ten years."

"That's a hot one," laughed Garnish.

"It's true," insisted Pepper. "What about that hamburg?"

They sauntered over to the Palms and ordered. The chatter went from baseball to basketball to college football and back to baseball. The hamburgs came and pretty soon it was 6 o'clock.

"What time did you say that broadcast was?" Pepper asked Garnish.

Six-thirty," said Garnish. "How about another hamburg?"

"I thought it was 6:15," said Pepper. "We got plenty of time."

"Sure," said Spike. "I'm ordering another 'burg. Do I have to twist your arm?"

"Nope," said the Wild Hoss. "And don't spare the ketchup."

Babe Kraus

Upon the death of Babe Kraus (Ch. 17), I was moved to write a eulogy for the Geneva Times. It ran on September 10, 1966 under the original column logo I had bequeathed to my successor as sports editor fifteen years earlier, and was later reprinted in the Hobart alumni publication.

Babe Kraus is gone and a chapter of Hobart history spanning two full generations has closed. A chapter? Better, a book.

This Gibraltar of a man brought a rugged, competitive spirit to Hobart 40 years ago, and as the seasons came and went, that spirit mellowed only a little, as it does in mature men. But behind that ruddy, strong face and beneath that thatch of snowy hair with its orderly wave there was a vast strength and a deep serenity.

Babe Kraus was a giant and a winner when he came to Geneva as a college boy, and his athletic feats were prodigious. He could kick a football halfway to Canandaigua, and when he piled into the linemen they, in the words of Art Kenney, "stayed hit a long time."

And it is actually on record that, when he was a young ball player in his native Fulton, Babe Kraus hit the longest home run ever recorded in Oswego County. He smote an unsuspecting pitch over the center field fence, and the ball, landing in an empty coal car in a passing freight train, came to rest in West Virginia, a few hundred miles beyond the reach of outfielders.

Babe's life was in athletics, and his devotion and leadership in his favorite sport, lacrosse, took him to the top of his profession as a coach and administrator. He was, in the parlance of sports writers, the dean of U.S. lacrosse coaches, and the sport honored him on his 30th coaching anniversary by moving the revered North-South game from the sacred precincts of Maryland for the first time some years ago, and staged it at

Boswell Field. This is somewhat akin to moving the World Series to Oakland because Casey Stengel lives there.

But for all Babe's winning, which was considerably more than his losing, he never lost sight of the true objective of a coach—molding fine young men out of all kinds of boys. He taught them how to block and pivot and feint and pass, plus all the strategy of his vast experience, but he also taught them the meaning of athletics and how it was important to them in a world that so often permits true values to get out of perspective.

During the periods of athletic eclipse at Hobart—and there have been many seasons when Hobart teams struck no fear at all into the opposition, and many more when Hobart teams were distinguished only by mediocrity—some people used to complain about the athletic setup. What Hobart needed, they said, was some new blood in the athletic department. What they never considered was the fact that up in his office Babe Kraus, the director of athletics, was setting up schedules and talking to coaches 12 months of the year with the objective of giving Hobart boys—good athletes and the many guys who just liked to play football or lacrosse or basketball—a full season of competition with other colleges that had the same attitude on the proper balance between the classroom and the locker room.

He was a tower of strength when it came to preserving valuable relationships with Union, Hamilton, Rochester and other traditional rivals. He also knew the value of injecting the variety of a trip to such campuses as Wagner, John Carroll, Thiel, Juniata or Norwich for some honest perspiration in combat.

When the University of Buffalo promoted itself to a major-league football schedule, Babe turned to his list of sympaticos and the schedule retained its balance. When the president of the U. of R. sauntered into the dressing room after a Hobart game and permitted himself to be shocked at the sight of some skinned knees, a black eye and a few puffy lips, his unfortunate remarks were picked up by the press, and a rich and treasured rivalry was fractured. During the storm of words and statements Babe Kraus kept his poise and sat back to wait for the storm to blow over, which he knew it would and which it did.

353

Babe knew what he was doing all the time, and when he strolled across the campus between his office and his house, he looked like just what he was, a giant inside and out. On the practice field he'd see all the mistakes his teams were making, and he would point them out to a bystander and then add, "They're good guys and they'll do all right on Saturday."

On Sunday nights Spike Garnish, Eddie Tryon, Bob Teague and the others would drop by the house, and Marg would push the Sunday papers aside and inquire whether the mood was beer or coffee. Babe rarely moved from his favorite chair, the pipe that was as much a trademark as his white mane was forever planted in that great countenance, and the stories would unfold, the games would be replayed, the old punchlines would be reviewed with another laugh. It was Babe, the pivotal man in the room, the leader of the panel, whose poise and unruffled serenity seemed to set the scene.

Hobart boys who played for Babe, hundreds of them across the years, paused last week when they heard the news. They let their thoughts drift back to those muddy days on the practice field when they were tired and it was getting dark, and Babe stood there, showing them the way it should be, a boulder-like silhouette on the sidelines, sometimes raising his voice, but quick to forgive. Scattered around the world are others who haven't yet heard, and when they do, they will pause and remember an incident, a story, and the familiar pipe.

Babe has gone, and someday there will be a proper memorial on the campus. When it is put in place, it should be a symbol of strength combined with serenity, representing power in perspective with stability. That was Babe Kraus's unchanging contribution to a changing world.

Appendix

Notes

Gordon W. Bryant

Gordon Bryant died in Watertown on June 24, 1984, at age 84 with the distinction of being an active newspaperman longer than anyone on record in New York State. He joined the Watertown Times three weeks after his 17th birthday, hired as a high school senior to help answer telephones on Election Night, 1916 as editors tabulated returns in the presidiential race between Woodrow Wilson and Charles Evans Hughes. After graduating the following June, he became a cub reporter for the Times. He was covering the obituary and hospital beat when he joined the U. S. Marines. After serving in France, he returned to the Times. He was promoted to covering city hall and sports, advanced to the copydesk and then became assistant city editor. He was city editor from 1932 to 1956, when he was named executive editor, a post that included the position of managing editor. He became an editorial consultant in 1977 and served in that capacity until his death. His association with the Times spanned 68 years. A four-column head on the prestigious back page of the paper crowned his obituary, and inside there was a full page of tributes written by a dozen newsmen—former reporters and copydesk editors he had trained before sending them on to other journalistic triumphs.

Henry J. Leader

Henry Leader left the AP in 1956 to join the Gannett News Service bureau in Washington. Later that year he moved to New Jersey as editor of the Plainfield Courier News. In 1958 he returned to upstate New York as general manager of the two Gannett papers in Utica, the Press and Observer-Dispatch. He later became publisher.

Henry was severely injured in an automobile accident in 1964. Extended hospital stays caused his early retirement in 1965, cutting short a brilliant newspaper career. He died in 1972 at the age of 63.

Henry's quick mind and instant grasp of story situations made him a newspaperman's newspaperman. He began his career on the Syracuse Herald-Journal, served as editor of a string of nine weekly newspapers in the Syracuse area, and returned to the daily field as telegraph editor of the Little Falls Times and later as a rewrite man for the Troy Record. In 1936 he began an eight-year stint with the same Utica papers he was to head two decades later. As their correspondent in nearby Rome, N.Y. he showed his talent so well that he was brought into the main office as state editor. He joined the Associated Press in Albany in 1942, and after serving in most of the slots mentioned in Chapters 15-17 in this narrative, became state editor and an outstanding political writer and columnist.

A. M. Learned

Al Learned was named managing editor of the Schenectady Union-Star in 1953. In taking the new position, he again brought Charlie Bennett with him as city editor. When the Union-Star was taken over by new ownership several years later, Al returned to Geneva, where he became head of the Hobart College News Bureau. He resumed his active community life in church work, Kiwanis, choral groups and other civic and fraternal organizations, and remained an active volunteer in many causes after retirement.

Thomas O. Paine

Tom Paine resigned as a senior vice president and group executive at General Electric to become president of the Northrop Corporation in California. When he retired from Northop, he formed his own consulting firm in Santa Monica, using it as a base to pursue his lifelong interest in the U. S. space program and in submarine history and technology. He maintains his own private Submarine Warfare Library, which has become one of the world's most authoritative source for researchers in the submarine field. That project was largely motivated by his experience in 1945 as executive officer of a U. S. Navy prize crew entrusted with sailing the innovative Japanese submersible aircraft carrier, the I-400, from Tokyo Bay to Pearl Harbor following the surrender of Japan ending World War II. At this writing Tom is chairman of the fifteen-member National Commission on Space, based in Washington, where he had a key role in the writing and preparation of that body's vividly illustrated 200-page report, *Pioneering the Space Frontier,* published in 1986.

Albany AP Bureau

When the Capital Newspapers moved to their new building in Colonie, the AP and UPI were assigned appropriate space with modern comforts. The AP retains the same office in the Capitol press section.

Geneva Daily Times

The Geneva Times is now officially the Finger Lakes Times. After Learned, "G. B." hired several managing editors, one of whom, George Northridge, in earlier days was one of the few newsmen ever fired by the Watertown Times. Upon the death of G. B. Williams at 91, his only child, Sam Williams, who, estranged from Geneva as a young man, had lived the life of an international drifter, returned to take charge of the paper despite never having had a day's experience as a newspaperman. In subsequent years, despite a new plant and the addition of photo facilities and modern production techniques, the paper has attained no recognizable distinction, one of many mediocre small-city dailies. Sam Williams died in 1987, and as this was written (1988) the newspaper reportedly has been offered for sale.

Watertown Daily Times

With a new building, modern production facilities and a new look typographically, it continues to be recognized as a newspaper of unusually high quality. Its dominance in northern New York has never been challenged. John B. Johnson succeeded his father at the death of Harold B. Johnson in 1949, and preserved the emphasis on full coverage. John B. Johnson, Jr. handles the day-to-day administration on the editorial side. The Times added a Sunday edition in 1986.

Index

Granite, Md., 298
Grasse River, 54, 56
Greenbush Area News, 308-309, 311
Grenier Field, 120
Grier, Roger, 312
Guilderland, N.Y., 277-278, 290, 309
Gutoff, Reuben, 236

Hagerty, James C., 217
Harman, Mit, 148, 150, 164
Harmon Field, Nfld., 96-120
Hearn, Bernard (Barney), 148-149, 151
Hearst Corp., 176, 192, 253-256, 275-276, 285, 309, 312, 315, 320
Herald-Tribune (New York), 22
Helderberg Sun, 273, 276-280, 282, 285, 307-312
Herkimer, N.Y., 202-204
Hilchie's Hardware, 283, 285
Hiss, Alger, 204
Hobart College, 131, 145-146, 167, 348, 350-352
Holder, Lee, 291
Holliday, Fred, 35-38, 51, 78
Hornell Tribune, 225
Hudson River, 177, 277, 307, 309
Hunt, Richard P., 213
Hurlbut, Robert, 104-105
Hutton, Ina Ray, 67

Illingworth, Robert, 314
International News Service, 15, 176

Jackson Heights, N.Y., 95
Jenkins, Joe, 150
Jennings, Mildred 139-141
Jensen, Robert, 188, 215, 227
Job Corps, 294-300, 319
Johnson, Harold B. 15-17, 34, 44, 78, 81, 130, 280
Johnson, John B., 16-17, 31
Jones, David P., 248
Jones, Johnnie, 189

Jones, Kay (Parker), 181, 187-189, 197, 202
Jones, Reginald, 236-237
Justice, Dept. of, 310

Keesler Field, Miss., 91
Kelly, Edward, 220-222
Kelly, Joe, 124-127
Kennedy, Scoop, 63, 65, 67-68, 71, 73
Kennedy, William, 194-195
Kenney, Arthur, 168, 350
Kent, Milton F., 241-243, 246
Kimball, Frederick, 16
King, Robert G., 263-265, 270, 275-280, 283, 291-292, 305, 315
Klestinec, Al, 164-166
K-Mart, 283, 286-287, 291
Kohinke, Bertram E., 267-268, 299
Konstanty, Jim, 59-61
Kraus, Francis L. (Babe), 145-146, 150, 167, 352-354
Korean front, 142, 187

Labor Dept. (U. S.), 294, 296, 298, 319
Lady, Ben, 160, 345-347
LaGuardia Field, 95, 120
Lake George, 246-247, 261
Lake Michigan, 93
Landon, Harry F., 16, 20, 33-34, 38
Landsman, Milton, 84, 86
Larkin, Walter, 46, 51-52
Latham, N.Y., 257, 276-277, 309, 312
Leader, Henry, 181-190, 198-202, 218, 280, 325
Learned, A. M., 128-129, 135-136, 138-144, 198
Legislative Correspondents Association (Albany), 222-225, 322.
Legislature (New York State), 179, 231
Lennon, Howard, 124

Tupper Lake, N.Y., 19
Tye, Vincent, 113-120

Union College, 197
U. S. Corps of Engineers, 65
United Press (UPI), 15, 77, 175-176, 195, 215-216, 220, 334
Utica, N.Y., 6, 15, 83-86, 202, 215
Utica Observer-Dispatch, 7, 187
Utica Press, 6, 187, 202-203

VanWoert, Dr. Irving, 273
Vento, Stephen, 111, 113
Volz, Louis, 56
Voorheesville, N.Y., 277, 286, 302

Waldorf, Tex, 29-30
Wall Street Journal, 334
Washington, D. C., 95, 106, 214
Washington County, N.Y., 204
Washington Post, 15, 227, 322
Waterford, N.Y., 309
Waterloo, N.Y., 139

Watertown, N.Y., 3-20, 31, 44, 46, 86, 128-129, 148, 165, 179
Watertown Daily Times, 3-20, 31-86, 107, 125-127, 130, 136-137, 177, 282, 302, 334
Wayne County, N.Y., 162
Weaver, Warren, Jr., 223
Webster, Clarence, 126-127, 137
Welch, Jack, 236-237
Wells, Robert, 123-124
West Sand Lake, N.Y., 208
West Winfield, N.Y., 202
White Plains, N.Y., 324
Whitzel, Raymond, 56-58, 74
Wilbur, John, 86
Willette, Felix (Phene), 152-153, 155, 166, 346
William Smith College, 131
Williams, George B., 130-135, 138, 280
Woodstock, Md., 298

Zanke, Len, 156, 164, 166

Credits

AP bureau files/Albany, 203
Author's collection, 28, 72, 80, 92, 151, 166, 197, 223, 225, 226, 255, 258, 262, 269, 271, 279, 289, 297, 300, 303, 304, 309, 317, 321
Barbara Boynton, 2, 88, 122, 174, 277
Capital Newspapers, 320
Dictionary of American Slang, 328
Geneva Historical Society, 132, 140, 161
Harmoneer, 96, 98, 102-103, 108, 111, 112, 114, 117, 121
Hobart College, 146
Dorothy Leader, 184, 198, 216
A.M. Learned, 139
Massena Museum, 36, 43, 57, 65
New York State Assembly, 221
New York State Dept. of Commerce, 211, 214, 219
Thomas Paine Associates, 244
Hy Rosen/Albany Times-Union, 301
Warren Hunting Smith Library/Hobart College files, 134, 142, 146, 155
Watertown Daily Times, 5, 8, 12, 14, 16, 18, 33, 66, 125
Arthur J. Westcott, 41, 47, 48, 64

Media Rare

Makes a great gift!

To order *Media Rare* as a gift, simply fill out names and addresses and add $1.50 to the book price ($11.95) for mailing. We will enclose the gift card.

ORDER FORM

Please send *Media Rare* to:

_____
Name

Media Rare $11.95
Postage 1.50

_____
Street

_____
City, State and Zip

_____
Name

Media Rare $11.95
Postage 1.50

_____
Street

_____
City, State and Zip

Check enclosed for $ _____

Gift of _____

Mail this form with your check to:

Chandler Press
P.O. Box 268
Maynard, Mass. 01754